A NEW HISTORY

OF SCOTLAND

For Lexie and Davina

A New History of Scotland

MURRAY G.H. PITTOCK

SUTTON PUBLISHING

First published in the United Kingdom in 2003 by
Sutton Publishing Limited · Phoenix Mill
Thrupp · Stroud · Gloucestershire · GL5 2BU

Reprinted in 2003

British Library Cataloguing in Publication Data
A catalogue record for this book is available from the British Library.

ISBN 0-7509-2786-0

Typeset in 11/14.25pt Photina.
Typesetting and origination by
Sutton Publishing Limited.
Printed and bound in England by
J.H. Haynes & Co. Ltd, Sparkford.

Contents

PREFACE

This book is a brief one-volume study of Scottish history; its purpose is to provide a general synthesis which will enable the reader to turn to further specialist reading if desired. In itself it is intended to be complete, if not comprehensive, and to take full account of the rapidly developing achievements of primary historical scholarship, which not all short histories do. In addition, the present writer aims to provide a particular focus from different points of view on critical periods in Scottish history, among them the Reformation and the Wars of Independence. This book is not simply a narrative history, though it can be used as such; rather it adopts different perspectives in examining critical developments in Scottish history from economic, religious, geographical and cultural perspectives. I have tried to be sensitive not only to the *mentalités* of the past but also to their terminology, and have used forms of names appropriate to their period: Gaelic forms for earlier Scotland, giving way to increasingly English forms of names for places and offices from the time of David I (r. 1124–53).

ACKNOWLEDGEMENTS

A New History of Scotland is naturally indebted to the work of many scholars including Michael Lynch, whose 1991 history was the first truly modern one-volume history of Scotland, and Tom Devine, whose intense grasp on the circumstances of modern Scotland is truly impressive. I have benefited greatly from talking with both of these scholars, and with Edward Cowan, Colin Kidd and Richard Finlay among my colleagues in the Glasgow-Strathclyde School of Scottish Studies. The work of Geoffrey Barrow, Archie Duncan, Bruce Lenman, Allan Macinnes and James Mitchell has also been influential, as have conversations with Ross Mackenzie (who began it all), Alexander Broadie, Thomas Clancy, Jonathan Clark, Cairns Craig, Owen Dudley Edwards, Frank McLynn, Donald Meek, Jamie Reid-Baxter and Fiona Watson. (Endnotes give full reference to the first citation within any given chapter; subsequent citations are to author and date.)

This history could not have been completed without the unfailing friendship and support of Jeremy Black, whose generosity is extraordinary. I am indebted to Professor Black and Dr John Koch of the National Centre for Advanced Welsh and Celtic Studies, Aberystwyth, for reading this text, and especially to Dr Gordon Barclay, whose advice and support with the first chapter was extremely important. I also owe a special, complete and continuing debt of thanks to my wife, Anne, and daughters, Lexie and Davina, to whom this book is dedicated. The faults that follow are my own.

Bearsden, January 2002

ONE

EUROPE, THE WORLD AND SCOTLAND BEFORE THE SCOTS

INTRODUCTION

Globalisation, according to the sociologist Ulrich Beck, creates 'proximity over distances and distances within proximity'. Increasingly, the cultural, social and political intimacies we now have are voyeuristic, not experiential. From afar, politics and other dramas, some real as starvation, some vacuous as soap opera, are injected into the lives of those who do not know their own neighbours. The intense locality of cultural interpretation, which once invested a familiar landscape with stories, now tends to preserve its life only as a representation of the heritage of an area to those who visit it or view it from afar.[1]

And yet this is an age of nationalism. Countries as diverse as Estonia and East Timor have recently come to political independence, and others such as Catalonia and Flanders have gained increasing autonomy. This process may be rooted in national histories, but it is also energised and supported by the disenfranchisement of electorates and political groupings in an era of capital migration, cultural relativism and the centralisation of existing states eager to hold on to as much of their power as possible. Where states and nations move to share power rather than compete for it, as is to an extent the case in the European Union, this is typically due to a perceived over-arching commonality of interest ('our common European home'). Countries which do not identify with this commonality (England), where it has ossified (Scotland), or who have reason to be historically suspicious of their neighbour's motives while lacking power themselves (Denmark) tend to be those most sceptical of this process. European integration, however represented, is at the least intriguing: an ambitious project to reconcile national revolt against globalisation with the process of globalisation itself, in an international grouping nonetheless committed to principles of subsidiarity in the organisation of power. In this, it is perhaps the only major idealistic project left in first-world politics which is not confined to a single issue of moment. From the Balkans to the Faeroes, Europe, the cradle of the nation state, stands at the crossroads of the national and global trends of our own day.

Scotland is on the edge of Europe, as it is represented by dominant states and populations; at the edge of the world (*in finibus orbi*) as the Milanese ambassador to France put it in 1474. It is an ancient state long subsumed in a modern one, the United Kingdom, to the extent that until 1900 at least, Scots abroad were happy to be called 'English'. In the James Bond films of the 1960s and early 1970s, Sean Connery, despite his long-standing Scottish nationalism and clear accent, continues happily to answer to this description. It is therefore not much wonder that Scotland is still (though less than before) confused with England by Americans and other Europeans. This book is not concerned with Scottish nationalism in its various forms; but it is important to be clear enough intellectually to recognise that the very fact of reading (and writing) a history of Scotland, particularly one which continues after 1707, is an acknowledgement of the country as a discrete place, a somewhere with continuity enough still to be recognised on the surface of the planet, and thus not simply a location of the imagination, or the divisive, flexible and historically challenged theories of nationalism which reflect the symptoms of globalisation without historicising the process which has brought their own theories into the arena of debate. I have no time to deal with these in detail here, but such issues are more broadly treated in my *Scottish Nationality* (2001) and *Celtic Identity and the British Image* (1999). The important thing to note is that the idea of identities as constructs is one which itself is a response to the erosion of both natural and cultural boundaries, and is itself part of the process it seeks to explain. Scotland's cultural distinctiveness, which in 1960 saw people work on Christmas Day and celebrate New Year for half a week, is, by many measures, less than it was. Scotland's natural boundaries have, thanks to improvement and the railway age, long seemed so nugatory that they are often forgotten, even by historians. Britain itself seems but a small island in a world photographed from orbit, an image which it is all too easy to forget was unknown less than half a century ago.[2]

Yet to understand Scotland's historical past and the present fruits of that past as distinct, we must understand the natural features which helped to make a separate country in northern Britain possible, and the only way to do this is to travel the roads of the past. History is basically an explanatory story, a tale born of questions: that is what the Greek word means, and that is what Herodotus, the earliest Greek historian, was – an asker of questions and a teller of tales. Such a history is a literature of the past, born both of the past's sources and the present's imagination. Since the Enlightenment in particular, the quest for a scientific, accurate and scholarly history has made differing kinds of history more possible and has removed the practice of history from that of literature to a greater degree, to the extent that history as story, narrative history, can seem quite elementary and inadequate to a modern professional historian. The history of a country must nonetheless be to some extent a story, but in the history that follows, the reader will encounter different kinds of historical approach: the economic, cultural, social, military and geographic pasts of Scotland will not be neglected.

When Sir Walter Scott described his country in *The Lay of the Last Minstrel* (1805) as 'Land of the mountain and the flood' he was assuredly presenting Scotland in the picturesque mode popular in the Britain of his generation, but he was also stating a truth easy to overlook: that rocks and water have been crucially important features in the formation of the human settlement of Scotland before history, and in its development as a nation within history. In this sense, the geography of Scotland is a key measure of what Fernand Braudel identified as *la longue durée* which made the Scottish nation possible, and to a degree controlled the patterns of its historical events. In the section which follows, it will be seen that Scotland was almost an island in the mind of the ancients and in some of the major conflicts of its history: peninsular in a sense hard to acknowledge today. The minds of the past, the *outillage mental* identified by Lucien Febvre, can hardly be explored fully in the confines of a short history such as the present one, but the lived experience and mental apparatus of vanished centuries will be two of the more important watchwords of this narrative. What E.P. Thompson has called in another context 'the enormous condescension of posterity' is one from which Scottish history has too often suffered. All history is posterity, but it ceases to condescend when it visits the past as another country. Any history of Scotland must be one where the imagined country of its present readers does not exist in the mind of the past. And yet, for all that, 'knowledge of history' is, in Lord Acton's words, 'choice of ancestors' – insofar as we choose the past we want to portray, history is imagination and interpretation. What follows attempts to engage with the alien quality of the past, while accepting that the reason we want to read a history of Scotland at all is because there was, and is, and probably will be a place called Scotland, which by name and culture owes a direct debt to those who in the past called themselves Scots, whatever (and this I hope to show) they meant by it.[3]

GEOGRAPHY AND SETTLEMENT

Millions of years ago, Scotland was separated from England by sea, but this fact is less important to its separateness in historical time than are the geological events of the last 20,000 years. Unlike England (where the south escaped), Scotland was deeply and entirely covered by glaciers in the last ice age. As the ice receded, millions of tons of ground-down rock was washed out of the mountains to form the river-terraces and rolling hills of the lowlands, in a landscape originally far more bare and bleak than that we know today. Mountainous formations combined with water discharged from the melting ice in the glens and sea lochs to create a distinctive land formation covered with woodland, 'oak, ash and elm' in the south, 'birch, rowan and pine' in the north, though the idea of a 'national' Great Wood is perhaps a romantic myth. Marshland was common in the flatter areas, but the glaciers also left vast expanses of well-drained sand and gravel behind them.

Wolves, bears, lynx, vipers and wildcat roamed a land also populated by deer, boar, wild oxen and many seals. Scotland's fauna resembled that of Scandinavia and Canada slightly more than that of southern England. Both the southern uplands and the highlands rose from the plain, the latter almost reaching the coast in the north-east at a place called the Mounth, but a greater natural boundary than either was the now invisible frontier formed by the moss of the Forth at Stirling, which made the land to the north a 'virtual island'. As Peter McNeill and Hector MacQueen note in their *Atlas of Scottish History to 1707* (1996), it was the marshlands which separated the Firth of Forth from the western mountains and which cut off northern Scotland from the south. Fording the Forth at Stirling was the only clear route north until the moss 'was drained almost a century after the Union', which is why controlling Stirling was so crucial for most of Scotland's history. Stirling was the 'brooch' which pinned the country north and south of the Forth–Clyde line together. North of it in the early centuries of Scotland's historical existence lay 'Alba', the Pictish and early Scottish core; south of it, land over which Scots, Britons and Northumbrian Angles competed, and where the only significant Anglian settlement of Scotland took place. To read Scotland's history along the Highland Line, which runs from Aberfoyle to Dunkeld and Dunkeld to Ballater before retreating to the west, is less informative than understanding the geographical boundary of

Forth–Clyde, only 60 km wide, and narrowing to a point at Stirling. As the Roman historian Tacitus wrote:

> The Clyde and the Forth . . . are separated only by a narrow neck of land. This isthmus was now firmly held by garrisons, and the whole expanse of country to the south was safely in our hands. The enemy had been pushed into what was virtually another island.
>
> (*Agricola*, ch. 23)[4]

Along the frontiers of this 'virtual island', the Romans built the Antonine Wall, Wallace fought at Stirling Bridge in 1297, and Bruce at Bannockburn in 1314. In these two battles, water and marsh helped to give inferior Scottish forces victories which defined the existence of the Scottish state, while as late as 1645 victory at Kilsyth on the same frontier gave Montrose brief control of Scotland. Throughout history to 1707, most of the greatest defeats suffered by Scotland or its predecessor polities took place south of this line, and their most critical victories often occurred on it or north of it. The famous early English *Mappa Mundi* at Hereford Cathedral shows Scotland north of Forth–Clyde as peninsular, connected to the rest of Britain by a mere isthmus. While this exaggerates the geographical reality, it is an important insight into the medieval mind. Scotland is some 35 per cent of the landmass of Great Britain (England 56 per cent, Wales 9 per cent), and 75 per cent of Scotland lies north of Forth–Clyde.

Human beings were in what we now call Scotland in 8000–7000 BC, shortly after the ice receded. These were Mesolithic (Middle Stone Age) hunter-gatherers and fishers, living in caves (mainly in the west) or constructing tents or windbreaks from poles and skins, nomadic in their pursuit of food (which included significant quantities of nuts and vegetables), but using a large range of tools. As their numbers grew, the lack of bison, reindeer and mammoth in Scotland may have acted as a catalyst towards the development of farming. By *c.* 4000–3500 BC Neolithic farmers began to control and tame the land. Plants were no longer merely gathered but also grown, and animals began to be reared (rather than hunted) for meat. There is also evidence of 'human management' of Scotland's woodlands. It is a matter of debate how far these changes were due to local development and how much to incomers from continental Europe: animals and cereals were both imported. The main tool used by the farmers was the axe, and axe blades were manufactured in Orkney and near Killin in Perthshire, whence they were possibly traded 'over considerable distances' within Scotland, although it is important to be aware of the dangers of an anachronistic reading of any Neolithic 'trading', which was not conceived of in terms of market efficiency. Scotland's early farmers found land travel in the dense forests and mountains difficult, and tended to travel by water. Waterways were to remain more important than land travel in parts of Scotland until the later Middle Ages. On land, complex buildings appeared. At Balbridie in Aberdeenshire there is a Neolithic building with a 240 square metre floor area, built in *c.* 3600 BC, which is both sophisticated and similar to other northern European structures. A similar building has been found near Callendar.[5]

Even in *c.* 4000 BC, distinct regional differences were emerging in what we now call Scotland, but was then part of the network of interrelated areas of cultural practice throughout the island of Britain, for which there can be no grand narrative of nationality that remains true to its sources. Yet subsequent identities may have been influenced by the regional distinctions of the remote past. In the north-east of Scotland the dead were buried (probably after the removal of flesh) in timber structures which were then sealed under long mounds of earth or stone; in Angus and East Perthshire similar timber structures were sealed under round mounds, but some cremation took place; immediately to the south-west, in Stirlingshire, stone chambers were covered (but not sealed) by stone cairns. The division between the north-east and Angus/Perthshire in the later Neolithic is marked by the almost mutually exclusive distribution of two types of ceremonial site – henge monuments to the south and the so-called recumbent stone circles to the north, implying by their different architecture different religious practices and (possibly) social structures. These complex regional varieties indicate that there was quite possibly a profound spiritual dimension to the life of Neolithic people.

The farmers cleared woodland with their axes, built timber houses, and planted wheat or barley on the land until it was exhausted, while their livestock grazed around. Pottery appeared for the first time. Most of these settlements left little long-term evidence of human presence, but in the later Neolithic settlement at Skara Brae in Orkney the farmers' houses were built of stone dug into the earth, and roofed with turf lined with wood or bones, to protect the community from the driving winds on the island. These houses, concealed by sand until the nineteenth century, seem at first sight remarkably modern in their furnishing. There are stone dressers, recessed beds (still a feature of Scottish architecture up to the nineteenth century) and wall cupboards. Peat burned in a central hearth, and its smoke rose through a hole in the roof. Food and water were kept in underfloor containers. The void between the stone inner and outer walls was packed with earth, and sunken stone-lined passageways connected the houses with each other. The farmers who lived there kept sheep and cattle, hunted deer and fished. At Maes Howe, 15 km from Skara Brae, a complex stone tomb was built, indicating a developed ritual life among the settlers on the mainland of Orkney, while at Calanais (Callanish) in Lewis, there is another ritual complex.[6]

Skara Brae cannot be regarded as necessarily typical of later Neolithic dwellings (indeed even elsewhere in Orkney there is an example of seaweed thatch to set against its turf): but it is better preserved, having been abandoned by 'about 1500 BC', being perhaps overwhelmed by a sandstorm. By this time, bronze had been in use on the mainland for some 500 years, possibly brought by settlers from continental Europe. Whether or not it was imported, the use of bronze spread rapidly. A warmer climate had helped farming and encouraged population growth, with land cultivable up to 300 m in places: indeed, 'land may have been used as extensively and populated as densely around 1000 BC as it was in AD 1300'. Many of the workers in the new metal clustered in Strathdee and Strathdon, following much the same style of life as their Stone Age ancestors, planting crops and raising livestock, including pigs. They used a wider range of tools and utensils, and smelted bronze into daggers, spears, swords, chisels and other tools in charcoal furnaces, while making a range of ornaments, armour and utensils from sheets of bronze, and even gold. Because tin was needed to mix with copper to make bronze, and because Scotland was without tin, trade had to be extensively developed in order to keep the Bronze Age people supplied with their necessary raw materials. The nearest tin was in Cornwall and Scandinavia, and other metals (such as gold) or goods had to be traded in exchange. Mobility was aided after *c.* 1000 BC by the development of the wheel. Given the importance of artifacts to trade in a moneyless society, the craftsman's status must have been high. Indeed, the later Scottish state remained without its own coinage until the twelfth century, although Celtic coins from the south and Roman issues circulated by the later Iron Age. The Celtic coinage of Gaul and south-east Britain was itself ultimately modelled on the Macedonian coinage of Alexander the Great's father, Philip (r. 359–336 BC).[7]

By 700 BC, iron had begun to be used in Scotland. The components of iron were commoner than bronze, but it required skilled workers, blacksmiths, to smelt it, as its melting-point was higher, and had to take place in a furnace ventilated by bellows. Craftsmen also continued to make artifacts of bronze and gold, and wool and leather were also worked. These users of iron became known to history (though not originally to themselves) as Celts, and they began to live in the ways later recorded for an earlier posterity by Roman authors. In their domestic lives, like their predecessors, the Celts built wattle and daub houses (a technique still in use until early modern times) and a thatched roof was supported on beams over a central hearth on a clay floor. In parts of Scotland with few trees, buildings might be of stone. These living conditions were not very different from those at Skara Brae, and the Iron Age Celts too were farmers, though perhaps more given to raising livestock than crops, a fact possibly connected with their warlike society. Dwellings were frequently gathered together in one of the more than 1,500 hillforts in Scotland (half of the British Iron Age total – Wales has many of the rest), which ranged in size from some 5,000 square metres (0.5 hectares) to 10 hectares or more (the Roman town of Pompeii, which had a population of up to 30,000, covers just over 30 hectares). Eildon Hill north has 16 hectares of enclosed defences and 500 houses, though it is not clear that these represented a permanent settlement. Houses were clustered together on the top of the hill surrounded by a massive wall of rubble faced with stone, up to 5 m thick, laced with wood and crowned with a wooden palisade. These forts, as their name suggests, were ill-adapted to defend low-lying arable land from raids, but livestock could be withdrawn within the circuit of their outer walls, a stronghold for the moveable wealth of the people.

Such a society may itself have been the result of deteriorating climatic conditions, which led to hill-farming becoming more marginal, increased population pressure on arable land, and promoted fortification and the circulation of weapons, including the bow, known since the Neolithic period. Hillforts were not the only means by which settlers protected their jobs and communities. In the crannog, or loch dwelling (inhabited as late as the 1600s in some cases) an artificial island was constructed on a raft bounded with timber posts on which a house was built in the wattle and daub manner, but on a large scale, being up to 165 square metres in area. A harbour was made on the loch side of the raft, and a causeway on the land side to the farmer's fields from whence the settlers could withdraw to their crannog if under threat. Hundreds of crannogs survive in Scotland; they could of course be used for occupation as well as defence. On lower-lying land in the north and west, often near the coast (though there are inland examples), another defensible dwelling, the broch, was built from *c.* 100 BC: a stone tower up to 15 m high with a low entrance, 'multiple internal floors' and an inner courtyard of some 50 square metres, too small to shelter livestock. The broch (like the crannog) was possibly a house for elite farmers: it certainly foreshadows the design of the later Scottish tower house. More than 500 brochs survive in areas from Shetland to the Rhins of Galloway, though the bulk of them are in Orkney, Shetland, the Hebrides and round the Pentland Firth coast – prime targets for the sea raiders, whether Romans, pirates or others, whom the broch builders feared. Brochs continued to be used up to *c.* AD 800, and were occasionally used for defence against the Vikings as late as the twelfth century. In the fertile lowlands, increasingly being developed by farming, timber roundhouses were equally common, being built up to 18 m in diameter, with roofs up to 10 m high.[8]

Crannogs, hillforts and brochs were features of social organisation in early Scotland which depended significantly on the mountainous quality of the country's geography and its generous helping of inland waterways, sea lochs and coast – Scotland has appreciably more coastline than England and Wales combined. Though crannogs and hillforts are found elsewhere in Britain, Scotland has a strong concentration of the latter, and brochs are unique. This was the 'Land of the mountain and the flood', the two key features of Scotland's geography of settlement which helped to form a nationality. In a country with so many defensible strongholds by land and water, tribal conflict and emulation were hardly likely to disappear swiftly.

ROMAN SCOTLAND

Following two inconclusive raids by Julius Caesar a century before, Rome undertook a serious invasion of what was to become the Roman province of Britannia ('Britain', but not to be confused with the whole island) in AD 43, with the 2nd (Augusta), 9th (Hispana), 14th (Gemina) and 20th (Valeria Victrix) legions under the general command of Aulus Plautius. Each legion was the size of a modern brigade, divided into 10 cohorts (battalions), each divided into 6 centuries (companies) of 80 men, except for the first, the *Cohors Millenaria*, which had ten. Subsequent European (and now global) military organisation to this day follows the Roman model, from the lance-corporal's fire team (the Roman squad of eight) through the captain or major's company and lieutenant colonel's battalion to the brigade, although in an age of smaller armies the legion was deployed more like the modern major-general's division than the brigade. Even Napoleon's invention of the army corps, with multiple arms under one command, was foreshadowed by the Roman use of auxiliary units within the legionary command chain. By AD 50 England to 'Trent, Severn, and Dee' lay within the Roman frontier.[9]

'Britannia', the title of the Roman province, has, as Norman Davies and others have argued, underpinned both the historic description and modern notion of 'Britain'. For commentators on the classical world such as Harold Mattingley, the Roman province can seem isomorphic with 'our island', while as Norman Davies points out, Roman Britannia occupied barely a third of the British Isles and half of Britain proper. The extent to which Great Britain has been (and is often still) defined in terms of customs and culture from south of Hadrian's Wall will become clearer as this book progresses. To the Romans, the island was a patchwork of tribes. Ptolemy (Claudius Ptolemaeus), the second-century Alexandrian geographer, identified them in a map of the island of Britain which in Scotland 'depended largely' on information gained in Agricola's campaigns. Ptolemy placed the Novantae in Galloway, the Selgovae in the Borders, the Votadini in Lothian and Damnonii in Central Scotland, with various tribes between Forth–Clyde and the Moray Firth, of whom the Caledonii were the chief. Caledonia became the name the Romans gave to this entire region, though whether it actually developed towards political unity, or was merely given a group identity as the unconquered 'other' is still a matter for debate. During the Roman occupation of Britannia, the Caledonians became called the 'Picts' (possibly *picti*: painted ones). The language they spoke differed from that of tribes like the Votadini (the later Gododdin), who, like other Britons, spoke an early form of Welsh. There were also probably Gaelic speakers in the south-west and elsewhere, but this group is not readily identifiable from Roman sources – one of the reasons that an 'invasion' of the Scots has been posited. Yet the Gaelic myths and such early evidence as there is suggests a long-standing settlement of the 'sea-divided Gael' in Antrim and Argyll, Dál Riata. Many problems remain in analysing the linguistic and ethnic make-up of early Scotland, with mixed language elements evident in a variety of places in the country.

Gnaeus Julius Agricola (AD 40–93) had been a young military tribune at the defeat of Boudicca's (Boadicea's) Iceni revolt in AD 60. As governor of the province of Britain from 78, he sought further military glory in the conquest of Scotland (though it has recently been argued that Roman forces had already begun to penetrate there), and even considered an attack on Ireland. Both areas were marginal military goals for the Empire, the pursuit of which perhaps hastened Agricola's recall in 84. In AD 78, he began by re-conquering north Wales and Ynys Môn (Anglesey), advancing on the east coast to the Tay in 80. The next year, he fortified the crucial Forth–Clyde line: the Votadini, with their fortress on Eildon Hill, submitted, and Agricola built a Roman fort near it at Newstead. In 82, Agricola was in Galloway and Ayr, and in 83 marched up the east coast north of Tay with his fleet in attendance, closing off the eastern glens with forts. In AD 84 came his victory over the Caledonians at Mons Graupius, possibly near the Moray Firth, possibly at Bennachie near Old Rayne in Aberdeenshire. As at Nechtansmere in AD 685, an invader sought control of Scotland north of Forth–Clyde by the east coast route, but unlike Ecgfrith, Agricola was victorious. After his recall to Rome in AD 84, the northern forts were soon abandoned, including, in 87, the 'great fortress at Inchtuthil', where 1,000,000 nails were buried to deny them to the Caledonians. Over the next twenty years, forts from central Scotland to Corbridge in Northumberland were burnt. The 9th Hispana, sent north to relieve the garrisons, may have suffered a severe defeat at the hands of the Caledonians and their allies.[10]

A clear-cut northern frontier was a necessity, and one was created shortly after AD 120 by Hadrian's Wall, which ran from the Tyne to the Solway, followed in AD 142 (after a campaign which reached into Angus) by the Antonine Wall on the Forth–Clyde line from Old Kilpatrick to Cramond. Although troops were withdrawn from the Antonine Wall after a generation, and it was not occupied after the death of Septimius Severus (whose reign saw a scorched-earth policy in southern Scotland) in AD 211, Rome continued to have some control between the Tyne and Forth, although it was sufficiently uncertain for three imperial campaigns to be necessary in the third and fourth centuries AD. Forth–Clyde remained the key frontier which separated Scotland from 'Britannia' and the Roman world, the Roman view of Britain as 'a double-headed axe' bearing sufficient witness to its distinguishing geographical importance. As the present author argues in *Scottish Nationality* (2001), Roman control in Scotland between AD 80 and AD 400 foreshadows that of Northumbria from AD 650 to AD 1000 – a tenuous grasp in the south combined with an inability or unwillingness to deploy the resources necessary to venture a prolonged attack on the north, easily accessible benorth Forth only by the vulnerable east coast route.[11]

Tacitus identified the Caledonians as Germanic, an ethnic characterisation subsequently far more influential on the theories of the Enlightenment than his equally unlikely identification of the Silures of Wales with the Spaniards. The German predisposition to freedom, identified by Tacitus as a propagandistic counterweight in his history to the Roman autocracy and corruption he saw in his own day, was used after the Reformation to bolster ideas of Protestant Anglo-Saxon manifest destiny. In Tacitus, it is found most famously in the speech the Roman historian attributed to the Caledonian leader Calgacus at Mons Graupius, who claims to represent 'the last of the free', and famously accuses the Romans of making a desolation and calling it peace: *'Solitudinem faciunt pacem appellant'* (*Agricola*, Tacitus, ch. 30).

Yet the distinctions which were to divide Scotland and England into two separate kingdoms within one island were not, and would never be, essentially ethnic, despite the eighteenth- and nineteenth-century historiographical fascination with Anglo-Saxon 'invasions' as creating a genetic transformation as well as a cultural change in England. Indeed, as the recent publicity over the DNA links between Stone Age and modern inhabitants of Cheddar Gorge makes clear, it is more than possible that underlying genetic differences within groups are very limited over time, in Scotland as well as in England. Instead, there were two great differences: the first geographical, where the mountains and waterways of Scotland both influenced its social organisation and forced into similar moulds Anglo-Saxon and Roman attempts to subdue it. Like Agricola in the first century, Athelstan marched up the narrow lowland east coast route shadowed by his fleet in the tenth, while without this source of intelligence, supply and military intimidation, Ecgfrith and the host of Northumbria perished there in AD 685. Scotland's geography was deeply influential both on internal society and external invasion.

Secondly, just as the Roman province of 'Britain', which at no time included much of Scotland, became influential on the historic notions of Britain and Britishness which still endure (in a history which begins with 'Roman Britain', how many children can discern that the Roman province occupied only half the modern state?), so the frontier of Britannia at Hadrian's Wall still exercises a profound hold on modern identity. In England, 'the other side of Hadrian's Wall' is still a term (inaccurately, since 80 km of England lies north of it on the east) used to identify the otherness of Scotland. It was the Wall which divided non-Roman from Roman Britain, and which historically placed Scotland in almost the same relation to the Roman world as Ireland. As John Koch wisely remarks, 'I now believe that the more important division [in Britain] . . . was not the Welsh West against the Anglo-Saxon East, but the surviving ancient division between an ethnically mixed extramural North (the precursor of Scotland) and an ethnically mixed intramural South (the old Roman province)'. 'Alba', 'cognate with Albion' and once the name of the whole of Britain, became the Celtic name for its free northern half, and thence for the successor-kingdom of Scotland.[12]

By AD 200, even allowing for Roman bias, 'it is possible that the first steps were . . . taken towards the creation of a single Pictish kingdom uniting the peoples south of the Mounth [where the mountains almost reach the sea near Aberdeen] under one war-lord'. The Picts have long remained a mystery: even in the twentieth century, writers such as John Buchan (in his story 'No-Man's-Land') could identify them with the fairies. Rather than being a mysterious separate people, as has been sometimes suggested, it is most likely that the name indicates a collective identification of a group of Celtic tribes. If the Picts were not Celtic, as some still suggest, they were not thus differentiated by the Romans. The extent to which they differed ethnically or culturally from the Welsh-speaking Britons who were found in Scotland, or the Gaelic-speaking Celts who might already have been settled in the west is a moot point. It has certainly been suggested recently that the distribution of P-Celtic (Brittonic/Welsh) roots in

Scottish place names (e.g. at Traprain, Fintry, Pencaitland, Perth and Pluscarden), from the north to the south of the country indicate a Brittonic presence in Pictish culture and language. The Picts certainly developed a 'distinctive and unifying culture', which their monuments and art still proclaim. They could also ally with the other peoples north of the Wall (as they did with the Scots in the fourth and fifth centuries) to attack those south of it. By *c.* 400, apart from the Scots in the far south-west of Argyll and the Britons of southern Scotland, Pictish culture predominated throughout the country.[13]

By the end of the third century, the Romans were finding the defence of Hadrian's Wall more difficult, and it was overrun in 367 as part of a general attack on the Roman Empire in Britain, being finally abandoned in 400. The Picts came south by sea, while the Votadini pushed south into Northumberland, to 're-emerge as the Gododdin' in the history of the Dark Ages, although John Koch argues for a less ethnically Celtic Gododdin in the struggles of the sixth and seventh centuries. The Scots, already established in Argyll and Antrim in Ireland, attacked north Wales by sea, while in Galloway, a Roman-derived line of petty kings may have flourished. The Roman world was breaking up, and new polities forming.[14]

ANGLES, PICTS, BRITONS AND SCOTS IN ONE CHURCH

As early as the fourth century, Romano-British influence in Scotland south of Forth–Clyde may have led to the establishment of 'territorial bishops'. However, the Celtic saint conventionally known as Ninian (possibly Uinnian) is credited with evangelising the south-west of Scotland, southern Fife and Angus in *c.* AD 400–500 (now thought more likely to be later than earlier), while St Columba/Colum Cille (521–97), a nobleman of the Uí Néill who came to the Argyll kingdom of Dál Riata from the Gaelic Scots in Ireland across the sea in AD 563, founded the famous monastic community at Iona. He reputedly carried his missions into central and northern Scotland, although the conversion of the northern Picts is perhaps better attributed to Columba's followers and another Gaelic saint, St Donnan, martyred on Eigg in 617. The presence of *cill* names in Gaelic, indicative of a church or Christian burial ground, attests to the early success of Columba's mission, which also helped to create, as in Ireland, a literate community capable of high cultural achievement, such as the magnificence of the Book of Kells, probably composed on Iona and now at Trinity College, Dublin.[15]

Ninian's church in the south-west was known as 'Candida Casa', the 'white house', later known as *hwit aern* in the Saxon tongue, 'Whithorn' today. Although differences of practice evolved in the area of the church evangelised by the Celtic saints (such as those over the dating of Easter resolved at the Synod of Whitby in 664 in which not even all the Celts were in agreement among themselves), it is nonetheless important to note that the church whose word and authority they spread was Catholic, whatever special pleading for its proto-Reformed character was subsequently made (and can still be found, as in the board guides for tourists at Dunkeld Cathedral).

It is certainly important to note that the Columban mission from Iona was not a 'national' mission in any Pictish or Scottish-Irish sense, although it was to become the founding mission of Scottish nationality in a way more profound than even that of St Patrick in Ireland. For the present, however, kingdom and kinship ties were flexible and fluctuating. In AD 635, one of Columba's followers Aidan went from Iona to be a bishop in King Oswy's Northumbria, where he remained a popular figure until his death at Bamburgh in 651. Likewise St Columba was supposed to have appeared to King Oswald of Northumbria in a dream in 634, prophesying him victory over Cadwallon of Gwynedd. Although there is a greater Anglo-Saxon nationalism visible in the writings of the Venerable Bede (*Ecclesiastical History of the English People*, 731), this tends, as Donald Meek has argued, to centre round the argument over the dating of Easter, rather than being self-consciously 'English' as opposed to 'Scottish'.[16]

Nonetheless, Columba's mission boosted the status of kingship, and thus of a single, 'imperial' kingdom, where the king was sovereign. The Cenél nGabráin were a kin-group of the Scots of Dál Riata who had become dominant by the time of Columba, and the saint had a close relationship with them. Adomnán claimed that Columba had laid his hands on King Áedán mac Gabráin of Dál Riata (r. 574–*c.* 608) in 574, and this even was later depicted as similar to Samuel's consecration of Saul and David, anointed kings of Israel as a state and single kingdom. Áedán not only inflicted defeats on the Picts, but may have flouted the authority of the High King/*ard-rí* of Ireland over the Dál Riata Scots, so his claim to such sovereignty is a historically interesting one. In 580, he raided as far as the Orkneys, and in 582 attacked Manaw round Stirling, the lynchpin of central Scotland, control of which was in the following century to be a major goal for those interested in dominating north of Forth–Clyde. He also fought in Man and Ireland. In *c.* 598 and *c.* 603, Áedán was defeated by Pictish and Anglian forces respectively, but such defeats, combined with his earlier campaigns, suggest that he was seeking overlordship over a wider kingdom. Columba's involvement in his claim to rule, stressed by Adomnán, the saint's successor, is thus potentially an important one. Adomnán himself was involved in state affairs: his *Lex Innocentium* of 697 made important humanitarian changes to the conduct of war and other risky businesses, including provision for the protection of women and 'partial culpability for industrial accidents and dangerous workmanship or manufacture'. It was adopted by kings throughout Dál Riata, Pictland and Ireland.

It is arguable that the Columban support for the Cenél nGabráin kin underpins a good many of the later premises of Scottish nationality. By the time of the Declaration of Arbroath (1320), the status of Scotland as the oppressed Israel defended from imperial aggrandisement by Judas Maccabeus was a standard trope for national identity. Combined with a classical tradition derived from Sallust and Tacitus, it became the model for a defensive patriotism which distrusted Empire but was passionately attached to the liberty of the Scottish nation, and which persisted into the Enlightenment (see chapters 3 and 5). Moreover, in laying hands on a king of Dál Riata, Columba was arguably laying the foundations for the political supremacy of the Gaelic-speaking Scots-Irish, of whom he was one. In 918, Columba was the 'protector of Constantín's army . . . his staff Cathbuaid (meaning "battle triumph" in Gaelic) was carried south' with the Scottish forces. In 1314, it was a relic of St Columba which the Scottish army carried with them into battle on the make-or-break occasion of Bannockburn. On the

23

other hand, Columba was also deployed by the Norse against Scots' attempts to recover the Western Isles. Overall, however, the ascendancy of great Gaelic saints among the evangelisers of Scotland contributed to the growing influence of Dál Riata. Dunkeld and Cennrígmonaid/Kilrymont (St Andrews) became the main religious centres in Pictland, the latter established for a relic of St Andrew by Óengus mac Forguso (r. 729–61), although it was already a royal Pictish 'burial-place'. In Strathclyde, St Kentigern/Mungo became bishop of Glasgow in the early seventh century.[17]

By AD 600, a number of polities were beginning to take shape in Scotland. There was a predominantly Gaelic-speaking group of independent kingdoms (Dál Riata), in the west, dominated by the Cenél nGabráin of Kintyre, with a number of other kin-groups: the Cenél Loairn of Lorne, the Cenél nÓengusa of Islay and the Cenél Comguill of Cowal, of which the most prominent was the Cenél Loairn. The high king (ard rí) of Dál Riata was chosen by a group from the chief kins of Cenél Loairn and Cenél nGabráin, and was inaugurated at Dunadd in Argyll, by 'placing his foot in a footprint carved in the rock'. His Gaelic-speaking subjects inhabited the complex of sea, island and peninsula in the south-west. Like the Picts, they were seafarers and traded to Ireland and France. Dál Riata 'held lordship over Irish territory in Antrim' (lost in 639), although to complicate the picture the Picts may also have had control of some of the statelets in Dál Riata. In 736, Óengus mac Forguso, king of the Picts, defeated the Cenél Loairn, and it has been supposed that they may have fled to Moray, where an alternative set of dynastic claimants to what was by then the kingdom of Scotland existed up until the twelfth century.

These Scots were part of the common world of the 'sea-divided Gael' which can be glimpsed in the stories of Deirdre and Naoise, Cú Chulainn and Aoife or the Fenian cycle, and which endured until 1700, and they had customs and social organisation in common with their brethren in Ireland. Like them, they had a hierarchy of loose control and obligation reaching up from the *rí tuaithe*, local or under-king, via the *ruiri* (king of a group of the former) and *rí ruirech*, regional over-king, to the *ard-rígh*, the high kingship. As will be clear later in this book, it is more than likely that the great territorial earldoms of Scotland in the Middle Ages, however overlaid they were with feudal practices, bore a clear relation to the inheritance of Gaelic social organisation. There are many flaws in the persistent use of the nineteenth-century term, 'the clan system', but one of the greatest of them is an inability to distinguish between the great regional magnates, chief of the Name, and 'chieftains' such as Cameron of Lochiel. In later centuries, the grants of heritable jurisdictions, the kinship basis of Scottish society *as a whole*, and the huge 'fighting tails' which noblemen such as the Marquess of Huntly could put into the field, all speak of the continued power of regional magnates, notwithstanding the many moments of change and crisis in the nature of that power, as under Robert I or James II.[18]

By AD 550–600, however, this Gaelic-speaking kingdom had not yet fully developed. The Scots shared Scotland with at least one predominantly Pictish kingdom in central and eastern Scotland and another in the north. These Picts 'lived in extended settlements with underground stores (the 'souterrains') and buried their dead in stone-lined graves under mounds of earth and cairns of stones'. Their symbol stones, many probably carved by 'a small group of specialists' are the most visible sign of their presence in today's Scotland. They were by no means, however, the closed and mysterious people of earlier archaeology, being open to both Northumbrian and Gaelic influences; indeed, by 800 there was perhaps little difference between the Picts and Scots.

In south-western Scotland there was the British kingdom of Strathclyde in the west, bordering on Rheged by Hadrian's Wall; in the east were the Gododdin and the beginnings of an Anglian incursion from the south. John Koch describes the land between Forth and Tees in 600 as 'largely Celtic, but peacefully influenced at its upper levels by a small aristocratic Anglian minority'. The implication of this is that the famous attack by the Gododdin on the Anglians at Catraeth/Catterick in *c.* 540–600, commemorated in the earliest piece of territorially Scottish literature (in early Welsh), was not an ethnic conflict as conceived by traditional histories, but rather an attack by a 'brittonicised pagan Anglian generalissimo' on another group with mixed Brittonic and Anglian speech and manners. The mixture of cultures within the elites of emerging polities was certainly complex, with extensive intermarriage, leading to (usually transient) dynastic unions; a king such as Oswiu of Northumbria might even speak Gaelic.[19]

Whatever the nature of the underlying conflicts however, the newly coalescing Northumbrian polity began to push north, in what is still best termed an Anglian invasion. In 603, Áedán mac Gabráin of Dál Riata was defeated by the Angles at Degsastan in a conflict which Alfred Smyth insists 'can be viewed as a struggle between German and Scot'. Din Eidin/Edinburgh was stormed in 638, and Strathclyde, despite

King Owain's victory in Strathcarron in 642 over a Dál Riata already weakened by the victory of the Uí Néill at Mag Rath which had ended its lordship in Antrim, found itself in its turn unable to withstand Northumbrian power, and fell under its influence from 655 until the battle of Nechtansmere thirty years later. By 650, the Northumbrians controlled Scotland to the Forth, their presence shown in place names such as Tyninghame and Haddington. As their forces reached the Solway, Strathclyde became isolated from Welsh-speakers in the south, and the Anglians, already moving into the power void in Manaw left by Dál Riata's and Strathclyde's defeats, moved to settle in the southern coast of Fife. In 672, Ecgfrith of Northumbria defeated the Picts. In 681, the Northumbrians attacked as far north as the coastal fortress of Dunottar, 25 km south of Aberdeen, and established a bishopric at Abercorn. Fife was a county which 'was to ancient Caledonia what Kent was to England – a rich vast peninsula of farmland offering a secure base to the would-be conqueror'. But Fife was frontier territory beyond Forth–Clyde, and to hold it securely it would be necessary to prevent a descent by the Picts from the higher ground which ran along the coast. The Picts were 'under siege' in Strathearn in 683, and Ecgfrith continued to push north with the warband of Northumbria.

At Dunnichen, not far from Forfar and a little inland in Angus, their road passed between the high ground of Dunnichen Hill on the left and marshland on the right, Dunnichen Moss or Nechtansmere. Here, in one of the two or three most decisive battles in Scottish history, Bridei son of Beli's (r. 672–93) Pictish-Brittonic army charged down from the high ground and swept the Northumbrians into the moss:

few escaped. Just as at Stirling Bridge in 1297, Inverlochy in 1645 or Killiecrankie in 1689, a descent from high ground against an enemy trapped by water was decisive. The mountain and the flood ended Anglian intrusion north of Forth.

Bridei son of Beli was Owain of Strathclyde's brother, and it is possible that the dynastic links between the royal houses of Pictland and Strathclyde may have meant that Bridei was able to unite the strength of their warbands, but whether or not this was the case, Nechtansmere changed the shape of Scottish history. The bishop of Abercorn fled to Whitby, Northumbria fell back to the Forth, Strathclyde re-emerged into independence. Subsequent battles in 698 and 711 which saw neither side gain an upper hand, led to the establishment of a frontier, possibly at the Pentland Hills. North of this, the Pictish king Óengus mac Forguso (r. 729–61) may have transitorily united all Scotland between Forth–Clyde and the Moray Firth, when he allied with Northumbria to subdue the kingdom of Strathclyde's stronghold at Dumbarton and sacked Dál Riata. Victory at Nechtansmere placed Scotland once more out of the conqueror's orbit, and although the frontier lay at the Antonine rather than Hadrian's Wall, Alba, consolidated by resistance, was on the verge of becoming a state in a recognisable sense. One last ingredient was missing: the Vikings.[20]

TWO

NECHTANSMERE TO LARGS: TERRITORY, IDENTITY AND LANGUAGE

TERRITORY

As the most powerful realms in the northern part of the island, the Pictish and Northumbrian kingdoms continued to have both cultural and diplomatic links in the eighth century. Alliance with the Northumbrians enabled the Picts to extend a sphere of influence both into Strathclyde and Dál Riata itself after 740, although this prompted King Óengus to ally with the Britons against Northumbria. Among Óengus's successors, Constantín (r. 789–820) gained enough power to set up his son as a king in Dál Riata, and by the beginning of the ninth century 'the power, prosperity and machinery of the Pictish kingdom laid the foundations for the Scottish one that would take its place'.[1]

By this time, however, both kingdoms were facing a fresh threat in the shape of Viking (principally Norse but also Danish) attack and immigration, which encroached on both the Pictish north and the Scottish west, where the Vikings attacked in 794, five years after the first raid on Saxon Wessex. In 795, following attacks on Northumbrian ecclesiastical centres at Lindisfarne and Jarrow, the Vikings 'devastated Skye and Iona: the latter's sanctuary was to be attacked twice more by 806'. Given the importance of the Abbot of Iona, this was a serious threat to the religious identity of Dál Riata and perhaps the other Scottish kingdoms.[2]

Heavy Scandinavian settlement took place in the north, in Orkney, Shetland, Caithness and Sutherland from 800, with the *jarl* of Orkney becoming by the middle of the century the central figure in what was to be a semi-autonomous polity. By 850, the Norse were in the Hebrides, and in 892 Sigurd the Mighty, 1st *jarl* of Orkney, defeated the Mormaer of Moray, the great steward or *rí ruirech*, under-king in the north of the new Scottish kingdom. For the next four centuries, Norwegian power was to have a significant effect on the course of Scottish history, and not only on the west coast, where the decisive encounter which recovered Man, the inner Hebrides and Largs, was not fought until 1263, and where Rothesay Castle on Bute fell to the Norwegians as late as 1230. Caithness and to an extent all Scotland north of the Great Glen was under Viking influence up to AD 1000, while Scandinavian settlements in the western mainland reached up the banks of the Clyde. Not only did Orkney and Shetland/Hjaltland belong to Norway until the fifteenth century, but Norse influence was felt on the mainland too, with Aberdeen being raided as late as 1151. In northern Scotland, the story of the Norse settlement from 891 is told in the *Orkneyinga Saga*.[3]

If the Vikings caused problems for the Picts and Scots, this was even truer for Northumbria. After Lindisfarne was raided in 793, the Northumbrians were under frequent threat from the Vikings, culminating in the defeat of King Osbert in 867 and the establishment three years later of the Danish kingdom of York/Jorvik in Deira (southern Northumbria), after many years when a vast *wicinga here* (Viking army) had harried deep into Anglian territory. Many Anglians were driven north of Tyne into Bernicia, Northumberland and south-east Scotland, where there may also have been 'Anglo-Danish' settlement. The Northumbrian polity between Tees and Forth was any case in decline. In 827 Egbert of Wessex declared himself *bretwalda* (overlord of Britain – i.e. the Roman province, though from this Wales was now excluded, being separated from England by the dyke built under the orders of Offa of Mercia (r. 757–96) and the earlier Wat's Dyke), thus beginning a continuous period of southern domination of the English kingdom. Earlier kings in Northumbria had also used the title; it indicated little in the way of practical overlordship, being more of a statement of being first among equals, but the fact that no monarch from outwith the House of Wessex could claim it again spelt the beginning of the end for Northumbrian power.

Strathclyde continued to be independent, but whereas the Pictish struggles with Northumbria had delivered Scotland north of Forth–Clyde from Anglian power (including Dál Riata in the west), Northumbria remained powerful in the south in the eighth century. In 731, an Anglian bishopric was established at Whithorn, and in 752 the plain of Kyle was conquered by the Northumbrians, whose hold on this area was nonetheless uncertain, beginning to disintegrate after 800. Even so, Brittonic Strathclyde was under persistent pressure elsewhere; driven out of West Lothian, it probably retreated to a western stretch of territory within Renfrewshire, Lanarkshire, Dunbartonshire and the Ayrshire and Galloway coast, where by the ninth century it was vulnerable to the Vikings, who took Dumbarton Rock, its fortress capital, in 871. Eighteen years later, Domnall II mac Constantín of Scotland attacked Strathclyde, and the kingdom was reduced to effective dependency on the Scottish crown. It continued to have an quasi-independent existence however, with a new royal centre based at Govan on the Clyde, until the beginning of the eleventh century.[4]

The Scots were driven east (though they were by no means immune to attack there) by Viking pressure on the western seaboard. They had already fought intermittently with the Picts, and by a combination of intermarriage and political conflict (the exact proportions of which remain in doubt) the two polities became integrated. There is evidence of joint kingship from the early ninth century under Constantín (who placed a 'new ecclesiastical foundation' at Dunkeld) and Óengus II mac Forguso (r. 820–34). Kenneth MacAlpin/Cinaed mac Ailpín (king of Dál Riata from 840) traditionally became joint king of Dál Riata and at least southern Pictland from 843–7, including Fortriu (Kinross, East Perthshire and Fife), which had some of the best agricultural land in Scotland, and the Pictish centres of Scone and Abernethy. Given the converging history of the two peoples, it is likely that Cinaed's success was less of a radical disjunction than tradition alleges. In 849, as another Viking host appeared on the western seaboard, the relics of Iona and other western islands were transferred to mainland Scotland, with St Columba's 'bones and treasures' being moved to Dunkeld ('Fortress of the Caledonians') in what is now Perthshire. The king's court moved with them to Scone, 30 km to the south, a likely Pictish centre which was certainly a Scottish royal centre by

906, a place of 'assembly' where laws were promulgated. Struggles with the Vikings for central Scotland continued: Cinaed's son, Constantín I mac Cinaeda (r. 862–77) fought the Danes at Dollar in Clackmannanshire in 875, and was killed by them two years later. His nephew, Constantín II mac Aeda (r. 900–43) contained the threat to the new kingdom's heartland in defeating the Vikings in Strathearn in 904. In his reign, the new emerging kingdom of Scotland, called 'Alba', can be discerned as bordered by the Moray Firth, the Forth and the central Highlands, with Vikings in the north and west.[5]

After the defeat of Northumbria by the Danes, the new larger Scottish kingdom had the opportunity to extend its frontier beyond the Forth, although the new kingdom's aggressive intentions were already plain under Cinaed mac Ailpín, who attacked Northumbria 'no fewer than six times', burning Dunbar and Melrose. Domnall II mac Constantín (r. 889–900) attacked Strathclyde, and his successor Constantín II mac Aeda (r. 900–43) pushed south of Forth into Lothian, possibly advancing to the Tweed. By this time the Danes of York were under pressure from a renascent Anglo-Saxon polity, the kingdom of England, led by the dynasty of Wessex under Edward the Elder (r. 899–924) and Athelstan (r. 924–39), who retook York in 927, after an interval when the incumbent Danes had lost control to Norse adventurers. Constantín and his Strathclyde allies were also Edward's military inferiors, and the Scottish monarch acknowledged Edward as 'father and lord' to avoid trouble. This formula was a painless route to peace with a superior foe which gained him nothing but 'a nebulous claim to suzerainty, and usually a personal suzerainty at that, not one yielded in perpetuity'.

However, such acknowledgements, repeated more than once throughout the centuries, formed ammunition for English claims to feudal overlordship of Scotland under the Plantagenets and Tudors. Athelstan in fact seems to have believed in his right to the subjugation of Scotland (which made a submission to him in 927), naming himself not merely *bretwalda*, but *basileus*, 'emperor'. Eadgar the Peaceable (r. 959–75) also later claimed to be 'king of the English, and of the other peoples dwelling within the bounds of the island of Britain', a possible statement of entitlement to the island and not merely the Roman province. To make matters more complicated, however, a contemporary chronicler, celebrating the House of Wessex's victory over the Vikings, wrote that 'Britain is now called England, thereby assuming the name of the victors'. The word 'Britain' can never be read back into the Middle Ages in the clear terms we might expect, and neither can the formulae adopted by Scottish kings in negotiation with their stronger southern rivals.

Such forms of words appear to have mattered little to the Scots, and this was clear when Athelstan's forces raided Scotland as far as Dunottar near Stonehaven in 934, in order to try and keep Constantín under control, taking his son as hostage. For his part Constantín, with the support of Owain MacDomnuill of Strathclyde, concluded an alliance with the Danes of York, Olaf Guthfrithson of Dublin and Aralt of Man in support of his invasion of England in 937 in an attempt to turn the balance of power. It ended in disastrous defeat at Brunanburgh, possibly on the southern frontier of Northumbria in the Wirral or Humberside, by the Anglo-Saxon forces of Athelstan, who thus triumphed over Scot and Briton, Norse and Dane in a single battle, becoming the preeminent *beaga brytta*, lord of the rings, a title which evinced the powers of patronage (and hence authority) of Saxon noblemen.[6]

Constantín withdrew, but Scotland remained stable enough to allow him to retire to an abbey in 943, being succeeded by Mael Coluim (Malcolm) I macDomnuill (r. 943–54), the first Scottish king to explicitly identify himself with the kingdom's founding saint, being 'servant of Columba', who had already been the protector of the Scots army under his cousin and predecessor, Constantín. Scotland had benefited from the conquest of Northumbria by the Danes, and although the new kingdom of England centred on Wessex was a more formidable military threat, it was a far more remote one. This cut both ways: if the kings of England cared little for territory in Scotland, and were unlikely to pursue extended campaigns there, it was also the case that Scotland could no longer hurt the core territories of England in Winchester and the south. Unless ruled by a strong king such as Athelstan, however, England might lack the military will to defend the old Northumbrian territories, and one Scottish king after another took advantage of this. Eadmund (r. 939–46), Athelstan's brother, may have in 945 ceded 'Cumbria' to King Mael Coluim, an area probably to be identified with the old Northumbrian territories of west and south Ayrshire and Galloway rather than Cumberland and Westmorland in northern England, on the fairly meaningless condition that the king of Scots 'be his helper both on sea and land'. Far from being helpful, Mael Coluim raided to the Tees in 948, by which time Eadred (r. 946–55) was struggling to recover Jorvik from Eric Bloodaxe of Norway, finally succeeding in 954. In the same year, the Anglian Earl of Northumbria gave up Edinburgh to King Idulb mac Constantín (r. 954–62) on regaining control of York, while Eadgar, king in Mercia and Northumbria from 957 and of all England from 959–75, ceded Lothian to Cinaed II mac Maíle Coluim (r. 971–95) in 973. This cessation was reputedly accompanied by an act of Scottish 'homage' which remained contentious right up to the debates on Anglo-Scottish Union in the early eighteenth century. The tale was that Eadgar had been rowed on the Dee at Chester by eight kings of whom he was the overlord, including the King of Scots, and this remained into the twentieth century a narrative building-block in the story of England's historic rise to ascendancy over the whole island. Whatever was the case, Lothian was retaken by the Northumbrians by 1000, but this was to be the last period of Anglo-Saxon control. Mael Coluim II mac Cinaeda (r. 1005–34) found his way clear to winning back what is today south-eastern Scotland for good, faced as he was by the weak Aethelred II Unraed (the uncounselled, r. 978–1013; 1014–16) in the south. Moving south of Tweed, Mael Coluim laid siege to Durham, and at Carham in 1018 he and his Strathclyde allies (henceforth integrated into the Scottish kingdom following the death of its sub-king Owain in the battle) defeated the forces of the Earl of Northumbria to establish Scotland as a single kingdom from Caithness to the Tweed, although both Moray and Galloway (see below) remained (as Northumberland itself and Cornwall did in medieval England) less than fully integrated.[7]

Whatever the transient successes of English monarchs against the Scottish kingdom in the north, from now on the territorial target of that kingdom was the conquest and integration of as much (and preferably all) of historic Northumbria as possible, as far south as Hadrian's Wall, which would thus have restored the old frontier between Roman Britannia and non-Roman Alba. Control over Northumbria repeatedly remained a goal for the kings of Scots, at least until Alexander II mac William renounced the right to its earldom in 1237. Mael Coluim attempted to go further than the Wall in integrating the Welsh-speakers of Cumberland and Westmorland, but was driven back by Cnut (r. 1016–35), whose forces reached the Tay in 1031. Once again the Scottish king backed down; once again he lived to fight another day, and a pattern became established whereby a weak or absent English king would risk facing persisting Scottish raiding (if not attempts at wholesale military conquest) in the northern counties, a shape of events which arguably lasted until the defeat at Flodden in 1513. From the reign of Mael Coluim II to that of David I (1005–1153), Scotland controlled Cumberland and Westmorland as often as not. It was a test of Scottish kingship: Donnchad (Duncan) mac Crínan's failed siege of Durham in 1040 was followed by his defeat in battle by Macbethad mac Findláich (r. 1040–54/7), of whom more will be heard in the discussion of Moray in the *Identity* section below.

Despite having gained Macbethad's throne with the aid of forces supplied by the Earl of Northumbria (whose warriors may have gained estates in southern Scotland as a reward), Mael Coluim III mac Donnchada Cinn Moír ('big head' or 'great chief') (r. 1054/7–93) became a persistent raider of northern England; nor did the Norman Conquest in the south put an end to his activities. Mael Coluim's hold on the northern part of his kingdom was strengthened by the death of Thorfinn the Mighty, the *jarl* of Orkney, who had gained ground from Macbethad in the north, in *c.* 1065: Mael Coluim married his widow Ingibjorg, who died in 1069. Although in long-term decline, the earldom of Orkney still married twice into the Scottish royal house in the eleventh century.

In the south, William I the Conqueror (r. 1066–87) could overpower Mael Coluim in the field, forcing him to submit at Abernethy in 1072, but he could not control him, though Mael Coluim's dynastically threatening marriage to Margaret, grand-daughter of King Eadmund (r. 1016), sister to Eadgar Aetheling and heiress to the House of Wessex, might have rendered this desirable. Mael Coluim's ability to contract such a marriage and to sustain attacks on England in the face of Norman power shows how little any intermittent Scottish promises of submission meant. Both Saxon and Norman England had the military force to defeat other opponents on the edge of their realms or beyond them: Gruffydd ap Llywelyn in 1063, Earl Morcar in 1071, Count Robert and the House of Rollo in 1106. In each case, the defeat was devastating. With Scotland it was otherwise. Mael Coluim's submission at Abernethy, the old Pictish centre on the Tay in 1072, was followed by another to Robert of Normandy, the Conqueror's eldest son, in 1079 at Falkirk. However, this latter agreement seems to have comprehended a border on Tyne and Solway, which the Normans reinforced by the building of Newcastle and the castle at Carlisle by the close of the century, the latter taken from Scotland after yet another incursion (and submission) in 1091. Repeated Norman attacks failed to settle the problem of Scottish aggression, and the new English dynasty's aims for their northern border remained modest ones.

In the medieval world of European power politics, the early Normans tried another tack in attempting to subject Scotland ecclesiastically to the Archbishop of York, whose 1072 claim to be metropolitan of Scotland (which it is possible that Mael Coluim and Margaret supported) would have prevented the country's attaining the full status of a separate sovereign kingdom, held of the king directly from the Pope. Instead, Scotland would have been part of the province of England's northern archbishop. Although York's metropolitan rights in Galloway were not finally overturned until 1355, this was the culmination of what was a long and successful struggle by the Scottish bishops to promote both the ecclesiastical and political consequence of their country. Much of the latter indeed depended on the former, for without recognition by the Papacy, Scotland's kings would lack rights to the anointment due to the sovereigns of states rather than underkings. Thus Columba's laying his hands on Áedán MacGabráin of Dál Riata in the sixth century provides an ideological under- pinning to the claims of the Scottish Church to symbiotically support the independence of the nation in its own separateness from external obedience to any bishop short of the Holy See. Eventually, in the early fourteenth century, entitlement to the 'full rites of anointing and coronation' were at last acknowledged by the Church as an endorsement of the Scottish king's status.

By this time, Scotland's position had long been recognised as controversial. In 1080, according to an English source, the Archbishop of York failed to gain the assistance of his Scottish 'subject' bishops in consecrating a new Bishop of Durham, while in 1101 Paschal II wrote 'to the suffragans of the archbishopric of York throughout Scotland': the Scottish bishops are recalcitrant, but apparently a due of obedience is owed, and the Pope confirmed York's primacy in 1122.

Yet when Henry II (r. 1154–89) demanded an 'oath of obedience' to the English Church by Scottish bishops, Pope Alexander III denounced it as 'lay interference' in his *Super Anxietatibus* of 1176, amplified by the *Cum Universi* of 1192, both of which indicated that the Treaty of Falaise (see below) had little effect in the ecclesiastical sphere, as did the Papacy's offer of a 'golden rose' to William in 1182 as a sign of kingly right. However, a subsequent attempt by Alexander II mac William to request crowning and anointing in the coronation service in the manner of imperial sovereign rulers was opposed by the Pope under English pressure in 1221 and 1233. Yet in 1251 the Papacy rejected 'an English petition that the Scottish king might not be crowned or anointed without consent of Henry III', an explicit attempt to control the kingdom on the sensitive point of its sovereignty. By this time significant gains had been made by the native church. By 1192, all but one of the Scottish dioceses (Galloway) had been declared free of English episcopal overlordship, and since the country still lacked a metropolitan, it became a 'special daughter' of the Papacy, even maintaining cross-border ambitions, for 'the bishops of Glasgow claimed ecclesiastical jurisdiction' in the once-Scottish territories of Cumbria into the 1260s. In 1225, a 'national provincial council' of the Scottish Church was established, and in 1249–50, the canonisation of Queen Margaret gave the Scottish crown a saint of its own to match Edward the Confessor or Eadward the Martyr, and helped to consolidate the links between political and ecclesiastical independence. St Margaret was to remain an important focus of Scottish nationality into the eighteenth century, and her cultus has arguably indeed undergone something of a small revival in the twentieth.

Margaret herself died in 1093, three days after hearing of the death of her husband at the siege of Alnwick, where he was still freebooting in his mid-sixties. She was buried in a small church in Dunfermline which was consecrated as an abbey by her son David in 1150 (and had been so titled since 1128), and after her canonisation it became a major pilgrimage site. Mael Coluim's brother Domnall III mac Donnchada Báin ('Fair Donald') succeeded him, but in 1094 William II of England (r. 1087–1100) who had just built a castle at Carlisle to help keep the Scots out of Cumbria, had the power to place his client Donnchad II mac Maíle Coluim (Ingibjorg's son) on the throne. The Scots rose up within a year. In 1094, Maelpetair, Mormaer of Angus killed Donnchad at Mondynes, near Stonehaven. Domnall III was restored, only to be finally deposed and blinded by Rufus' second puppet Eadgar, son of Mael Coluim, who held 'the land of Lothian and the kingdom of Scotland by gift of my lord, William, King of the English'. A similar fate awaited Count Robert of Normandy after his defeat by Henry I in 1106, the Norman royal house in England echoing the practice of its Scottish daughter. On his death, Domnall III became the last Scottish king to be buried on Iona. Eadgar ruled for ten years (1097–1107), possibly allowing 'further English settlement in Lothian'. In the west, Magnus Barelegs asserted Norwegian control over the Western Isles and Man through his powerful intervention of 1098, which led to a treaty 'recognising that all the islands off the west coast of Scotland between which a galley could be sailed with its rudder shipped belonged to Norway'. Eadgar's successor, Alexander I mac Maíle Coluim (r. 1107–24), another of Margaret's sons, sought to distance himself from Anglo-

Norman power by moving the core of his kingdom 'north to Scone and Gowrie, the heart of Celtic Alba' and by revolting against ecclesiastical obedience to York, although he was obliged to campaign with Henry I (r. 1100–35) in Wales.[8]

Scotland was thus only able to maintain itself uncertainly in the face of Norman power. David I mac Maíle Coluim (r. 1124–53), who had previously ruled southern Scotland under his brother Alexander, adopted a policy of Normanising Scotland under the control of the King of Scots, by inviting minor league Norman adventurers into the country to develop it upon lines which could compete with England a kingdom in which David had no inconsiderable stake. In 1114 he had married Maud, widow of the Earl of Northampton and daughter of the Earl of Northumbria, and through her gained title to lands throughout England, including the honours of Huntingdon and Lancaster. As king, David controlled Northumbria 80 km south of Newcastle, and had ample lands elsewhere in England, but this apparent power was also a weakness. David had conquered much land (he even planned an attack on York in 1149) and won more by negotiation and his support for the Empress Maud against King Stephen, but he also acquired extensive estates by marriage. There was an ambivalence in his English possessions, which were both those of a successful sovereign king of a foreign country, and also the inheritance of a mighty English magnate. Such ambivalence was not unusual: English territories in France were acquired by both routes, but France could not usually compel English homage. As an English magnate, brought up in the Norman court of England, David owed homage to his liege-lord Henry I, just as Henry owed homage to the King of France for his lands there.

But whereas France was across the sea, the bulk of David's lands were contiguous both to his own kingdom and to the Norman realm of England, and the duty he and his successors owed as English vassals could be conflated by English monarchical propaganda with feudal rights over Scotland itself. Thus when Alexander III mac Alexander (r. 1249–86) came to London in 1274 and 1278, pressure was placed on him to elide the difference between his status as English vassal and Scottish sovereign, and in October 1278 the following encounter occurred:

> At Westminster, Alexander, king of Scotland, did homage to the Lord Edward [Edward I, r. 1272–1307], king of England, son of king Henry, in these words: 'I become your man for the lands which I hold of you in the kingdom of England for which I owe homage to you, saving my kingdom'. Then said the Bishop of Norwich: 'And saving to the king of England, if he has right to your homage for the kingdom'. To whom at once and openly the king replied, saying: 'To homage for my kingdom of Scotland, no one has a right save God alone, nor do I hold it save of God alone'. (*Register of Dunfermline*)

It is perhaps indicative that this pressure came from an English bishop, for it was, as indicated above, the ecclesiastical attempt to control Scotland which was the most incessant. The English and Scottish minutes of the above encounter differ, but it is clear that Alexander did not do 'homage and sworn fealty explicitly for his realm'.[9]

Scotland and England had already been in repeated conflict in the twelfth and early thirteenth centuries concerning feudal rights in each other's territories, and both Henry I and

II (r. 1154–89) took kings of Scots with them on campaign, though whether in the latter case (that of Mael Coluim IV mac Henry (r. 1153–65), knighted by Henry II at Perigueux in 1159, as Henry had himself been knighted at Carlisle by David ten years earlier) this was in recognition of feudal authority over the Scottish king as English lord or Scots king is not altogether clear. In any case, Mael Coluim returned the Northumbrian territories won by David to England at the Treaty of Chester in 1157. His brother William mac Henry the Lion (r. 1165–1214), who made Scotland's first treaty with France in 1168, and in the far north consolidated his kingdom's control over the whole of the Scottish mainland, was captured by the English in an attempt to regain Northumbria in conjunction with the rebellion of Henry II's eldest son.[10]

William was released in 1174 under the terms of the Treaty of Falaise, which bound Scotland to English over-lordship until dissolved by the Quitclaim of Canterbury in 1191, when Richard I Lionheart (r. 1189–99) sold his feudal rights for 10,000 merks (£6,660) to finance the Third Crusade. Under the terms of Falaise, Scotland was an explicit fief, English garrisons were to be placed in five Scottish castles, including Stirling on Forth–Clyde, and hostages were to be surrendered to the English crown. The bishops of Scotland 'were forced to agree that their church would give such obedience to the English church as it owed by right and custom' though 'they were able at once to lobby successfully at the papal court against this claim'. The point about Falaise though was that it was necessary and regarded as a gain by Henry II, for had Scotland truly been under English over-lordship as the propagandists later claimed, such a treaty would have been redundant. Indeed by 1200, William was able to describe any duties he owed to John (r. 1199–1216) as 'saving only his own rights', an anticipation of Alexander III's words to the Bishop of Norwich in 1278. By the Quitclaim William was to be only 'liegeman for all the lands for which his predecessors were liegemen of our predecessors', a formula retaining a useful degree of ambivalence from the English point of view. In 1192, William, who contributed to Richard's ransom, even offered 15,000 merks for Northumberland, but was refused. He was more successful against Harald Maddadson, *jarl* of Orkney, who was forced to submit to William in 1197 and 1202, stalling his intrusion into Ross. Nonetheless, William remained in debt to English power. Having been granted the 'lordship of Tynedale' by John, as well as troops to help suppress trouble in Moray, the ageing Scottish king was still vulnerable to Plantagenet demands. His ambition in the north of England had led him to pay a heavy price, one compounded by his payment of 15,000 merks (and two of his daughters) to John by the Treaty of Norham in 1209 in order to stop England's building a castle at Tweedmouth.[11]

When King John's government in England went into decline, Alexander II mac William (r. 1214–49) made a last attempt to impose Scottish authority in Northumbria. In 1215, the Northumbrian lords paid him homage, as did the Yorkshire barons at Melrose the following year, while Alexander marched to Dover to in his turn give homage for the northern counties to the King of France, who had a claim to the English throne. The barons of Magna Carta adjudged Northumberland, Westmorland and Cumberland to Alexander. John's death in 1216 put an end to this plan, and Alexander had to yield Carlisle in 1217 and return to allegiance for his English territories. This was to be the end of Scottish claims to England's northern counties, a situation formally resolved when Alexander quitclaimed Northumberland, Westmorland and Cumberland by the terms of the Treaty of York in 1237, which finally established (except for the possession of Berwick) Scotland's southern frontier. Alexander had internal troubles to deal with as well, notably unrest in the province of Galloway following the death of its lord in 1234 'without a male heir'. By this time a greater stability in the Anglo-Scottish relationship had been established by Alexander's marriage to Henry III's (r. 1216–72) sister, Joan Beaufort, in 1221. Following her death in 1238, he married Marie de Coucy, scion of the great *sires de Coucy* of France, who regarded themselves as greater than the most powerful of the titled nobility: *'Roi ne suis,/Ne prince ne duc ne comte aussi;/ Je suis le sire de Coucy'.*[12]

Alexander II also attempted to gain control of the Hebrides, seeking to buy them from Norway in 1244. Although he died without accomplishing this, his son Alexander III mac Alexander finally wrested control of the western isles (including Man but excluding the outer Hebrides) from Norway by the 1266 Treaty of Perth which followed the Battle of Largs three years earlier, where Haakon IV's (r. 1217–63) forces had been brought to a losing standoff. By the terms of Perth a small payment and annuity (which remained unpaid) was involved for the western islands, but this could have been little more than a face-saving exercise on Norway's part. A distant Norwegian kingdom, now very much a second-rate power, had shown that it could not effectively defend such far-flung (and, in any case, semi-autonomous) provinces. Apart from Berwick, its doubtful control over the outer Hebrides and the continuing Norwegian presence in Orkney and Shetland, Scotland (with the exception of the ownership of Man) occupied the territory in 1266 that it occupies today.

LANGUAGE AND IDENTITY

Although the Picts formed a large part, possibly the majority, of the inhabitants of the kingdom of Scotland, Gaelic soon became its dominant tongue, and by the Wars of Independence the Pictish contribution to the nation of Scotland was marginalised, both in the submission made by Baldred Bisset to the Curia in 1300–1 and by the 1320 Declaration of Arbroath which succeeded it. Bisset's account was also 'the first extant Scottish account of Scottish origins to cast Scotland rather than Ireland as the Scottish homeland', emphasising the (fictional) transfer of the Stone of Destiny from Ireland.[13]

Gaelic became the predominant language evinced in place name and other evidence throughout Scotland, excepting only Orkney, Shetland, parts of Caithness and Lothian and the eastern Borders. In Orkney and Shetland, the vast bulk of place names are Norse, and a form of the language, Norn, survived in Orkney until the seventeenth, and Shetland until the nineteenth century. Scandinavian influence is also notable in the place names of Caithness, Sutherland and the north and west Highlands. In Berwickshire and Lothian, Anglian names are strongly present, but are almost unknown elsewhere – this territory was that most completely integrated into the Northumbrian kingdom, being a part of Northumbria from c. 600–1000. By contrast, the retreat of

Brittonic speech south of Forth–Clyde in response to Northumbrian intrusion is implicit in the fact that, while 70 per cent of place names show Brittonic influence in West Lothian, this is true of only 35 per cent in Midlothian, close to Edinburgh/Din Eidyn, the fortress captured by Northumbria in 638. Welsh probably remained the language of Clydesdale and Northern Cumbria, possibly as late as the twelfth century, and there is some evidence of hybridity between Pictish and Gaelic in place names.[14]

By 1100, then, Gaelic was the general language of Scotland outside Lothian, but in the century that followed it is likely that Anglophones formed a significant proportion of the population of the burghs. Non-Gaelic/Brittonic place names begin to occur north of Forth (and there is evidence of Anglophone speech even north of Tay) in the 1200s; by the 1150s, there were Anglophones in Strathclyde. Almost at the moment of its greatest extent, Gaelic began its long retreat.

This retreat was not principally one attended by conflict. Indeed, there was bilingualism (evident on the east coast in particular) and thus a long period when Gaelic and Anglophone usages could interact with each other. A significant number of Gaelic words entered what was to become Scots, as did many Norse ones. Gaelic imaginative literature and cultural conceptions powerfully influenced the forms taken by their Anglophone equivalents to an extent still largely unrecognised. Just as the great Scottish Norman earldoms had their basis in Gaelic and Pictish practice (see below), so Scottish literature and culture rest on the hidden substrate of Gaelic's long retreat. In the thirteenth century, people in places such as Dunfermline 'abandoned Gaelic names' for Norman forms, and Gaelic place names began to be translated in the north-east, though most modern place names had formed by 1250. Gaelic was still *Scotice*, the language of the Scots, in 1400, but a century later the move towards identifying it with Irish (as 'Erse') had begun. The Reformation and the wars of the seventeenth century ironically both completed the process of identifying Gaelic as alien and Irish, while at the same time alienating Scotland from its own historic links with the Gaels of Ireland across the sea, despite the fact that, as William Ferguson tells us, 'There can be no doubt . . . that the national identity of the Scots sprang from an early Gaelic tribal root that first flourished in Ireland'. Scotland was always an ethnically-mixed kingdom, but the influence of Gaelic was a profound and lasting one.[15]

There is little sign of ethnic conflict in the early Scottish kingdom. Although some of the Strathclyde nobility fled to Gwynedd at the time of Domnall II's attack in 889, this appears to have been an isolated occurrence. There is some evidence of anti-English and Norman feeling in the country as a whole in the 1090s and in revolts in Galloway in the following century, but on the whole the long-standing myth of 'Highland history', with its view of the native Gaelic-speaker retreating before the advance of Germanic speech and people is misleading, however much it has suited the different purposes of Enlightenment historians or Celtic romanticists. The retreat of the language must not be confused with an ethnic retreat, any more than in Ireland. Scotland was, outside the south-east, predominantly Brittonic or (more commonly) Gaelic in culture, and the fact that the Chief of the Name of Fraser or Ramsay or Stewart was originally 'Norman', while that of MacDonald was 'Celtic', seems to have made little discernible difference to the way they behaved.

Even at the 'Highland–Lowland' battle of Harlaw in 1411, the MacDonald of the Isles who marched south to defeat in Aberdeenshire was the son of 'Norman' Robert II's (Stewart) daughter Margaret, who bore the name of the 'Saxon' queen who was Scotland's patroness. She had married the son of 'Celtic' Angus Óg of Islay, and their son married Mary Leslie, of 'Celto-Norman' descent. At Harlaw in 1411 MacDonald was defeated by the forces of the Earl of Mar, who was the grandson of Robert II, but who had a 'Celtic' mother, and was Donald's father's nephew, and thus his adversary's cousin. Mar's territories were mainly Gaelic-speaking, and the Chief of the Name of Forbes was one of the 'Lowland' heroes of the occasion, although later sources seem to see the Forbes family as a 'clan'. While there is no need to deny the importance of the Highland–Lowland divide as a perception in early modern Scotland, to actually construct Scottish history in ethnic terms, as has so often been done and sometimes still is, is misleading to the point of fundamental misrepresentation, for Scotland was always a mixed polity, and the fact was frequently acknowledged. In general, Scots and Britons, Picts and Angles, participated in what appear to have been the relatively harmonious development of the distinctive political institutions of the kingdom of Scots.[16]

What were these institutions? First and foremost, there was the development of a unitary kingship, which itself may have derived both from an existing Pictish tradition of political unity and the need to maintain a common front in the face of Viking and Northumbrian aggression. In the same way, we might speculate as to whether England would have unified so early under the House of Wessex had it not been for the Danes. Both England and Scotland were mixed polities, and under David I (r. 1124–53) administrative changes were made, intended to bring the consistency of Norman practice to a loosely unified country, modernising and developing its institutions. Although the kings of Scots were not anointed until 1329, a ceremony of inauguration developed from early times: Charles II (r. 1651/60–85) was the last king of Scots to be inaugurated on the Moot Hill at Scone.

Patterns of lordship found elsewhere in Europe were superimposed on an underlying Celtic aristocracy by the Flemish and Norman servants of the monarchy. In many areas, change was superficial. The 'Mormaer', or 'great steward' of the king, probably derived from the under-kings of traditional Celtic practice, the *rí ruirech* under the high king, *ard-rígh*. The Lord of the Isles was *Rí Innse Gall*. On this traditional base were grafted the great territorial earldoms and lordships of medieval Scotland. It is 'likely, and in the case of Mar and Buchan it is known, that the man who bore the Latin designation of *comes* ('earl') was known in the vernacular as 'mormaer'. Fife, Atholl, Strathearn, Caithness, Mar and Angus were all earldoms arguably based not only on the territories of the old mormaers, but on the provinces of the Picts. The power of the Scottish magnates was regionally concentrated: although the power of the earls was curbed under the early Stewarts, as late as 1715 the Earl of Mar could not be stopped by the government from launching his Jacobite Rising because he was regarded as untouchable on his own land. By contrast, the holder of a nominal earldom in England would be more likely to hold land scattered throughout the country.[17]

In Scotland, however, lordships sometimes appeared merely to rationalise the *status quo ante*. Somerled (d. 1164), the Celto-Norse first Lord of the Isles, drove the Norwegians out of some of the western islands in 1156–8 and was killed in Renfrew fighting against Mael Coluim IV mac Henry. His son Raonall held Kintyre and Islay, while Dubhgall held Lorne, Mull, Jura and part of Bute. They and their descendants for a century 'owed allegiance to Norway for their island possessions, while they held their territories in Argyll from the Scottish crown'. Men from Somerled's lands fought under King David at the Battle of the Standard in 1138. This dual allegiance on the utmost fringes of both monarchies clearly put them in a powerful position, as was the case with the Lords of Galloway, masters of an inaccessible frontier zone for many generations. But Somerled and his descendants were no misty-eyed Celtic fundamentalists: Lord Raonall was depicted as a knight, offshoot of French chivalry, while MacDougall of Lorne wrote to Edward II (r. 1307–27) in French. Powerful as they were, these great western barons were part of the power politics of their day, not kings over a romantic *Tir nan Og*, a never-never land of wish fulfilment, as later Celtic romanticists have rendered them. As far as the principles on which they held land obtained, as Geoffrey Barrow observes, 'there is absolutely no suggestion that king, council or *capella regis* ('chancery') was conscious that grants and infeftments of landed estates in the Highlands or in the Isles differed in any fundamental respect from those made by the Crown elsewhere in the realm'.[18]

Perhaps the most important unifying factor in Scottish identity was the Church, not only through its faith but also through its politics and its language. Edward Cowan has suggested that the *lingua franca* of Latin speeded the absorption of the Pictish elite into the Scottish polity for example. As early as 909 according to the *Annals of Ulster*, the *Albanaich* united as one people against the Vikings under 'their miracle-working standard, the crozier of St Columba'. In 918 (see above), St Columba's staff was carried at the battle of Corbridge as a sign of his status as 'apostle' of the 'men of Scotland'. As such, it 'allowed a mixed army of Picts and Scots to fight together . . . as *Albanaich* against a common enemy'. At the Battle of the Standard near Northallerton in 1138, the Galwegians surged forward crying *'Albani'* (*Albanaich*) under the leadership of their Norman commanders. It is likely that the combination of the influences of the Gaelic-speaking saints and the long-consolidated separateness of Alba beyond the Wall were factors which, together with the internal practice of and external pressures for a unitary kingship, helped form the realm of Scotland.[19]

Margaret, Alexander I mac William and David I all contributed to the development of the Church, one in which the cult of the saints was certainly important. Earlier monastic foundations, such as those of the eighth-century ascetic Irish *Céli Dé*/Culdees, became merged into or replaced by the great Continental orders, as Scotland moved into the European mainstream. David not only founded the great Abbey at Dunfermline, but also those at Kelso (1128), Melrose (1136), Jedburgh (1138/54) and Dryburgh (1150). Into these houses Continental orders began to arrive: Benedictines to Dunfermline (then a smaller community) in 1070, Cistercians 'to Melrose in 1136', Valliscaulians to Beauly in 1230. They could absorb earlier monastic foundations: the *Céli Dé* community at Abernethy 'became Augustinian *c.* 1172' and that at Monymusk had conventional monastic arrangements by the mid-thirteenth century; but there was sometimes some conflict, as at Iona in 1204, when Lord Raonall's Benedictine monastery was destroyed by Irish traditionalists. The economic activities of the monks (such as farming) made an important contribution to Scottish society. At the same time, the founding of great religious houses represented such a major infrastructural investment that it was impossible that the political dimension could be ignored. William I mac Henry founded Arbroath Abbey in 1178, dedicating it to St Thomas à Becket in order to cock a snook at his then overlord, Henry, who was held responsible for the holy archbishop's martyrdom. The Church was an emblem of nationality and national pride which was of long continuity – even under the Picts there had been the beginnings of church building in stone. In the Scottish realm which succeeded it, as Thomas Clancy and Barbara Crawford point out, 'learned clerics . . . advocated an ideology which . . . supported the aspirations of kings'.[20]

Among the cults of the saints, not only did Columba provide a bedrock for the sovereign claims of the Scottish monarchy and Margaret a saint from that monarchy; Andrew, whose cult had been less influential in the ninth century, was also becoming increasingly important. St Margaret herself had revived his cult and provided 'free passage across the Forth' for his pilgrims at Queensferry. As Michael Lynch informs us:

By 1279, the seal of the Bishop of St Andrews bore the image of St Andrew crucified, and in 1286 it also appeared on the seal of the Guardians of the Kingdom, accompanied by the legend, 'Andrew be leader of the compatriot Scots'. By 1318, when St Andrews Cathedral was consecrated in a service of national thanksgiving 'for the notable victory granted to the Scottish people by blessed Andrew, protector of the realm' four years earlier at Bannockburn, the identification of saint and nation was complete.

St Andrew was also explicitly used as a focus of multi-ethnic unity, being presented as suzerain 'over all the peoples of Scotland, "the Picts, Scots, Danes and Norwegians"'.[21]

The monarchy was alert to the ethnic diversity of its subjects. Eadgar (r. 1097–1107) termed his people 'Scots and English', while later royal charters are directed to 'French and English, Scots and Galwegians', alike the 'worthy men' of the king. Saxon kings such as Eadgar had acknowledged similar diversities in the early days of the English kingdom. By the end of the reign of William I mac Henry the Lion, the king's subjects were being addressed 'without reference to their ethnic origin, shortly after Henry II had addressed his subjects as "English"'. It has been suggested that William's changing usage 'coincides with a prolonged revolt in Galloway'. Scotland was a medieval monarchy under a single king. Its people did not think of themselves as 'Scots' except under the lordship of that king. But the king was king of those within the bounds of 'Scotland', and hence those who lived within those bounds could begin to think of themselves as loyal Scots *while they lived there*. 'There' was not quite modern Scotland: for those in the far north or the western coast the king's sovereignty was still marginal, if present at all, while most of the islands were under Scandinavian sway. Although in the twelfth century one could not yet be a Scot in exile (though this concept had meaning soon afterwards), it is probably a mistake to think that no identity was conferred by living as the subject of a king in a united kingdom on land over which he ruled. By the reign of Alexander III mac Alexander (1249–86), the notion of a 'Scot' as at least partially separable from one who owed homage to the king of Scots for lands in Scotland was beginning to form, as was displayed in increasing sensitivity to land owned by foreigners. 'Wholly absentee landlords' were no longer acceptable, and attempts were made to buy out English holdings in Scotland, both clerical and lay, especially where these were held by southerners. Contiguous landholdings in Northumbria and southern Scotland do not seem to have attracted the same attention.[22]

The term *Scoti* itself originally referred to those who were either Scots or Irish: Brian Boru, the victor of Clontarf (where Domnall, son of the mormaer of Mar fought with him), is described as *'imperator Scotorum'* in 1004. In the eleventh century, the Papacy began to distinguish between Irish *Scoti* and Scottish ones, and although the Scots remained conscious of the linkage (Robert the Bruce described the Irish as *'nostra nacio'*, one of 'our nation'). As late as 1318, an Irish document identifies Ireland as *Scotia Maior* (as against the *Scotia Minor* of Scotland). Although by this time, Scotland had long been internally described as 'Alba', Scottish accounts themselves, as Dauvit Broun has argued, 'did not aim to endow Scots with an ancient history distinct from the Irish'.[23]

The Scottish monarchy developed, as did the English kingdom in the south, a foundation-myth, and the divergence between the two myths became one of the key points of distinction between the English and Scottish monarchies in the medieval and early modern periods. The English story, codified by Geoffrey of Monmouth in his *History of the Kings of Britain* (1136) was designed to give 'a precedent for the dominions and ambitions of the Norman kings'. Its basis was that Brutus, the great-grandson of the Trojan hero and legendary founder of Rome, Aeneas, had come to Britain, which was later divided between his three sons, Locrinus who had England, Kamber, Wales and Albanactus, Scotland. In Geoffrey's version of the tale, Locrinus as the eldest had authority over the other two, although an alternative version (the *Duan Albanach*) existed which posited Brutus and Albanus as brothers, it was ignored, or unknown to Geoffrey. The Scots, Picts and Irish appear in the Galfridian story as treacherous enemies of King Arthur, Brutus' descendant; disloyal subjects of the true 'emperor' of Britain, not merely the Roman province but the whole island, indeed, both islands of the British Isles. Arthur's story, as told by Geoffrey and in its other sources, was known as 'The Matter of Britain'. Since the historical Arthur (if he ever existed) was probably a Romanised Brittonic commander, there is a semantic elision between Arthur's status as a 'Briton' with rights over the Brittonic kinglets in the Roman province of Britannia, and his rights to the whole of the island. In addition, Arthur's status as a Brittonic hero gave him a Welsh identity which later English kings (Henry VII (r. 1485–1509) in particular) used to incorporate the patriotic sentiments of the Welsh elites within a fundamentally English polity.[24]

In Fionn, the Gaelic-speaking world had a rival to Arthur who was never so incorporated, and just as the Fenian cycle was widespread throughout both Scotland and Ireland, so the

Scottish monarchy developed a story of its Irish roots. A form which saw 'Gathelus . . . the *eponymus* of the Gael' marry 'Scota the daughter of Pharaoh' developed. The original story of Scota, daughter of Pharaoh, who brought Jacob's Pillow (see the account of Jacob's dream in Genesis 28) to Scotland via many countries including (finally) Ireland, was first developed in the reign of Constantín II mac Aeda (900–43), and modern scholars such as Edward Cowan believe that one of its initial purposes was that of reconciliation between Picts and Scots through the marriage of Scota and Gathelus. Jacob's Pillow was to be identified with the Stone of Scone or of Destiny: the coronation stone of a unified Scottish kingdom reputedly brought from the Middle East (via Tara, seat of the *ard-rí* of Ireland) but in fact quarried from the stone of Central Scotland. Constantín also 'married members of his family into the Viking war-bands' to cement this aim of one consolidated kingdom. Under Alexander II mac William, the Pictish king-list was added to the Dál Riata list to make a (far too long) single list which implied that instead of ruling as competing kings, these monarchs, Picts and Scots, had sequentially held authority over a unified territory. Although as the Middle Ages progressed, the Scottish monarchy's reliance on explicitly Irish roots diminished or were excluded for political reasons, they never quite disappeared, while both Scottish and Pictish descent were emphasised, particularly after the origin-myth was revamped under William the Lion. The prominent role of the *seanchaidh*/bard who recited the royal genealogy at the coronation of Alexander III mac Alexander is indicative of the importance of this unifying symbol of a monarchy, which, though it presided over several peoples, had a Gaelic identity at its core. John Bannerman has argued that the Gaelic bards made an important contribution to Latin culture in terms of the ideas they contributed to Baldred Bisset's *Processus* and the Declaration of Arbroath twenty years later.[25]

If the notion of monarchy was a unitary one, however, there were rival dynastic pretensions from outside the house of Cinaed Mac Aílpin, possibly ultimately deriving from the Cenél Loairn of Dál Riata, and certainly rooted in Moray. In 900, Domnall II mac Constantín and in 954 his son Mael Coluim I MacDomnuill were both killed fighting in the north, as was King Dubh mac Maíle Coluim in 966. From conflict of this kind the notion has grown up that Moray was a semi-separate kingdom, but in fact the case appears to be that it harboured a rival dynasty, whose claims became particularly pressing in the eleventh century, for 'up until the time of Mael Coluim II (1005–34) one king of Alba was recognised from the Cromarty Firth to the Firth of Forth'. The house of Moray probably saw themselves as having 'the right to a say in the choosing of kings' and may have found this frustrated when Donnchad succeeded in 1034. Subsequently Macbethad, the son of Findlaech mac Ruardri, Mormaer of Moray, succeeded as king in 1040, when he killed Donnchad in battle near Elgin, at a time when Moray itself was under threat from the Vikings, perhaps a reason for Macbethad's pressing of his claim to the southern core of the kingdom. Although Macbethad was a successful king, Donnchad's son Mael Coluim III mac Donnchada Cinn Moír forced Macbethad back to Moray with English help, where in 1057 he was killed by Mael Coluim's forces at Lumphanan in west Aberdeenshire. Macbethad's stepson Lulach succeeded him in Moray but was killed at Rhynie in March 1058. Subsequently

Mael Snechta succeeded, being described as *'rí Muireb'* ('king of Moray') rather than (as previously) mormaer, and ruled in the north from 1058–85. His title, however, seems to have been a sign not of success but of failure: the preservation of a limited ambition under Scottish overlordship.

Discontent in Moray had by no means come to an end, however, for under David I and Mael Coluim IV, Mael Coluim of Moray was a renewed source of trouble, not least from his marriage to the sister of Somerled, the first great Lord of the Isles. In 1157, Mael Coluim of Moray was released from imprisonment in Roxburgh Castle and granted the earldom of Ross in a move surely designed to merge the greatest mormaer's power with the new successor-system of 'feudal' earldoms, but even this did not finally end unrest in the province, Domnall Mac Uilleaim of Moray revolting again under William I mac Henry, and being defeated. This ended the threat posed by the house of Moray to the Scottish succession, although it did not end fear of the north, for as late as 1230 a dynastic claimant from Moray, 'an infant heiress . . . had her brains dashed out against the Mercat Cross of Forfar'.[26]

Why was such a prolonged dynastic challenge possible? First, there was no tradition of automatic primogeniture in the male line. The Picts used a matrilinear succession to the crown 'in cases of dispute', while Scottish kings in the early period could be chosen from among male collateral relatives by the *derbfine*, still the name given to the court at which the Lord Lyon King of Arms rules on succession to the chieftainship of a clan. The tanist/tanaiste (from *tanaise*, 'second, next') was the heir-elect, chosen by the process known as tanistry. The heir-elect (who may have at times been king of Strathclyde) thus had an incentive to kill his predecessor. The practice of 'alternating succession between collateral branches of the royal kin group' in effect compounded this problem. Between 900 and 1000, Constantín succeeded his cousin Domnall, was succeeded by Domnall's son Mael Coluim and only then by his own son Indulb. In 962, Mael Coluim's line was reverted to, and his son Dubh became king, to be succeded by Indulb's son Cuilein in 966. In 971, Cinaed, Dubh's brother (who tried to regulate the succession), succeeded, to be succeeded in his turn by Cuilein's son (Indulb's grandson) and then by Dubh's line once more. This kind of difficulty was not unique to Scotland. In England, the sons of Henry II rebelled against him, and his eldest, Henry, was even crowned king in his father's lifetime. However, the consensual nature of the Scottish succession certainly encouraged trouble when the consensus broke down.[27]

The monarchy's grip was increased by conferring favours, and by monastic foundations such as those of David I, who also developed commerce through the first establishment of burghs by royal charter, conferring on Scottish towns with an active economic life a jealously-guarded historic right to a status protected by Article XXII of the Union, and only lost by local government reorganisation in 1975. In the early centuries, however, distinctions between 'royal', 'baronial' and 'ecclesiastical' burghs were not so clear as they later became.

Scotland's distinct legal system had an early origin, the first recorded laws of the country being promulgated by Domnall I (r. 858–62) at Forteviot. Although there were many local variations (Galwegian law survived into the thirteenth century and Norse law in Orkney and Shetland until 1611, while aspects of udal or land law in these islands continue to be operative to the present day), the central administration of royal justice tended to move these into its orbit over time. From the reign of David I onwards, royal power was circulated throughout the newly monetised economy of Scotland, as the country gained a distinctive coinage of its own for the first time – a sign of sovereignty, and a powerful means of circulating the royal image. Monetisation in its turn undermined the nature of serfdom as a bond in kind. As part of the Normanisation procedures of David I mac Maíle Coluim and his successors, regional sheriffdoms were introduced, on which the later counties came to be in part based: there was a system of 'one sheriffdom for each county' up to the 1800s. Sheriffdoms were less effective, and in the early days were absent, from the west and north-west Highlands.

Above the rank of the sheriffs (an office which 'tended to become hereditary in certain families' after an Act of 1305 stipulated that sheriffs should hold office for life) were the King's Justiciars, who went on circuit dispensing royal justice. At first two in number (for 'Scotia' and Lothian), by the death of William in 1214, there were three justiciars: one for 'Scotia', north of Forth, one for Lothian and one for Galloway. The justiciar for 'Scotia' 'may have been associated with an earlier Celtic office of king's *breitheamh*' (see below). Eventually there was only one Justiciar, who became described as Lord Justice General, today the senior judge of Scotland, 'presiding . . . over the High Court of Justiciary'. The role of the justiciars helped to ensure consistent practice throughout the kingdom, though Galloway, with its 'primitive code of blood-payments commensurate with the injury complained of' did not begin to be fully absorbed into the system of royal justice until the 1200s. By this time, traditional justiciary offices from the earlier period were being merged into the king's justice, as was the *breitheamh* or judge of the customary law in earlier times, who survived as the 'dempster' or 'doomster' of the later Scottish courts, an office only abolished in 1773, and which may have long survived in its original form in the western isles.[28]

Consistency in the administration of justice was the spine of a body politic which by the twelfth century had become liable to the imposition of customs and other duties. The commonality of the duties payable to the king was the obverse of the commonality of the king's justice, 'the king's law, common to all his kingdom'. This commonality was associated with the king's feudal status as lord, before whom all were vassals. The lords under the king might offer the service of so many knights (or, in the island west, 'a galley of so many oars') in military tenure, later 'ward holding', while there were also forms of holding for nominal service ('blench ferme') and the most common, 'feu ferme', where feu duty – a monetary payment – was payable to the superior by the vassal. This last remains the basis of Scots landholding law today: although the feu duty has usually been redeemed for a lump sum payment, the superior retains certain rights over the property. Feu duty could be merged with its 'Celtic' predecessor, 'cain' ('tribute'), a payment due to a feudal superior, and 'usually paid in cattle and other farm livestock, and in certain basic foodstuffs'. Subinfeudation – the creation of a new layer of feudal tenure by extending the 'chain' of obligation – remains competent in Scotland, but disappeared in England in 1290. Traditional 'kin-based land ownership began to mutate' into these new modes of landholding. In Fife, 'the feudal earls co-existed and shared power with a collateral line which represented older . . . kin-based structures of lordship'.

Justice remained devolved to regional magnates in medieval and, indeed, early modern Scotland. Although sheriffs, burgh courts and justiciars combined to dispense royal justice, courts of barony and regality developed in the hands of the great landlords, where justice was dispensed by the inheritors of the regional (*ruiri* or *rí ruirech*) and local (*rí tuaithe*) kingships of Celtic Scotland, in a system where 'community cohesiveness' was 'operating downwards from the regional magnates'. Feuds might be dealt with by 'heads of kins'; disputes over land by the 'feudal overlord'. Scottish society was a 'striking' hybrid of Celtic and Norman systems. Local courts of the baronial kind had more or less disappeared in England by 1300, but the long inheritance of the power of regional magnates in Scotland was only brought to an end by the British abolition of heritable jurisdictions in 1747. Before that, regality courts might on occasion try any case except that of treason, while even barony courts had the right of *furca et fossa*, 'pit and gallows', a capital power which represented in legal form the continued hold the baronial classes of Scotland had on their following. There were other local variations as well: the Clan Law of MacDuff in Fife being one example. In the upper Garioch of Aberdeenshire,a local settlement of Flemish wool growers was allowed to keep their own laws from the twelfth to the fourteenth centuries.[29]

Many of these administrative reforms may have been imported from Norman practice, but it is important to note that the traditional version of Scotland's early history as a state, wherein a pure 'Celtic' kingdom was 'adulterated' by the importation of 'Saxon' values under Mael Coluim III Cinn Moír and Queen Margaret, followed by 'Norman' ones under David I, needs to be qualified. The introduction of certain changes from abroad, even when accompanied by a cadre to implement them, does not necessarily constitute a major shift in the lived life of the people, or even their institutions. Mael Coluim II had arguably introduced Saxon ideas in the system of thanages at the beginning of the eleventh century, which in their turn descended into sheriffdoms, just as the mormaers became earls. While the counties of Scotland were not original to the 'Celtic' era of the kingdom, they nonetheless descended from the provinces once grouped round regional royal strongholds.[30]

LIFESTYLE AND LOCATION

Only a small proportion of Scotland's population of 250–500,000 lived in the towns, which were beginning to develop trading links with northern Europe, more accessible by sea than England, and even than parts of Scotland. Some parts of maritime Scotland, such as Galloway, with links to the islands and Ireland, had a completely different outlook on the trading world to others, such as the east coast burghs, who looked to Scandinavia, Germany and the Baltic. Most people lived on the land with their livestock in stone and turf chaumers (single-roomed houses) which in their internal living arrangements may not have differed much from the houses of the Bronze Age. In Shetland, where there was little wood, the Norse settlers lived in rectangular earth and turf houses, faced (like Skara Brae) with stones to keep the wind out. The house could be entered by two doors: one into the living quarters with a central fire for cooking smoking up through the roof, the other leading to the livestock. The livestock area was paved for cleaning, but the living space had an earthen floor to help retain heat. The farmers who lived there ploughed the land in long strips and kept sheep and cattle. Their artifacts, particularly those of bone and metal were of a high standard, as the surviving set of Lewis chessmen demonstrate.

On the Scottish mainland, people still lived outside the towns in small settlements with houses of wattle and daub, wood founded on stone or (rarely) stone itself, generally rectangular now rather than round, but sharing the lifestyle of their Bronze and Iron Age predecessors and their living space with their animals. They ploughed with oxen, planted barley and oats, and, as time went on, paid a systematic rent of food or *corvee* duty to their landlord, a chief for whom they might fight, later a lord to whom they owed armed service. Although there were slaves in Scotland in the eleventh and twelfth centuries, by the fourteenth even the poor were no longer serfs in the sense of 'being legally tied to the land'. French visitors were, in fact, 'much put out by the upstart nature of the Scottish peasantry'.

The 'ploughgate' of some 42 hectares was often called a *davoch* north of Forth–Clyde, a word of Pictish origin. Oxen drew the ploughs, and oats, barley, and occasional wheat and rye grew on the land, which was divided into single rigs or strips, 200 m by 5 m, a single run of the plough. Rigs, which ran downhill, helped to answer 'a main problem of Scottish agriculture, that of drainage'. The landholding was divided into infield (arable, possibly with some pastoral) and outfield (the poorer land). Only infield was liable to tax.

Pigs might find food in the woods, though not presumably in the royal forests, founded by David I on the Norman model from the 1130s. Such roads as existed were of beaten earth, and served as a means of communication within the settlement rather than between settlements. Craftsmen such as joiners or blacksmiths supported the farming infra-structure. In the fermtouns, 'joint-tenants' clustered in a little settlement on an allotment, with 'common grazing' and other rights. In the kirktouns, houses of wattle and daub clustered round a central church, sometimes of wood but often as time went on of slate and stone. Some of these, such as the eleventh century St Regulus/Rule's tower in the monastic complex at St Andrew's Cathedral or the round tower next to Brechin Cathedral in the Irish style, still survive. The monasteries and abbeys tended to be in the larger burghs, where a wider variety of economic activities took place. The power of the cathedrals themselves was not what it was to be in the later medieval period, since the bishops did not on the whole have fixed seats of authority until the twelfth or thirteenth century. As the cathedrals of medieval Scotland began to be built, in St Andrews from 1160, in Glasgow, Aberdeen and elsewhere from the thirteenth century, schools began to grow up round them: the High School of Glasgow (1124), Aberdeen Grammar School (c. 1256/63) and others in smaller burghs, such as Ayr Academy (1133). Grammar schools could 'have the status of an ecclesiastical benefice', and at Aberdeen the school was in the gift of the Chancellor of the Cathedral.[31]

The burghs, with their Flemish, French and Anglophone populations, began to develop 'the settlement and com-munity of privileged merchants and craftsmen' before 1200.

They grew up on 'livestock routes' (as at 'Rutherglen, Peebles, Roxburgh') 'or at good river-mouth harbours' ('Berwick, Montrose, Aberdeen'). Cult, royal or military centres might also be given burgh status. Most of them were without stone houses until the fourteenth century at least. In twelfth-century Aberdeen, post and wattle buildings of some 7.5 × 3.8 metres were divided between human and animal occupation in much the same way as country dwellings. Their trading took the form (as in England) of weekly markets, combined with the fairs, which served as occasional seasonal markets, most usually in summer. Few burghs were fortified. Under David I, royal mints were set up at Carlisle, Roxburgh, Berwick, St Andrews, Perth and Aberdeen. By the time of Alexander III, although Carlisle was in English hands, Inverness, Montrose, Forfar, St Andrews, Kinghorn, Stirling, Glasgow, Renfrew, Edinburgh, Lanark, Ayr and Dumfries had been added to the list of mints. Burghs helped speed the circulation of coin, but Scottish inter-regional trade depended largely on the circulation of English coin: Scottish coin is in a minority in surviving hoards.[32]

Scotland as a whole was growing in prosperity. The warm climate of early medieval Europe up to *c.* 1300 was surely one reason for this: Kelso Abbey had 'over 100 hectares of tillage' at 300 m above sea level. Figures for thirteenth-century clerical taxation indicate that the east coast from Fraserburgh to Berwick was generally fairly well off, while tax assessments on estates confirm this picture for Fife and Lothian. The revised tithes ordered by Pope Nicholas IV in 1290 (the Scottish ones were allocated to Edward I!) show that Fife, Lothian, much of Angus and Aberdeen city were assessed at roughly the same level as the diocese of

Winchester, while Glasgow and the west were on an approximate level with Carlisle, and higher than the bishoprics of Lichfield or Exeter. Only the dioceses of Ely, Lincoln, Norwich and the archdiocese of Canterbury show markedly superior prosperity to the bishopric of St Andrews on the Papal assessment. Scotland in 1286 was not a rich country, but compared to England its situation was far superior to the depths it would reach in the years immediately before the Union. Alexander III's realm was an effectively organised and relatively affluent small European kingdom. It was about to face one of the two defining political crises in Scottish history.[33]

THREE

SCOTLAND 1286–1560: NATIONALITY, *MENTALITÉS*, POWER AND THE COMMONWEAL

GOVERNING SCOTLAND

Both the sons and the sole daughter of Alexander III mac Alexander died in their father's lifetime: a dangerous situation for any medieval kingdom to find itself in. In February 1284, the magnates of the Scottish kingdom accepted Alexander's infant grand-daughter, Margaret of Norway, as his heir. Two years later, on 18 March 1286, Alexander III was killed when his horse fell over a cliff on a ride in the dark from Edinburgh to Kinghorn on an impulsive dash to the side of his young wife Yolande. The Estates (see below) of Scotland offered the crown to Margaret, in the meantime electing six Guardians on behalf of the community of the realm: 'the Bishops of St Andrews and Glasgow, two earls and two barons', who 'represented the major political factions . . . and Scotland both north and south of the Forth'.

Alexander III had already broached the possibility of a marriage between Margaret and Edward I's (r. 1272–1307) son Edward of Caernavon (b. 1284), the future Edward II, and the Guardians pursued this possibility, though 'Papal dispensation' had to be sought because Edward I was Margaret's great-uncle. The Guardians sought to guarantee Scotland's status as a 'distinct kingdom in any such dynastic union', and agreed a preliminary treaty at Birgham, on the Scottish side of the Tweed in 1290. The Treaty of Birgham stated that in the event of Edward and Margaret's marriage, Scotland would remain a separate kingdom, 'divided . . . free in itself and without subjection', with the permanent preservation of its 'rights, laws, liberties and customs'. If Edward and Margaret left no heirs, the kingdom of Scots would revert to her nearest heir. Edward's team insisted on reserving the English king's rights, which were not spelt out, but simply those which 'in any just way ought to pertain'.

In May 1290, Edward sent a ship to Norway to fetch Margaret, but the Norwegian king insisted on using his own fleet. She fell ill at sea, and died on Norwegian territory in Orkney in September. There was now a crisis in the succession since there was no clear heir to the Scottish throne. Edward saw his opportunity, and even before the competition for the throne began, seized Man for England. Eventually, thirteen competitors for the throne declared themselves (including Margaret's father, the King of Norway), and Edward gathered a group of them at Norham, where he held a Parliament in May 1291. The Scots were unwilling to attend in numbers, eventually sending a small delegation.

Edward asserted at Norham that he was 'overlord of Scotland'. He secured for himself the claim that his task was not to arbitrate between the competitors but to judge their causes: a fine distinction, but one which placed the English king in a superior, rather than a neutral position. The Guardians agreed to accept Edward's authority on these terms for the duration of the competition, but he had every mind to make it permanent. Accordingly, the Guardians, who resigned their office into Edward's hands in 1291, had a different conception of what they were doing to his. Those who were to compete for the crown likewise accepted the English king's overlordship, a condition he demanded of them. Robert Bruce the Competitor, grandfather of the later king, was the first to do so, John Baliol the last. Some objected; Robert Wishart, the patriotic Bishop of Glasgow, argued in 1291 that 'the realm of Scotland was held directly of God alone'. Edward's claim to superiority had ecclesiastical as well as political overtones: he had already nominated the Bishop of Durham to act in his interest in Scotland.[1]

When the competition for the crown began in earnest, there were four significant claimants. John Baliol, Robert Bruce the Competitor, John Hastings of Abergavenny and Count Florence V of Holland were all direct descendants of Henry mac David (d. 1152), the son of King David I mac Maíle Coluim (r. 1124–53). Baliol, Bruce and Hastings descended from Henry's youngest son, David; Florence from his daughter, Ada. This should have written off Florence's hopes of the crown straight away, but he lodged a special claim: that 'Earl David had resigned the right which he and his heirs might have in the throne to his brother King William the Lion and his heirs'. William was also supposed to have 'designated his sister Ada as heir'. The documentation for this extraordinary claim was absent, although eventually a version of Earl David's resignation of rights did turn up.[2]

Hastings' claim was one which threatened the integrity of the kingdom of Scots itself. With little chance of a claim to the whole kingdom succeeding, he 'pointed out that the kings of Scots were neither crowned nor anointed and drew attention to other grave defects of Scottish kingship', arguing that therefore Scotland could be divided like a feudal estate – he requested a third of it. This still could not bring Hastings' cause to the forefront, but it marked a dangerous precedent. As opinion consolidated around the claim of John Baliol, whose mother, Devorguilla, was Lady of Galloway, Bruce's lawyers changed to a version of the Hastings claim in order to gain support from Florence and keep out Baliol. This side of the cause fell when it was decided by the Scottish assessors (Edward had appointed only a minority among the 104 assessors as a window dressing of equity for the power he was exercising behind the scenes) that Scotland was 'a true kingdom' and could not be divided like a 'feudal lordship'. John Baliol was confirmed as king of Scots, and was 'inaugurated on St Andrew's Day', 30 November 1292. Edward offered English land grants to the major Scots magnates in order to consolidate their indebtedness to him.

The conditions placed by Edward on John Baliol's tenure of power and the degree of subsequent English interference were alike onerous. Edward kept the right to interfere in the king of Scots' (or 'Scotland' as John sometimes used, imitating the English style) jurisdiction, intruding into the Scottish court process and forcing the 'personal attendance of the king of Scots to answer for his judgements' in cases of appeal, such as when John appeared humiliatingly before the English Parliament at Michaelmas 1293. In 1294, John had to accompany Edward in his war against France.[3]

Such humiliation was too great for many. Leading members of the Scottish nobility began to take matters out of John's hands. In July 1295, a 'representative council' of twelve, consisting of 'four bishops, four earls and four barons', took matters into their own hands, concluding a 'mutual defence treaty' with France in October and becoming 'accessory to the Franco-Norwegian treaty' of alliance; thus King John's government earned Scotland, at least on paper, the protection of France. This date is traditionally taken as the beginning of the Auld Alliance between the two countries, although this can be projected back to the reign of William the Lion if not earlier. In any case, King John was emboldened by this independent foray into foreign policy. In response, Edward marched north and sacked Berwick with bloody ferocity, while the Scots responded by burning Northumberland to Hexham, where they may have committed reciprocal atrocities. On 27 April 1296, the incomplete (because Bruce the Competitor refused homage and service to Baliol) feudal host of King John fled in disarray before the Plantagenet forces at Dunbar. John submitted to King Edward at Montrose on 8 July, abdicating his throne at Brechin on the 10th, and was stripped of both the spiritual and physical attributes of his royal authority, memorably becoming in subsequent tradition 'Toom Tabard', 'empty coat'.

In recent years a school of revisionism has taken hold, which points to Baliol's domestic achievements, such as the plan to extend sheriffdoms into 'Skye, Lorne and Kintyre in 1293', and stresses the difficulties he faced with a divided kingdom and powerful opponent. But by every measure of medieval kingship, John Baliol was indeed 'Toom Tabard', a busted flush. He was unable to extend his realm, defend his people, administer justice according to his own laws and not those of another, or keep order without external interference. Unlike earlier kings of Scots who had been forced into temporary feudal inferiority to England, his was structural and bid fair to be permanent. After 1296, he made no attempt to lead the Scots even when out of confinement, and his son was a willing English pawn in attempting to destroy their kingdom until the middle of the next century. It may be that none of the other competitors would have been any better: but this can never make John Baliol a good king of Scots.[4]

Although the Scots forces had treated the English as feudal equals, Edward treated them as rebels against his lordship. Edward sought documented control over feudal Scotland, whether it had opposed him or not. In the infamous Ragman Roll of 1296, 'certain and well-defined classes of persons who held property in Scotland were required to provide written and sealed instruments of homage and fealty'. Edward wanted a secure hold on the entire class of feudal superiors, and their expressed loyalty. By no means everyone signed. Perhaps most noteworthy, given the role of the church in defining Scottish identity, was the fact that only three of Scotland's twelve bishops did homage. The patriotic clergy were to be the ideological, if not the military, heroes of the Wars of Independence, in their own way more important than Wallace and almost as important as Bruce. Given the speed of his victory in 1296, Edward can have expected little further resistance from the natural leaders of Scottish society. He appointed the Earl of Surrey to administer Scotland, who in his turn delegated authority to Walter Amersham the Chancellor, Hugh Cressingham the Treasurer and the three justiciars, Ormesby (Lothian), Mortimer ('beyond the sea of Scotland', a telling phrase for north of Forth) and Skoter (Galloway). Based at Berwick, Cressingham's writ can hardly have run north of Forth–Clyde, and likewise Ormesby was the justiciar with the greatest real power. The English king 'took with him Scottish nobles and knights captured at Dunbar' to France on campaign in August 1297.[5]

By this time Robert Wishart, Bishop of Glasgow and James the Stewart (steward) of the realm were offering covert support in the west for a rising against English power. This can 'hardly be doubted', as Geoffrey Barrow observes, also noting that 'Wishart, Lamberton [later Bishop of St Andrews] and Wallace . . . set the preservation of the independent kingdom of Scotland above the question of who should be its lawful king.' Together with Robert Bruce, Earl of Carrick (grandson of the Competitor and descendant of Fergus, Lord of Galloway), they 'rallied their forces to resist English occupation', Bruce telling the 'knights of Annandale' that 'I must join my own people and the nation in which I was born'. They may have intended to restore the Guardianship to themselves. In May 1297, William Wallace (the name originally referred to Welsh or British ancestry) (1270/2–1305), a vassal of the Stewart in the west of Scotland, killed Sir William Heselrig, sheriff of Lanark, and this outrage was followed by an attack on the court of the English justiciar at Scone. In the same month, Andrew de Moray, nephew of Sir John Comyn, Lord of Badenoch and former Guardian, called out the burgesses of Inverness to a rallying point at Castle Ormond, high on the northern shores of the Moray Firth, and with the men of Inverness attacked Castle Urquhart on Loch Ness. The invaders, who had little settled power in the north, retreated to their castles, but even there they were not safe: those at Elgin, Banff and Inverness fell to de Moray that summer. The young Robert Bruce of Annandale, born in 1274, joined the rising in the south, and together with the Stewart and the Bishop of Glasgow, spun out negotiations with the English to allow Wallace to gather strength. Both de Moray and Wallace, no doubt stung by Edward's brutality, declined to offer the courtesies of feudal chivalry to their English opponents. This has obtained a bad press for Wallace in particular in some histories to this day. The reality of the case was that savagery begot savagery, as it usually does in war.[6]

Negotiations could not be spun out long. English financial control, and the ability of the occupiers to raise taxes in Scotland, was under severe threat. In July 1297, Hugh Cressingham wrote to London saying that it was impossible to raise taxes and that the English were confined to the castles. Wallace, gathering men in Selkirk Forest, emphasised the point by 'laying siege to Dundee Castle in August'. A month earlier, Moray's army had taken back the north of Scotland as far as the Spey. In the south, English power forced the overt submission of the Stewart and the other nobles on 7 July, but they probably continued to lend support to Wallace and de Moray, who had rendezvoused at Dundee and now prepared for a descent on Forth–Clyde.[7]

On 11 September 1297, a major English force under the Earl of Surrey reached the Forth at Stirling, intending to cross the river that separated northern and southern Scotland. The bridge was narrow, but Surrey, with heavy cavalry and men at arms, was confident that no Scots would dare attack. His men began to cross.

High above, on the Abbey Craig, standing amid the ruins of an Iron Age hillfort which had once served the same military purpose at an earlier stage in the landscape of Scottish history, Wallace and de Moray stood with a sizeable army.

When a substantial proportion of the English had crossed, with others still on the bridge, a charge was ordered. The Scottish infantry poured down the slopes of the Abbey Craig. Trapped between the mountain and the flood, the English army was defeated and severely mauled. Cressingham, who might have expected to be ransomed given his rank, was killed and skinned, in a vicious metaphorical *reprise* of his skinning of Scotland through taxation. The Anglo-Norman's skin was cut 'into small pieces and carried about the country as tokens of liberation'; Wallace was said to have had some of it made into a purse, another grim metaphor for English fiscal oppression. De Moray was badly wounded, but his and Wallace's armies had carried the day. The Stewart and the Earl of Lennox, who had nominally submitted to the English, attacked them as they retreated.

Who were in these armies? Who were their soldiers? Edward had gained the support (on parchment, at least) of the vast bulk of the feudal nation. This should have ensured that no troops could be raised, unless the nobles revolted from their allegiance to him.

This situation has led to the long and at times apparently ineradicable misconception (seen in *Braveheart* (1995), a film from which the crucial role of the bishops is entirely absent) that the Scots who fought with de Moray and Wallace were volunteers from among the poor and ordinary people of Scotland, who deserted their feudal allegiance to save their nation; while the nobility betrayed their country, with even the best of them offering only grudging and unreliable support. While it is true that some of the 'Scots lords' suggested the possibility of submission ahead of engagements such as that at Stirling Bridge in 1297, the armies of that year could not have been brought to the field without their help, even though their more exposed position made it easier for Edward to bring them into temporary obedience or conditional submission. Cressingham suggested that the earls were complicit in raising Wallace and de Moray's army, and the brother of the late Earl of Fife joined Wallace. At Stirling Bridge, it was the Stewart and the Earl of Lennox who harried the retreating English rank and file and baggage train with their cavalry, while when Wallace raided Northumberland it was probably with the support of the Earl of Strathearn. When Edward's might destroyed Wallace at Falkirk in 1298, although his cavalry fled, there is, as Geoffrey Barrow argues, no need to suppose noble treachery. Among those who probably died on the battlefield was MacDuff of Fife, 'fighting at the head of the men of that earldom'. In addition, it has been argued that Wallace's own defeat at Falkirk was a product of his 'conservatism' in seeking a pitched battle: and it is noteworthy that Wallace on his own was considerably less successful in the field than in combination with the noble de Moray, who had died shortly after Stirling Bridge, possibly of wounds sustained at that battle.[8]

Falkirk as a battle was much more than a sideshow for English power. When Wallace's and Edward's armies met there on 22 July 1298, the army deployed by the English king 'was larger . . . than any other before the seventeenth century'. The schiltrons (pike squares) of Scottish pikes stood firm, even after the Scottish cavalry had fled, but, after they were thinned by longbowmen, the knights could ride them down, and the battle ended as a rout. However, had Wallace not taken the field, it is likely that the logistical problems of and internecine tensions within the Plantagenet army might well have prevented its concluding a successful campaign. Even in the sixteenth century, attempting to subdue Scotland was an expensive business; in Edward I's day, it weighed heavily on England's resources, and all for the sake of a country with less wealth than one of the provinces of France.

Edward failed to follow up Falkirk effectively. There he had deployed and led in person a huge army, which had almost collapsed internally before gaining its victory. He had won back Scotland as far north as Forth–Clyde, but temporarily and at a price. England lacked the ratio of force to space necessary to hold Scotland if all her other military commitments were to be maintained. From 1299 to 1303, the Guardians of Scotland (see below) held the country north of Forth–Clyde, and sometimes south of it.[9]

Robert Bruce the Competitor died in 1295 in his eighties. His son, Earl of Carrick in the right of his wife the Countess Marjory, who died in 1304, surrendered his claim to his own son Robert. Young Robert Bruce, who fought in Wallace's Rising, now became heir to his family's claim to the throne. The position in Scotland was however drifting in Baliol's favour, particularly after Bruce lost his Guardianship in 1300, after two years. In 1301, Baliol was 'released from papal custody and returned to his ancestral estates in Picardy' in France. The time seemed ripe for a restoration, to which Bruce could not easily be party, and after which he would probably never be trusted even if he were. Consequently, at the turn of 1301/2, Bruce came into King Edward's peace, indeed making a humiliating submission recognising England's absolute overlordship, and married that same year Elizabeth de Burgh, daughter of the Earl of Ulster, Richard, who had already handed over Man to Edward. However, the prospects of a Baliol restoration at the hands of the Guardians almost immediately collapsed.

Following the treaty with France in 1295, Philip IV (r. 1268–1314) had been assiduously lobbied by the Scots throughout the 1290s, and in 1299 wrote praising their defence of their country's liberty. At the same time, England was locked in intermittent war with France, and, as a consequence, was unable to effectively subdue Scotland, with whom it was forced to make repeated truces. In 1302, French pressure secured a nine-month truce in the Anglo-Scottish war, and the restoration of Baliol must have appeared increasingly likely. But France also had her own military commitments, and these were soon to turn to disaster. On 11 July 1302, the 'massacre of the French feudal host at Courtrai' by the foot soldiery of Flanders may have foreshadowed Bannockburn, but it also led France to withdraw to lick its wounds. King Philip was out of the fight to help Scotland, while his quarrel with the Papacy compounded the problem. On 20 May 1303, he made peace with England on terms which excluded the Scots, leaving them bereft of allies – the time had come to subdue the northern kingdom.[10]

Edward I and his army marched north in 1303–4, capturing patriot strongholds as they went. Scotland was quickly subdued. In February 1304, Wallace and his forces were defeated by Plantagenet troops 'at Happrew in Stobo, a few miles west of Peebles'. The last Scottish army in the field had been defeated, and English forces could now drive Sir William out of his last redoubt, Selkirk Forest. In March, Edward convened a parliament at St Andrews, and in April laid siege to the last stronghold in Scottish hands, Stirling

Castle, whose small garrison under Sir William Oliphant made a heroic resistance in the name of King John. Even after Sir William expressed a willingness to surrender, Edward ordered his great trebuchet, War Wolf, to pound the fortifications for a day just to see what damage was done. Modern experiments indicate that unless its crew could be pinned down by archers, the trebuchet, a giant spring-loaded catapult which fired huge rocks, could easily destroy dressed stone once it found its range.

After the submission of the nobility, Edward pressed the Scots magnates to hunt down his hated opponent, in a pursuit which 'bore every mark of a personal vendetta'. As Fiona Watson observes, 'Edward may well have felt most uncomfortable with Wallace's ideas of liberty and nationalism'. Scotland was to be no more a kingdom but a 'land', and its nobles could have their lands restored in return for direct homage to Edward. Most saw no alternative to pursuing this route, but some, including the Guardian John de Soulis, already in exile, did not surrender. Wallace made one last attack, in the ancient heartland of Abernethy, in September 1304, and then was on the run until he was betrayed by Sir John Menteith in summer 1305, tried as a traitor against a king whom he had never owned as lord, and butchered at Smithfield on 23 August.[11]

Meanwhile Bruce, while officially in Edward's peace, had made a secret 'band' (bond of support) with Bishop Lamberton of St Andrews, in June 1304, which was to be 'a solemn bond of mutual friendship and alliance against all men'. Sir John Comyn, Lord of Badenoch, the son of the earlier Guardian who had been a competitor in 1291 before withdrawing in Baliol's favour, also made some kind of compact with Bruce. Either he or Bruce reneged on the compact, and during a discussion between them at Greyfriars Kirk in Dumfries on 10 February 1306, Bruce (with or without the help of Sir Roger de Kirkpatrick, who is alleged to have said 'I mak siccar' ('I'll make sure')) slew Comyn before the altar.

On Lady Day (25 March) 1306, the tenth anniversary of the beginning of the War of Independence. King Robert I FitzBruce was crowned at Scone. It was a new beginning, but 'less than a third of the magnates' sided with him 'and more were actively hostile' – the new king had not only the pro-English, but the pro-Baliol factor to contend with. Comyn and his father had been Guardians for ten years between them, and were solid Baliol men. John Comyn, Earl of Buchan, the murdered man's cousin, had been 'often leader of the Scottish army', in the war, and Isabel, his wife, performed a supplementary coronation ceremony for Bruce on 27 March, thus exacerbating the divisions in the kingdom. Alastair MacDougall, Lord of Argyll and Lorne and the murdered man's uncle, would support the Comyns in the west. King Robert had civil war and war with the might of Plantagenet England on his hands. His hopes from diplomacy were vitiated by the sacrilege of Comyn's murder. His kingship was an act of futile desperation: even his wife thought he could not last the year.[12]

CONSTITUTION AND COMMUNITY, 1286–1560

A Scottish parliament first sat in 1235, and by 1326 representatives of the commons were included. In its early phase it 'was a unified bloc of the secular and clerical lords known as the "community of the realm"', a term which was to become an important part of the national history of Scotland. By 1357, the Scottish Parliament had assumed the beginnings of its late medieval and early modern forms, for it was in this year that the term 'Three Estates' (*'tres communitates'*) first appeared, by which the Parliament eventually became familiarly known. Subsequent developments included the Lords of the Articles who managed business on behalf of the Crown, and the Privy Council, which operated in Scotland almost as the equivalent of a cabinet.[13]

As Geoffrey Barrow has so compellingly argued, the constitutional developments which attended the period after Alexander III's death in 1286 deserve the closest scrutiny. In the interregnum, a number of Guardians, *custodes*, were 'elected' by 'the community of the realm'. The near-contemporary historian John of Fordoun (*c.* 1320–84) states that the Guardians were elected at Scone by the Scottish estates, at this time consisting of the lords spiritual and temporal of the kingdom. Six men were elected: the bishops of St Andrews and Glasgow, the earls of Fife and Buchan, James the Stewart and Sir John Comyn, Lord of Badenoch. Together they represented the country from the Great Glen to the south-west, and moreover indicated an attempt on behalf of the Estates to give equal weight to the bishops, earls, and lords or great officers of the Crown. The bishops technically continued to maintain their independence from the Church in England: ten of them owed obedience to the Holy See direct, with only one (Galloway) recognising York and two (Sodor and Orkney) recognising Trondheim in Norway.[14]

The job of the Guardians was to secure and administer the realm in the absence of the king. Their status, during their term of office, was equal to his, their seal stressing 'the royal dignity of the realm'. Its two inscriptions alluded to Scotland both as a kingdom ('the seal of Scotland appointed for the government of the kingdom') and as a nation ('Saint Andrew be leader of the compatriot Scots'). The Bishop of St Andrews and the two earls had responsibility north of Forth; the others south of it. This situation became destabilised when the Earl of Buchan died and the Earl of Fife was (in 1289) murdered. The Guardians were thus more vulnerable in 1290–1, and, although King John's Council of 1295 appeared modelled on an enlarged concept of guardianship, it was arguably not until after the rising of 1297–8 that the office was once again to appear politically central.[15]

Following the victory at Stirling Bridge in 1297, 'at a parliament held at Torphichen on 29 March 1298 . . . Wallace was formally elected guardian'. This event (which may have been a ratification of what had already occurred) showed that the Guardianship could be offered to someone outside the ranks of earls, lords and bishops: in this case, someone who had proved his worth militarily. This was of necessity a two-edged sword: after Falkirk, Wallace resigned the Guardianship, and by 5 December Bruce and John Comyn, the younger of Badenoch, each with a strong territorial hold on a different side of Forth–Clyde, had been installed as Guardians. The next year, the new Bishop of St Andrews, William Lamberton, joined them. Lamberton had custody of Scotland's castles, and 'symbolised through his presence the backing of the national church for the cause of independence'. Even though 'dissension and famine in the English camp' prevented Edward following up his victory at Falkirk, and the Scots controlled the area north of

Forth–Clyde, a major question remained unresolved. Who was to be king if Edward were driven out? Baliol was in Edward's hands, a discredited pawn, while Robert Bruce was young and free and Guardian of Scotland. Already the Community had ignored precedence in elevating the militarily successful Wallace into the Guardianship: it might appear a lesser step to put Bruce on the throne.

But in 1299 Baliol was surrendered by Edward into Papal custody, and to some must once again have appeared a credible king. In 1300, Ingram d'Umfraville, a Baliol supporter, replaced Bruce as Guardian, and in 1301, John de Soulis, another Baliol man, became sole Guardian. At the turn of 1302, Bruce submitted to Edward I, no doubt determined to evade involvement in any restoration of King John. De Soulis remained Guardian, an office he partly shared with John Comyn in 1303–4, when the Scottish polity was on the verge of collapse.[16]

The Guardians were active internationally as well as within Scotland, where exchequer, mercantile and judicial activity continued. Wallace and de Moray sent letters to Scotland's 'trading partners in the Hanseatic League' after Stirling Bridge, assuring them that the country was once more free to do business. A famous letter from Wallace and de Moray, sent to the merchants of Lubeck in 1297, attests to the Scottish kingdom's having been freed. Scotland nonetheless had limited Continental contacts, and was heavily dependent on France. The peak of the diplomatic war was in 1298–1303, before Philip IV's separate peace with England, and during it there was a considerable development in the discourse of Scottish nationhood. In 1300, following Scottish lobbying, Boniface VIII issued a bull which 'challenged Edward to produce evidence of his right of overlordship over Scotland'. It was received by Edward the following August, and a string of assertions, based on the Brut-myth in the Geoffrey of Monmouth version (which implied English seniority and overlordship within Britain), was offered in response in early to mid-1301. To these the Scots replied in the *Instructiones*, which in turn formed the basis of the *Processus*, put forward by Baldred Bisset, Canon of St Andrews and Professor at Bologna, who was entrusted by de Soulis and the Community of the Realm with the development and presentation of a statement of the nationality of the Scots, which he and two others put to the Curia in 1301. In it, Bisset opposed the Scota-myth to the Brut-myth, and also appealed to the 'independence and antiquity of the Scottish kingdom', symbolised in the Stone of Scone, and to 'universal law, that no kingdom or king should be subject to another'. Bisset's powerful statement, which underpinned the later Declaration of Arbroath, was designed from the history of nation-building rhetoric which had already taken place in Scotland. It was, as John Bannerman has argued, underpinned not only by the language of feudal Norman Scotland, but also by that of customary Gaelic Scotland.[17]

While in indisputed control of Scotland in 1304–6, Edward made some efforts to integrate the country into English constitutional practice. In September 1305, he called ten Scottish magnates to a Parliament 'which drafted an ordinance for governing Scotland in the manner of Ireland'. Scots were also included among the officers of the Crown. Edward was a punctilious administrator. He had already removed Scotland's government papers, the Scottish regalia, the Stone of Scone and the Black Rood of St Margaret in

1296; many of the papers were lost at sea. The king's purpose was not merely bureaucratic. Edward I had sought 'to seize or destroy any artefact or document relating to Scotland's past or its kingship, to erase any sense of Scotland as an independent sovereign nation', and the taking of the Stone of Scone and of Scottish governmental documents alike served this end. There were '65 boxes of Scottish documents, probably from Edinburgh Castle and Scone Abbey . . . still in English hands in 1323'.[18]

By this time, Scotland was once more effectively independent, and innovation in government practice was continuing apace. From the time of the Stirling Parliament at Cambuskenneth Abbey in 1326, burgesses (the commons) were admitted to Parliament, forming the third estate. Their admission may have been due to the role of the 'urban elite' as a source of taxation revenue. Within Parliament, business committees began to develop from the 1340s on, and from the 1450s a group called the Lords of the Articles began to form, whose role was to be an executive pushing through parliamentary business in the Estates. At first the Lords were 'more the servant of the Three Estates than of the Crown', but gradually they became the Crown's means of government, a role they had taken on by the middle of the sixteenth century, and which mostly endured until 1707. Parliament also 'emerged as the highest court in the kingdom'; its committees heard appeals, and by about 1490 'the Lords of Council and Session emerge as a specific central court of justice'.

The development of the king's status also betokened a centralisation of authority. After full rites of anointment were adjudged to the monarchy by right in 1329, Scottish kings became increasingly conscious of their own status. From the reign of James III (r. 1460–88), the king wore a closed crown, sign of a sovereign imperium which notionally put him on a level with the greatest monarchs of Europe. In the sixteenth century, the Honours of Scotland, crown jewels fitting for such a sovereign, were commissioned and used. As power became increasingly centralised, a royal household and administration developed, with a Chancellor and secretariat. The Chancery, run by the Chancellor and usually based in Edinburgh Castle, 'was the state's writing office, responsible for the promulgation of the royal will in the form of brieves, charters and diplomatic correspondence'.

Dumbarton, Edinburgh and Stirling Castles 'were set aside as royal residences' under James II (r. 1437–60). By the fifteenth century a 'keeper of the privy seal appeared, while the secretary looked after an even more private royal seal, the signet'. Writer to the Signet (WS) subsequently became a 'by royal appointment' mark for writers (solicitors) in the capital, which by the time of James III (r. 1460–88) was more or less settled as Edinburgh. A Master of the Royal Household looked after the (annually audited) central finance from the time of James I (r. 1406–37), while a treasury and exchequer also developed, as did a privy council, of which 'extensive . . . records' survive from the later fifteenth century. The separate justiciar of Galloway disappeared, and in 1532, the administration of justice was formally centred in Edinburgh by the creation of the College of Justice, a central court system, which originally had seven lay and seven clerical judges. The historical importance and social consequence of the sheriffs and justiciars were retained in the new system, which helped to contribute to the law's great status as a profession in Scotland, intimately involving as it did the power of the landed classes and their regional authority. The first Lord President of the Court was Alexander Myln, Abbot of Cambuskenneth. The abolition of most Norse law in Orkney and Shetland in 1611 further centralised the system, although not until the disappearance of heritable jurisdictions in 1747 did law finally become a profession independent of local magnate power.

On a local level, burgh administration became more and more recognisably modern (council minutes survive from Aberdeen from 1398) and sheriffs and local barons gained responsibility for conducting regular wapinschaws ('weapon shows') of fencible men, to 'check equipment'. Burghs of barony had 'their own trading rights and collection of tolls and customs'. Sometimes, as in late fifteenth-century Aberdeenshire, their development helped to open up an economic hinterland. The regulation of burghs and crafts within the burgh also helped to create a complex network of custom and observance linked with local festivals, while the administration of the burghs consolidated in the hands of burgesses and gilds, who controlled commercial activities. When differences in status became more codified in the fifteenth century, burghs of barony had more limited rights than royal burghs (they had no automatic right to be represented in parliament and no overseas trade rights, for example), but they might be raised to the status of royal burghs. Many burghs of barony were hardly viable as trading entities, while among royal burghs, trading boundaries could be confused.[19]

The great territorial earldoms and lordships of Scotland were a mixture of feudal tenure and the provincial rights of the old mormaers, though 'the strength of the earldom-province relationship must not be overstated' as there were 'pockets of Crown demesne, even seats of royal sheriffdoms' within the boundaries of earldoms. As Geoffrey Barrow notes, the provincial magnates were the 'great officers' of the Crown, not just 'great landowners . . . on whom the title of earl had been bestowed as no more than a mark of special honour'. The Earl of Surrey might have lands 'in Sussex, Norfolk and Yorkshire', but the Earl of Atholl had the right to summon the 'common army' of Scotland within Atholl, wielded judicial power in his province, and had customary rights which derived from his heritage as a provincial or under-king. As in the remote past, so to quite a late date in Scottish history, a lord might be measured not by his wealth alone, but by the 'fighting tail', which, in Atholl's case, was still up to 6,000 men even as late as the eighteenth century. In some cases, as in the Western Isles (and to a lesser extent Galloway), where the 'sub-king of the Hebrides' ruled, the great lords were semi-autonomous, but even in the Western Isles, feudal landholding largely prevailed, although practices connected to legal agreements varied. Community cohesiveness operated downwards from the great lords on a system whereby feuding was 'initially settled by the heads of kins' and 'lawsuits over land were initially dealt with by the feudal overlords', where these were not the same. As Alexander Grant notes, the hybridity of Scottish society wore a 'striking aspect', with its mixture of Celtic and Norman practices: 'the Celtic features of Scotland were deeply embedded in her social structure, her language and her customs'.[20]

The power of the great territorial earldoms began to wane under Stewart rule. In 1401, the territorial foundations of their power and influence were undermined by an Act which stated 'that all the baronies held within an earldom or lordship must in future be held directly of the Crown'. In addition to this legal change, a number of historical accidents and strong decisions benefited the power of the Crown. In 1425, on his return from England, James I (r. 1406–37) overthrew the power of the Dukes of Albany and 'the earldoms of Fife and Menteith were forfeited to the Crown, along with the ancient earldom of Lennox', Buchan and Ross having already reverted after the death of Albany's second son in France at the Battle of Verneuil in 1424. In 1429, the earldom of Moray 'passed to the Crown after the last earl had died without any male issue', and in the next twenty years so did Mar, Atholl, Caithness and Strathearn, both by forfeiture and lack of heirs. In 1428, a new category of lordship was introduced, that of the 'Lord of Parliament' (to this day the Scottish equivalent of the English baron), who was distinct from the old great territorial lordships: a member of the estates, rather than a great territorial magnate such as the Lord of Galloway or of the Isles, whose power was finally broken in the 1470s. Resentment at these changes helped to cost James I his life and caused problems for his successors. James II (r. 1437–60) had a long struggle to control both the Lord of the Isles and the great house of Douglas, which for the Douglases finally ended at the battle of Arkinholm in 1455, and for the Hebrides in 1493. As one historian observes: 'ultimately the attempt to balance ideals of service to the king and community with the maintenance of semi-detached power in large parts of the kingdom proved difficult to defend'.[21]

The dioceses of the Scottish Church which had developed by the twelfth century bore more than a passing resemblance to the shape of the old mormaer provinces, and like the great lords, they could hold rights not only of barony but of regality, which might give them the judicial powers of the crown in all cases save those of treason. Such a grant was made to the Bishop of Moray in 1452. At the time of the Great Schism (1378), when there was a Pope in both Rome and Avignon, Scotland, 'like France, Castile and Aragon, acknowledged the Avignon popes' remaining 'loyal to the last, Benedict XIII, longer than any other country'. The 'Great Schism also stimulated parliamentary authority over the Scottish church', and led to the division of the diocese of Sodor and Man between two bishops, since Man (held by England once more from 1333) adhered to Rome while Scotland stayed with Avignon; Galloway was finally regarded as an unequivocally Scottish bishopric from 1430. In 1468, Man returned to Scottish hands; in 1472, Scotland's ecclesiastical status was finally fully recognised by the elevation of St Andrews into an archbishopric, henceforth the metropolitan of Scotland; twenty years later, Glasgow followed suit. By this time, Scotland was a country burgeoning with religious houses, with the vast bulk of parish teinds being diverted to the support of these numerous foundations. Imported Continental practices of devotion grew and burgeoned.[22]

Thus by the later fifteenth century, there was a wide variety of careers and appointments in Church and State open to talent in Scotland. To take one illustrious example, William Elphinstone (1431–1514), an official of the Glasgow diocese, became Rector of the University of Glasgow in 1474–5. In 1478, he held senior administrative rank as Commissary General of St Andrews, and was also a member of Parliament and Lord of Council. In 1481, he was nominated Bishop of

Ross, but became in 1483 Bishop of Scotland's third richest diocese of Aberdeen, where he founded a university at King's College. In 1484–6, he was chief negotiator for peace with Richard III and Henry VII, and in 1488 Chancellor of Scotland. Removed from this office on the murder of James III, in 1492 he was back in secular office as Keeper of the Privy Seal, commissioner of Crown lands and auditor of the Exchequer. In 1513, he was nominated Archbishop of St Andrews and guardian of the infant James V, but died before he could take up these offices.[23]

IDENTITIES AND *MENTALITÉS*

Both the imaginative and literary representation of Scotland as female (a trope used also of Ireland *vis-à-vis* a male England) and the development of what has been called the school of 'defensive patriotism', can be found in the era of the War of Independence, from which they may date. The identification of Scotland as female, married to her king, who is properly the defender of her honour and independence, was a trope descriptive of Scottish nationality which survived into the Jacobite period. Although its origins may lie in Scots-Irish mythology, where Fionn's wife Grainne has been identified 'as one of the manifestations of the loathly hag who turns into a beautiful young woman in the narratives that deal with the Sovereignty of Ireland', it is found in history for perhaps the first time early in the Wars of Independence, when in 1291 Scotland was described as 'widowed' without her king. As a female, she could also be compared with the Church, the Bride of Christ, and whether or not this comparison was made, both the bishops of Moray and Glasgow told the people 'that fighting for Scotland was as good a cause as fighting against the Saracens'. Scots who failed to support King Robert were 'described as "English" by the later Scottish chroniclers'. Bruce himself in 1297 said that he was to return to his own people, while Bishop Lamberton wrote affectingly of the 'land of my birth' to Philip of France in 1309.[24]

What has been identified as the school of the discourse of valour or 'defensive patriotism', which stressed Scotland's status as a nation whose existence was defined in terms of its ongoing struggle for liberty, also had its roots in the Wars of Independence. It is 'no accident' that the poet John Barbour (c. 1320–95) 'puts into King Robert's mouth on the eve of Bannockburn the very words of Judas Maccabeus', while the same Jewish hero reappears in the Declaration of Arbroath (1320): a valiant defender of the integrity of the chosen people against the pagan Seleucid empire. In 1301, Scottish envoys at the Papal court had already 'compared Edward I to Antiochus, defiler of the Temple at Jerusalem in 169 BC'. The Scottish nation was thus likened to the chosen people of Israel, struggling against its oppressors.

This discourse of Scottish nationality developed both from Biblical sources and classical ones, including Sallust (whose *Bellum Catilinae* was quoted from in the Declaration of Arbroath, as Edward Cowan points out) and, from 'the late fifteenth century', Tacitus, who had contrasted the freedom-loving Caledonian/German tribes and the corruption of imperial Rome. This national self-identification tended to stress the nature of liberty as antipathetic to the claims of empire; in that sense it was used in a later age of both Corsica and America in the eighteenth century. In the fourteenth, the Declaration of Arbroath drew attention to the history of

Scottish resistance as a struggle for liberty: 'the warlike tribes of the Picts against the Britons and of the Scots against the Picts'. The Declaration quite extraordinarily suggested the provisionality of kingship and the centrality of the nation of whom the king was the elected, rather than anointed, ruler. The events of 1286–1314 had no doubt led many to see the sacral and inviolable nature of kingship in a different light, but what followed was nonetheless surprising. After praising Bruce, the Declaration states:

> But after all, if this prince shall leave these principles he hath so nobly pursued, and consent that we or our kingdom be subjected to the king or people of England, we will immediately endeavour to expel him, as our enemy and as the subverter both of his own and our rights, and we will make another king, who will defend our liberties: For so long as there shall but one hundred of us remain alive we will never give consent to subject ourselves to the dominion of the English. For it is not glory, it is not riches, neither is it honours, but it is liberty alone that we fight and contend for, which no honest man will lose but with his life.

The Declaration is one of the most remarkable documents of medieval Europe. In it the nation and the king stand as separate concepts: the feudal king's right lies in his performance. That its signatories were barons and not commoners matters little, the Bill of Rights of 1689 and the American Declaration of Independence were alike the products of an elite. Scottish political thought can be seen in this document, in some senses anticipating them both; indeed, it was probably to influence the American Declaration.

The Declaration of Arbroath formed part of a continuing tradition. John of Fordoun (*c.* 1320–84) stressed Scotland's history of liberty as resistance to the 'loathsome vale of slavery', and saw the nation as built on its moral martial quality of resistance to Roman, Briton, Saxon, Dane, Pict and Norman. Hector Boece (*c.* 1465–1536) saw the Scots as 'a nation-in-arms'. Later Scottish political thinkers such as John Mair (1467–1550) likewise argued that Bruce was king 'by virtue of the choice of the Scottish people' and endorsed the Declaration's view that 'the Scots asserted quite unequivocally that the community had the right to depose and replace their kings', an argument later developed by George Buchanan (1505–82). This may have been no mere theory. In the 1350s, 'the Scottish estates are said to have threatened to depose David II if he submitted to Edward III'. In 1385, an Act of Parliament 'commanded Scots soldiers to wear . . . the saltire' of St Andrew and the nation rather than the 'lion rampant' of the royal standard.[25]

Earlier in the fourteenth century, King Robert I's policies, which prevented Scots holding land in England, and forced English magnates to choose whether to hold land in England or Scotland, certainly underpinned the 'Scottish exceptionalism' arguably inherent in the Arbroath Declaration. Although it has been argued that Scots were more 'divided and uncertain' in their identity than patriot chroniclers such as John of Fordoun or John Barbour admitted, and though the English king might continue to grant lands in Scotland at times of English ascendancy, the Scottish loyalties of those living in the Scots realm were now extensible to those born there. In 1296, William of Bolhope, a Scot long resident in Alnwick, refused to recognise Edward I as his overlord and was put to death; in 1384, a Scotswoman living in England and married to an Englishman, 'lit a beacon' to warn the folk of Galloway of 'an impending English raid'. She was acquitted in an English court on the grounds of her being in the Scottish king's allegiance, as she was by birth, but not apparently by land, residence or marriage. Scottishness frequently expressed itself in such terms of defensive difference. It should not be overlooked, however, that in the climate of hostility between the two countries, there were some, like the philosopher John Mair (1467–1550), who argued for a united Britain (albeit as 'a union . . . of equal partners') in the 1520s. There was certainly (as surviving burgh records show) considerable, understandable and enduring anti-English hostility among the Scottish people after the Wars of Independence, but it should also be noted that this was not universal. Defining Scottish difference did, however, tend to involve definition against England, particularly as more and more Scots came to speak a form of English.[26]

Dauvit Broun has recently argued that Scots at the time of the Wars of Independence regarded themselves as having very close links with Ireland, having indeed an 'Irish Identity'. King Robert's appeal for Irish help in 1306–7, when he declared the Scots and Irish to be of one 'common language and custom' and 'sprung from one seed of a nation', and therefore requested Irish support in regaining Scotland's 'ancient liberty' becomes especially intriguing on this reading, as does Edward Bruce's attempt to secure the High Kingship of Ireland in 1316–18. Certainly, whatever later divisions occurred following the Reformation, Gaelic-speaking Scotland at least continued to identify to some extent with Ireland throughout the Middle Ages, and Broun's reading offers a route to deepening our understanding of this process.[27]

Within Scotland, 'the feudal principle that heiresses could transmit land and titles to their husbands allowed territorial aggrandisement on a large scale'. Greater and greater powers flowed to the big earldoms and lordships (at least until 1400, after which policies of royal centralisation provided a counterweight), but there were also distinct hierarchies in the localities, such as the council of the isles in the west. Many traditional practices continued, even at the highest levels: as late as 2 May 1349, 'the King's Justiciar, William, Earl of Ross' was present at the bishop's court in the 'standing stones' of Rayne in Aberdeenshire: a resort of ancient pagan significance still imbued with respect in the conduct of medieval justice.[28]

As regards the leadership of the country, many commentators, particularly in the nineteenth century, saw Bruce simply as a Norman, even an Anglo-Norman, whose ambitions were not national but simply personal and dynastic. This approach was particularly appealing to those who wanted to see the War of Independence under King Robert as a prelude to Union, rather than being an alternative to it. On this model (largely constructed after 1707), two great Germanic peoples (the Highlanders were largely excluded as 'Celts') with Norman aristocracies, united to form a nation (Great Britain) capable of leading the world. Now that Great Britain no longer leads the world, it is inevitable that this explanation should have diminished in its appeal. But more importantly, neither it nor its contrary (that Robert was a heroic Celt bent on war against the Saxon stranger) are sustainable. There were certainly elements in King Robert, as

Geoffrey Barrow has pointed out, of the 'potentate in the immemorial mould of the western Gaidhealtachd' [Gaelic-speaking area]; there was more in him of the Norman (though not altogether credibly Anglo-Norman) aristocrat. But what he was doing was defending an ancient nation against an invader, while looking after his own interests when required: not a Celtic nation, not a Saxon nor a Norman nation, but Scotland, a country, but one no longer only the land of the Scots. The more absolutist heroism of Wallace has long held a warmer place in much Scottish opinion, especially when (erroneously) linked to a belief in Sir William as some kind of medieval Red Clydesider, a view which can be traced back at least to his adoption by Romantic writers such as Robert Burns and Robert Southey. King Robert was not however the architect of the glorious defeat, that blessing of Scottish sentiment and curse of the Scottish intellect: he was a general and a leader of European stature, who with the help of many others, not least the bishops, made possible the Scotland that is still in evidence today.

The evidence does however favour a rehabilitation of the centrality of Gaelic Scotland to Bruce's achievement and subsequent Scottish political thought. Although anti-Highland prejudice grew from the late fourteenth century in response to political disturbance, the extension of Anglophone culture and (possibly) economic decline, Scottish patriot discourse continued to see the Gaidhealtachd as central to the nation's identity right up to the Jacobite period in the eighteenth century; indeed, the idea was revived by Sir Walter Scott. Hector Boece, a representative of this tradition, 'went out of his way to locate the well-spring of the nation's virtue in the Celtic west and north and to urge his compatriots to emulate the uncorrupted morals and manners of the Highlanders'. Uncorrupted morals and manners were the badge of ancient liberty in Tacitus's characterisation of the Caledonians and of the lost purity of Republican Rome when sovereignty was elective, before the days of empire. These features became embedded in the Scottish patriot tradition.[29]

BRUCE'S WAR, 1306–14

In the weeks after being crowned in 1306, King Robert struggled to gather troops in the face of imminent counter-attack. Edward had arranged to have Bruce excommunicated by Clement V, and appointed another member of the Comyn family, Sir Aymer de Valence, later Earl of Pembroke, 'as his special lieutenant in Scotland'. Bruce had some success in the north, but soon had to face Pembroke, who was hot on his tail. At Methven, the Earl of Pembroke's horse overran the king's positions at dusk, scattering the Scots, while in (probably) July, MacDougall inflicted further defeat on Bruce's forces near Tyndrum. Now driven out of both southern and western Scotland, Robert was a fugitive in Atholl and Breadalbane. Worse was to follow. He had sent his wife and daughters with the Earl of Atholl to the care of his brother Neil Bruce at Kildrummy, 70 km west of Aberdeen. But an angry Edward's arm was long: Kildrummy fell to English troops, Neil was hanged as a traitor, and the fleeing royal family were overtaken at Tain, the burgh where St Duthac was venerated, and treated abominably, the king's sister Mary being hung in a cage at Roxburgh Castle, while the Countess of Buchan was 'imprisoned for four years in a cage built of lattice-work' at Berwick Castle. Even Bruce's twelve-year-old daughter was due to be shut in a cage, but

Edward relented. Bruce's wife Christian and his sister were more leniently treated, but still imprisoned: the fact that the queen was daughter to the Plantagenet loyalist Earl of Ulster no doubt helped her. That winter, utterly defeated, Robert fled to Rathlin Island, and spent the next few months probably in Ireland or South Uist.[30]

Early in 1307, King Robert seems to have taken the decision to use a form of guerilla warfare against the English and their Scots allies, making his men into a mobile, rapid force which would move and strike unexpectedly swiftly:

> Based on the hill country of Carrick and Galloway, he would harass the enemy, spread panic among the English garrisons, recruit supporters until he was strong enough to break out towards the country north of Forth, where he could count on gathering many more followers. . . .

Robert's success with this policy was remarkable, and makes him and his commanders easily the most successful military leaders in the history of Scotland as an independent nation. Bannockburn was no one-off, except in the sense that it was a large pitched battle. Instead it was the culmination of years of almost unabated success, won first by the soldiery of Bruce's own lands in the south-west, then by an increasingly national army, for Edward I's harsh humiliation of Scotland led many to support King Robert who might have been at heart Baliol loyalists.[31]

After a disastrous start, when his brothers were overwhelmed by a MacDougall force in Galloway while Bruce was once again a fugitive from the English after landing at Turnberry, the tide began to turn. In April 1307, King

Robert's troops defeated an English force in an ambush in Glen Trool; on around 10 May, Pembroke was beaten at Loudon Hill by a heavily-outnumbered Scottish force; three days later, the Earl of Gloucester's troops fell to Scottish arms in Ayrshire. Edward's relieving invasion force, led by the king himself, moved slowly owing to his declining health; Edward died at Burgh-on-Sands on 7 July. His son (Edward II, r. 1307–27) led the army into Scotland, and received the homage of some Scottish nobles at Dumfries, but otherwise achieved little against the elusive Scots, and returned to London.

By the autumn of 1307, Robert was ready to march north, 'leaving a force' under his greatest commander, Sir James Douglas, to recover the Southern Uplands. Comyn-held Inverlochy fell to Robert's army in October, followed by Inverness and Castle Urquhart on the Great Glen. An unsuccessful attack on Elgin was succeeded by Robert's illness, worn out as he was by the privations of the field. But the Comyns, who opposed him in that part of the country, could make no capital out of it. Early in 1308, the king recovered, and he and his allies took several more northern strongholds before defeating John Comyn, Earl of Buchan's army 'on the road between Inverurie and Oldmeldrum' in May, an event followed by the 'herschip' or ravaging of Buchan that summer. The Earl of Ross submitted to King Robert; in June/July, Aberdeen surrendered. He had the north.

Almost immediately King Robert turned south, and at the Pass of Brander ambushed and defeated MacDougall of Lorne's forces by sending his own archers even higher up the 1100 m walls of Ben Cruachan than Lorne had sent his own men. MacDougall submitted to Bruce, though he proved untrustworthy, attending Edward II's Westminster Council in June 1309. Cupar fell, and King Robert retook Fife.[32]

By late 1308, Robert Bruce was successful enough to start to turn from fighting to the business of a civilian administration: 'surviving written acts of government' in the king's name begin at this time. He effectively controlled most of Scotland north of Forth, and much of the Southern Uplands and south west. In March 1309, the Scots Estates at St Andrews justified King Robert's claims as 'he has by the sword restored the realm', and an 'anonymous manifesto' laid stress on the history of 'military champions' who had defended the integrity of Scotland. By November 1313, Robert's power was so well established that his proclamation at his Dundee parliament gave those Scots who had not yet submitted to him a year to do so or face forfeiture.

By 1309, supplying the English-held castles of Stirling and Edinburgh 'was proving difficult and dangerous', but, further south, English power was entrenched at Jedburgh, Roxburgh, Berwick and many other strongholds. In the west, Edward Bruce, the last surviving brother of the king, found it hard going dislodging English garrisons from Galloway, where Dumfries did not fall until 1313. Banff, in the Comyn heartland, may have been taken in 1310. Once they were taken, Robert usually destroyed castle strongholds, thus making 'it nearly impossible to establish secure garrisons'. After his death, this policy was to prove of considerable benefit to the Scots who resisted Edward Baliol in the 1330s. In some cases (such as that of Dunstaffnage), Robert preserved the castle in order to secure his own control of Comyn/Baliol territory.[33]

Edward II responded to Robert's successes with an invasion force which marched 'deep into Scotland to little purpose' in

1310–11, reaching as far as Linlithgow near Edinburgh. Robert harried them, and Edward's forces finally withdrew in August 1311 with nothing accomplished. In response, King Robert raided England with ferocity, attacking Durham in summer 1312. More sophisticated than Wallace, Robert preferred to be bought off than to burn – one could always come again for second helpings. As Geoffrey Barrow tells us, by the time of Bannockburn:

> the four northern counties of England were close to exhaustion, either devastated or impoverished or both. The money which they should have paid to the exchequer at Westminster had gone, with two- or three-fold increase, to fill Bruce's empty war chest.

At home, Robert and his allies continued to pile success on success, taking Dundee in 1312 and Perth 'almost without a fight' in January 1313. The king launched a naval operation to recover Man (where Bruce had adherents and control of which was vital for 'the western seaways') in May and June that year. On Shrove Tuesday 1314 (19 February), Sir James Douglas took Roxburgh; the next month, informed by a local guide, the Earl of Moray's men climbed the rock of Edinburgh Castle and surprised the garrison. Saving only a few strongholds, the whole of Scotland was recovered from English rule.[34]

By this time however, a time bomb had been placed under Robert's success. His brother Edward had in 1313 chivalrously offered Sir Philip Moubray, the English commander of Stirling Castle, a year's respite from surrender, on condition that if he were not relieved by Midsummer 1314, he would deliver his castle into Scottish hands. Such a challenge was a matter of honour, and Edward II picked up the gauntlet. A feudal host was assembled and marched north: there were perhaps 15,000 foot and 2–3,000 armoured horse, knights and men-at-arms.

England had at its disposal two of the most effective weapons systems of the day, neither of which the Scots could match. Among its infantry were men carrying the Welsh longbow of 1.5–1.8 m, almost twice the size of the short native or early Norman bow carried by the Scots. At Falkirk, its use by Welsh archers had riven the sturdy spear formations of Wallace's schiltrons. Although English archers were not in 1314 trained to the levels they reached in the Hundred Years' War, the longbow was a devastating weapon, capable of firing up to 400 m at 12 rounds a minute in the hands of a good archer. Indeed, it is arguable that no more effective battlefield infantry weapon existed until the nineteenth century; the earlier adoption of guns was more of a reflection of fashion and on the cost and difficulty of training good archers. Scotland had nothing to match them.

Nor had King Robert the same number of heavy cavalry as were available to the greater powers of medieval Europe. Little could withstand the charge of 2,000 tonnes of man, mount and metal, lances outstretched, at 40–50 km/h. The massed pike formations of the Scots with their 3–4.5 m pikes stood a chance of doing so, which is one of the reasons why, at Falkirk, the archers had been employed to thin their ranks before the critical cavalry charge. Individually, English light bowmen and heavy cavalry were devastating: in combination, they were irresistible.

Edward Bruce's pledge of chivalry with Sir Philip Moubray was thus highly dangerous. King Robert had recovered his country from enemy occupation by sudden surprise attacks or contests with small forces. He had never faced, nor could he surely face, a large English army in open battle, such as he had avoided in 1310–11.

As Edward II and his forces approached Stirling, King Robert had under his command four brigades of infantry, each of about 1,500 men, and 500 (mainly light) cavalry. Edward's vast army was largely confined to the old Roman marching road, both by the ground and also by the fact that Robert had booby-trapped the soft land with pits and calthrops, which projected a spike wherever they landed. In the van of Robert's army in the New Park close by Stirling Castle stood the Earl of Moray's brigade, followed by those of Edward Bruce and Walter the Stewart (commanded by Sir James Douglas); the king's stood in the rear.[35]

The Earls of Gloucester and Hereford, leading the English van, made an early charge on 23 June across the Bannock Burn, during which King Robert killed Hereford's nephew, Sir Henry de Bohun, in full view of the Scots army. The pits and calthrops broke the charge, while another English cavalry force, under Sir Robert Clifford and Sir Henry Beaumont, were blocked in their attempt to reach the castle by Moray's schiltron. The Scots were, however, still on the defensive, and King Robert, true to his guerilla instincts, was considering withdrawing, before fresh intelligence and the morale of his troops led him to change his mind.

On the morning of the 24th, King Robert addressed his men, telling them (according to his contemporary, Bernard de Linton, Abbot of Arbroath, who was the keeper of the *brecbennoch* reliquary of St Columba, sign of Scottish nationhood) that their opponents were 'bent upon destroying us and obliterating our kingdom, nay, our whole nation'. Nation and kingdom were separate, but intertwined. The king also apparently invoked 'Our Lord Jesus as commander, Saint Andrew and the martyr Saint Thomas [à Becket]' to 'fight today with the saints of Scotland for the honour of their country and their nation'. It was not just their king for whom the Scots were fighting, it was Scotland herself, protected by the intercession of her saints: Andrew, her patron; Margaret, the queen; Duthac, at whose shrine the king's family had fallen into the hands of the English; Columba, whose *brecbennoch* reliquary was borne into battle before the Scots and whose reputed laying of hands on King Áedán of Dál Riata was a sign of the ancient sovereignty of the nation; St Kentigern, Columba's friend and founder of Bishop Lamberton's cathedral at Glasgow, the patriot bishop who had made that band with Bruce in 1304; St Fillan, King Robert's own patron; St Adomnán, early exponent of just war theory and all the rest. King Robert, who had killed John Comyn in a quarrel before the altar of a Dumfries church and seized the throne of Scotland for himself, would be vindicated in the sight of God and man if, with the intercession of the saints of the nation he lived to defend and rule, victory was won in open field against the feudal host of England under its king's direct command. The invocation of St Thomas, recorded by Bernard de Linton as abbot of the abbey dedicated to St Thomas à Becket by William the Lion, was surely significant – King Robert might have struck down Comyn, but Henry II's words had martyred the holy archbishop in his own cathedral. Plantagenet hands were stained with the blood of God's holy saint as well as that of the king's fellow-countrymen: now the martyr of Canterbury's prayers were called for to set Scotland free.[36]

The Scottish army lined up in its four brigades. In the van stood Edward Bruce, with his schiltron; slightly behind, the Earl of Moray, with his; falling back slightly further still, Sir James Douglas; in the rear, the King. The heavy cavalry under the Earl of Gloucester smashed into Edward's schiltron, possibly hindered by the boggy carse (although the battle may have been fought on the dryfield below it). For a moment there was chaos, then hand-to-hand fighting, as knights still on horseback slashed with sword or mace at the long spears and those who held them, no doubt bringing down soldiers in the front rank where the spear hedge had opened with the shock of the impact. But many, both horse and man, were impaled on the Scottish spears: Gloucester himself was killed, as was Comyn's own son.

Now another of Robert's great innovations in generalship was seen: the defensive formation of the schiltron, a static means of resisting attack, began to move. First Edward's, then Moray's and Sir James's schiltrons shifted forward, pushing back the knights in front and crushing them into those who followed. A ferocious stagnant mêlée ensued: the flower of English chivalry, with almost no room to manoueuvre let alone charge, crushed in the narrow space of the carse, fighting doggedly against the slow forward pressure of one then two then three thousand spearmen. Heavily armed and individually superb warriors, the knights often with many years' training behind them, the English van almost held its own against the press of the three schiltrons.

Now the English longbowmen poured a flanking fire into the massed phalanxes of pushing spears. Their position was, however, exposed. King Robert ordered Sir Robert Keith, Marischal of Scotland, to charge them with his cavalry, and they were broken and swept off the field after a few early flights of arrows. King Robert prepared to commit his reserve, commanded on the field by Angus Óg Macdomnuill of Islay, and as they joined the Scottish front, the English knights and men-at-arms began slowly to give way. At this point the lightly armed and non-combatant Scottish camp followers streamed over the brow of Coxet Hill, where they had been stationed. The English wavered: perhaps especially the infantry, largely kept out of the battle. As the poet John Barbour records, a cry went up from the Scots: '"On thaim on thaim on thaim thai faile"'. In a minute or two all was over. The English broke and ran: King Edward only just escaping the clutches of Sir James Douglas. The Bannock Burn and the Forth filled with the dead as defeat became a rout. The Scots captured the English baggage and the Earl of Hereford, who was subsequently exchanged for King Robert's queen, daughter and sister Mary.[37]

It was a critical victory, but Edward II would still not recognise Scottish independence. In response, Sir James Douglas sacked Hartlepool in 1315. But King Robert had plans further afield: and thus followed one of the most daring moves of the whole war, the attempt to install Edward Bruce as High King of Ireland, following an invitation on behalf of some of the native Irish, and to thus create an encirclement of England. In 1315–18, concerted efforts were made to enlist Gaelic Ireland's support. That Robert Bruce was a threat was well-realised: the king of Scots was now a countervailing power to Plantagenet imperialism. The Welsh commander Sir Gruffudd Llwyd wrote to Edward in 1316 stating that: 'the intention of the English' was 'to try and delete our name and memory from the land'. The Scots were conscious of this purpose, both with regard to the Welsh and the Irish, and the Bruces may have seen themselves as a useful means of countering it: Edward Bruce 'evidently hoped to become the overlord of Wales as well as Ireland', as more than one recent commentator has remarked.[38]

Robert's alliance by marriage to the earls of Ulster helped to create a power base for Edward's attempt. On 2 May 1316, Edward Bruce was crowned *ard-rí* of Ireland at Maeldun near Dundalk. As he was 'heir-presumptive to the Scottish throne', this action 'opened up the prospect of a dynastic union between the two countries, should the English be driven out of Ireland as well'. In 1317, an attempt was made to push south to drive the English out of Dublin, but the native Irish were divided. Even after Edward was defeated and killed near Dundalk in 1318, however, King Robert was unwilling to see 'English power become firmly established in Antrim or Down', whence it might be used as a springboard against the Scottish west, not least because of pro-English sympathies in the western isles (although there had also been strong support for King Robert there) and Galloway. As late as 1327–8, Robert crossed into Ulster to prevent this in a year in which his forces also attacked Northumbria in order to put pressure on the English.

Berwick was the last Scottish castle to fall into King Robert's hands, in 1318. Carlisle, Norham and Newcastle also fell to the Scots, and in 1319 Edward II responded to the taking of Berwick with another invasion force of 10,000 men, who were humiliated, retreating to Trent as Scots troops opposing them pushed into the Vale of York. A truce in 1319–21 was followed by a further invasion attempt of 1322 which reached Edinburgh, but lack of food forced a retreat.

The same year, Sir James Douglas routed the English in battle in Yorkshire at Byland.[39]

Neither King Edward nor King Robert neglected the international status of Scotland, an arena where England still held the upper hand, though defeated in the field at home. In 1319, four Scottish bishops were summoned before John XXII after resisting Edward's right to nominate 'ecclesiastical appointments in Scotland'. They didn't appear, an act which in itself might have betokened acceptance: instead the Declaration of Arbroath was the Scottish response. The attitude of the Papacy began to soften, and in 1324, John XXII finally recognised Robert's title. In 1326, Robert made a fresh alliance with France under the Treaty of Corbeil. Unsuccessful peace negotiations took place at York in 1324 (when the Scots tried to retrieve the Stone of Scone). After Edward II's fall in 1327, his queen Isabella and Mortimer, who had effectively usurped the government and dominated over the young Edward III (r. 1327–77) became prepared to negotiate, especially after the Scottish campaign of 1327–8, which 'appeared to be annexing Northumberland'. At the beginning of March 1328, England renounced claim to the overlordship of Scotland; by the Treaty of Edinburgh of 17 March 1328, ratified at Northampton on 4 May, Scotland was to be 'separate in all things from the kingdom of England, entire, free, and quit, without any subjection, servitude, claim or demand': token war reparations were offered by the Scots. In July, Bruce's son David married Edward III's sister, Joan. By English petition, the Papacy in October lifted its excommunication on King Robert for Comyn's murder; only the failure of England to return the Stone of Scone as agreed rankled: the Abbot of Westminster (like his successors) helping 'to frustrate plans' for its return. On 13 June 1329, six days after King Robert's death, a Papal Bull 'conferred' the 'right to coronation and anointing', long sought by the Scots and contested by the English. King Robert and his country had won.

On Lady Day 1330, twenty-four years to the day from his coronation, King Robert made his last appearance in battle. Sir James Douglas's small band of crusading Scottish chivalry were surrounded by Muslim forces at Tebas de Ardales in Spain, where a monument now stands to their bravery. Taking King Robert's heart in its casket, Sir James threw it into the thick of the Moors, reputedly crying 'Go first into the fray where thou wert wont to go' and led his cavalry in a last charge. The heart itself was returned to Scotland, together with the body of Sir James. Like Edward Bruce, Sir James threw away his life in the end unnecessarily: the skills of both of them would have been needed in Scotland in the decade that followed.[40]

PEOPLE AND CULTURE

About half a million to a million people lived in Scotland in the fourteenth century. The country was probably less affected by the Black Death of 1349–50 than England, where the population fell from some five to three and a half million, but nonetheless Scotland suffered greatly, losing perhaps 25 per cent of its people. The effects of population loss could not have helped a more general process of economic decline, which was already manifesting itself by the end of the fourteenth century. The falling temperatures of later medieval Europe affected Scottish harvests, and the greater marginality of much Scottish land may have meant that climactic deterioration had a particularly severe effect in Scotland. The wool market and export trade declined, and Scottish currency became less convertible abroad. At home, however, Scotland produced plenty of fish, meat and dairy produce, and was relatively free from the peasant radicalism so prevalent elsewhere in Europe. David Ditchburn and Alastair MacDonald have pointed out that the average height of those buried in monastic 'burial grounds' is only some 3–4 cm shorter than the contemporary averages: hardly a sign of widespread malnutrition, although such evidence is arguably more relevant for the middling sort or well-to-do.

City living was less developed than elsewhere, but by no means in its infancy. There were '70 or so burghs', none of which probably held more than 10,000 people, but then nowhere in England did either, except for London, Bristol, Norwich and York. Scotland was, however, notable for the number of its religious houses. By the early fourteenth century there were 30 abbeys and 56 other religious houses. By the fifteenth century, the Church in Scotland was firmly organised in twelve dioceses (Caithness, Ross, Moray, Aberdeen, Brechin, Dunkeld, Dunblane, St Andrews, Glasgow, Argyll, the Isles and Galloway) divided into around a thousand parishes. It was noteworthy that 'the national land assessment of 1366 valued Scotland north of the Forth higher than the south', and there is no reason to doubt that a large proportion of the population lived in the north of the country: still true in 1750, but totally changed today. Customs accounts, on the other hand, show a bias in favour of southern Scotland which widened steadily until by the 1530s it stood at nearly 75 per cent of the Scottish total. Edinburgh alone had over 50 per cent of the national export trade. The concomitant of this was that many other trading burghs faced decline.[41]

Until the reign of James III (1460–88) 'there was no fixed capital, and Perth and Stirling were as prominent as Edinburgh'. The court and Parliament were moveable feasts. Trade with the Low Countries was developing as early as the thirteenth century, and shipbuilding was already among the important industries. Scots were also beginning to gain a reputation as military experts as well as soldiers: between 1419 and 1424 there were 15,000 'engaged in French military service alone'; by the 1560s, they were appearing as far afield as Russia. Wool, hides, cloth, salmon and salt were among the main exports, trading into the Baltic, England, France and, more modestly on the west, with Ireland, Brittany and the Biscay ports. By the sixteenth century the wool trade had declined, while cloth and fish (and later, salt and coal) expanded significantly; by this time also, there was significant Scottish emigration to the Baltic.[42]

Signs of interest in education were early apparent. Not only did Scotland have three universities by 1560 (a fourth did not survive); the country also had an impressive network of grammar schools. Many Scottish academics worked abroad, notably at the University of Paris, and in the work of Duns Scotus (1266–1308) and John Mair (1467–1550) especially, made contributions of European stature. Scotus's powerful stress on human freedom is coming to be seen by some medieval scholars as at least possibly connected with Scotland's contemporary struggle in the Wars of Independence. In Scotland itself, the universities were very small affairs: but they provided a focus for a clerical and intellectual class whose profile and importance was growing;

they were also home to innovations, such as the Aberdeen medical chair at King's College, founded in the reign of James IV (r. 1488–1513), who also 'founded the Royal College of Surgeons'. Men like Laurence of Lindores (*c.* 1372–1437) who taught at St Andrews, Hector Boece, Principal of King's College, Aberdeen and John Mair himself, who returned to St Andrews in 1534, developed the intellectual profile of the country, as did the development of historical and imaginative writing mentioned below. Monasteries had their own schools, and an increasing general commitment to education was evident in the Education Act of 1496, which 'encouraged the attainment' of good educational standards 'by the sons of barons and freeholders'.[43]

Much of Scottish art and culture was directed towards the celebration of Scottishness and the distinctiveness of national identity and authority, from the open crown spires which symbolically stated the sovereign authority of Scottish kingship and its 'full Jurisdiction and fre Impyre', to the 'nationalist purpose' of the Archdeacon of Aberdeen, John Barbour (*c.* 1320–95), the Aberdeen priest John of Fordoun (*c.* 1320–84) and the Abbot of Inchcolm, Walter Bower (*c.* 1385–1449). As befitted the history of Scotland's independence, all three of these were churchmen.

Barbour's *Bruce* (*c.* 1375) was a particularly significant achievement, combining 'historiography and contemporary literary genres' in a poem which is both an epic and a romance, stressing the qualities of 'chewalry', 'leaute', 'pite' and 'curtesy' (chivalry, loyalty, pity and courtesy) among the Scottish knights, and thus stressing the scale of their achievement in the language of chivalric prestige and claiming 'Scotland's place in the ranks of fitting subjects for elevated literary treatment'. Yet Barbour also says that the 'symple yumanry' 'can be as good as a knight', and stresses that the *Bruce*'s special claim as a romance is that it is 'suthfast' (true) thus giving a 'doubill plesance' of romance and reality to the listener and of liberty to the Scots, for 'fredome is a noble thing'. In the late fifteenth century, Blind Harry's (*c.* 1440–95) *Acts and Deeds of Sir William Wallace* popularised the other major hero of the War of Independence; more polemical and populist than Barbour's poem, it proved enduringly popular, going through 23 editions by 1707.[44]

Royal progresses were times of excitement and celebration, when the burgh being visited made great efforts of expenditure and show to display its loyalty and enhance its claim to status. Queen Margaret's visit to Aberdeen in 1511, commemorated in William Dunbar's poem 'Blithe Aberdeen, thou beryl of all tounis' was greeted with a procession and pageants which

> Included the Salutation of the virgin, the Three Kings of Cologne, the Angel with the Flaming Sword driving Adam and Eve from Paradise, Robert the Bruce and the Stewart kings, and four-and-twenty maidens all clad in green, of marvellous beauty, with flowing hair, playing on timbrels, singing, and saluting the queen.

The Scottish monarchy enjoyed popular as well as high cultural celebration: 'Thomas Galbraith, a chaplain of the Chapel Royal . . . is recorded as singing ballads to the king during the New Year celebrations of January 1491', and this appears to have by no means been unusual practice.[45]

In poetry, Scotland was beginning to produce not only the great oral culture of the so-called 'Border' ballads (many of which in fact come from the north-east), but also figures such as Robert Henryson (*c.* 1430–1505) William Dunbar (*c.* 1460–1513) and Gavin Douglas (1474–1522), Bishop of Dunkeld and son of the Earl of Angus. Henryson's beast-fables and *Testament of Cresseid* provided a commentary on the grimness of life and the limitation and misery of human beings in magnificent verse, while Dunbar's versatility as a lyricist is matched by few writers in the history of English and Scots literature. Douglas meanwhile produced the first translation of the *Aeneid* into Anglophone vernacular, a vernacular he clearly wished to identify as Scots, a separate tongue from English, for Douglas specifically states his aim to 'Kepand na Sudroun, bot oor awin langage' ('using no English, but our own tongue'). Dunbar meanwhile extended the range of Scots with innovative borrowing from Latin and French, just as Chaucer had done in England.

Royal and aristocratic patronage operated in Scotland as elsewhere in Europe. The music of Robert Carver (1486–1568), Canon of Scone Abbey, showed that Scotland was capable of sustaining a major figure in early modern music and the resources to support him: Carver's masses for James IV, V and Mary (r. 1542–67) have recently been seen as carrying coded political messages for the monarchy. The monarchy itself contributed to the cultural process. Not only had James I been a considerable poet in his own right, but James III and IV were considerable patrons of the arts. The arts in their turn could critique the monarchy, as did the courtier Sir David Lindsay's *Ane Plesant Satyre of the Thrie Estaites* (1540), while James V, for whom it was performed, was an aficionado of the ballad and was reputed to go round in disguise as 'The Gudeman of Ballengeich' to hear what his subjects said of him, the song 'The Gaberlunzie Man' being attributed to the king in that persona.[46]

In the burghs, there were mystery plays, pageants and minstrels, and 'the Abbot out of Reason', a celebration of the Lord of Misrule. The wealthy had 'fore-houses' with 'fore-stairs' (houses overlooking the main street with a 'wooden gallery or balcony' reached by 'an outside stair') backed up by 'a quadrangle of buildings to the rear, surrounding a courtyard or close' and 'a long garden'. Greater houses had ornamental gardens, with art conferring status, such as James V's closed crown fountain at Linlithgow Palace. From their town balconies the gentry 'could obtain a fine view of . . . pageants, processions, and Royal progresses'. The better-off peasants had thatched or turved houses of around 8 × 4 metres with two rooms, which presumably allowed them to live separately from their livestock: there were even some pets. Farming was mixed rather than arable, and by the fourteenth century was on a considerable scale: Melrose Abbey and the Earl of Douglas 'both had some 15,000 sheep, putting them among the largest sheep-farmers in Europe', but most of the sheep were in far smaller flocks in the hands of peasant farmers. Even the comparatively wealthy had little by present-day standards, although at the highest level of society (for example, David FitzBruce's wedding in 1328) there could be cattle, sheep, eels, porpoise and sturgeon to eat. More usually, the diet of the Scots was based on oatmeal, bere barley, kail, milk, cheese, and mutton. A good idea of the property of a modest laird can be had from the list of 'spulzie' (plunder) from Petty in 1517, which lists a bed, chairs, stools, 10 ells of wool, 12 fustian doublets, 16 pairs of white hose, wine, meal, malt, wheat, 8 saddles, 2,000 candles and 40 stone of butter among the takings, as well as 24 halberds and axes, 10 dozen arrows, 8 steel bonnets and 18 swords.[47]

The currency was the pound of silver divided into 240 pence (still called '*d*' for *denarius* in the Roman manner) on the English model, and it retained parity of value with the southern currency 'until the 1370s', when it started a long decline which left it at six to the English pound by 1565 and twelve by the accession of James VI (r. 1567–1625) to the English throne in 1603. Although it subsequently sank very slightly lower, the official rate of exchange in accounts remained at 12: 1 until the pound Scots finally disappeared in the early nineteenth century, although 'bawbee', the Scots term for sixpence (and thus an English halfpenny) survived into the twentieth. Between 1583 and 1596 alone, 'the government made £100,000' out of the depreciation of the currency. The English pound was subdivided into the noble of 80*d*, less often into the merk of 160*d*: Scotland frequently used the merk. On the whole, the depreciation of the Scottish currency was a sign of a progressive relative weakening in the Scottish economy as the Middle Ages progressed.

The richest area of the country remained the east coast, particularly Fife, Lothian and the eastern borders, with the north and west Highlands the poorest of all. In urban Scotland, the burghs north and south of Forth 'contributed equally to national taxation' until the 1560s: thereafter the influence of what came to be known as the central belt became increasingly obvious. After a steady decline during the seventeenth century, by the time of the Union, the southern towns were paying three times the sum collected north of Forth. Within the southern burghs, Edinburgh had assumed a position of overwhelming dominance by the sixteenth century, with the vast bulk of the export trade. Within Scotland, people came to trade there from as far as Perth (80 km) or Dumfries (120 km). In 1499, Edinburgh exported 73,000 skins; by 1598, that total had grown to 401,000.[48]

DAVID II AND THE STUARTS

In 1314, Robert I 'decreed that all those who would not accept his peace or whose fathers had died in battle against him were to forfeit their lands and titles'. These were to be 'the Disinherited', who proved a fertile ground of trouble for his son and successor David II (r. 1329–71).

In 1330, Edward III of England threw off the tutelage of his mother and her lover, Mortimer, and set about making amends for what he saw as the embarrassing defeat (*turpis pax*: shameful peace) of 1328, and the resultant treaty of Edinburgh–Northampton he had agreed at sixteen. John Baliol had died in France in 1313, but his son Edward was willing to pursue the Baliol claim, and his English ally and namesake was ready to help him do so. David II was still a child, and the Earl of Mar was Guardian: but Mar's army was outmanoeuvred and defeated by English archers at Dupplin Moor in August 1332, and the Guardian was killed. Edward Baliol was crowned at Scone on 24 September, and in November recognised Edward III as 'lord superior' of Scotland, ceding the border counties to England. By the end of the year Baliol was forced to flee 'after he had nearly been captured at Annan'. In 1333, he returned with English support. Berwick was besieged, and the relieving army was destroyed at Halidon Hill on 19 July, where huge numbers of Scotland's nobility died in another incompetent attempt (as at Dupplin) to oppose spearmen to archers. The leaders of Bannockburn were dead, and their successors were inadequate.[49]

The Disinherited were restored, and Edward Baliol became king south of Forth; elsewhere, the country was in chaos, with the Earl of Atholl (the son-in-law of the disinherited Earl of Buchan) attempting to hold the north for Edward III and his Scottish ally. David II left Dumbarton with his queen for France in 1334, and French (and Fleming) support for Scotland proved a crucial irritant in plunging England into the Hundred Years' War. The men of Bute seized Rothesay Castle for Robert the Stewart, Sir Coilin MacCaluim made gains for the king, and the Earl of Moray and the Stewart both attacked Baliol's forces. At the first sign of weakness, many who had submitted to Baliol returned to David II, for time had moved on, and the Disinherited were now seen by many as intruders in England's cause, not the patriot partisans of an alternative dynasty. Scots fighting for England's cause were already being characterised as 'English', and moreover the Disinherited had to disinherit in their turn, expropriating King Robert's freeholders to create a class of the Pillaged. King Robert's destruction of Scottish castles also made it very difficult to create a sustainable bridgehead of English support, and the cost of rebuilding them for an occupying army was 'prohibitive'.

On St Andrew's Day, 1335, Sir Andrew de Moray defeated the Earl of Atholl at Culblean Forest near Ballater, and became Guardian of Scotland. Edward III responded by campaigning in Scotland as far as Aberdeen in 1336-7, where he burnt the burgh 'without the omission of a single house, although in all Scotland there were no handsomer houses', but he gained little, and turned his attention to the Continent. In spring 1338, Sir Andrew died, and Robert the Stewart replaced him as Guardian until 1341, when David returned and Edward Baliol 'fled across the border'. All of Scotland save a few border strongholds, and Man, lost in 1333, were now back in the hands of the Crown. Edward III had failed in his attempt to create a pale (a fortified frontier zone, as round Dublin in Ireland) of six Scottish counties beyond which he would rule the country through his Baliol vassal.[50]

By this time, the restored David II had found that there was another side to the French alliance, and when he marched into England in 1346, following the French defeat at Crecy on 26 August, not only was his army defeated 'at Neville's Cross near Durham', but he was captured. In 1347, Edward Baliol attempted to take advantage of this but a captured David's value as a political pawn to Edward III meant that it was now to England's advantage to recognise the Bruce claim, unless it was pursuing its own. In 1356, Baliol resigned his claim to Edward III, who used it as the excuse to launch another invasion.

After the defeat of the French at Poitiers in 1356, King David was released by the Treaty of Berwick the next year. By its terms, Scotland had to pay 10,000 merks per annum for ten years. After payments fell in arrears, it was proposed that the Scots should accept the English king or an English prince as their next king if David died childless. This king would be crowned 'King of England and Scotland' twice in two ceremonies, while Scots would hold guaranteed offices and the Stone of Scone would be returned to Scotland. In addition, the 1363 proposals stated that 'the name and title of the realm of Scotland shall be preserved and maintained with honour and with due distinction, without union or annexation with the realm of England'. David accepted these terms, but after debate the Scottish Estates rejected them in 1364. The very nature of the proposals, which recognised while effectively undermining the separateness of the kingdom of Scotland, made apparent the fact 'that Scotland could not be conquered by military force alone'.[51]

Robert the Stewart had manoeuvred against David in his latter years, and was disliked by him, but nonetheless succeeded in 1371, and became Robert II at the age of fifty-five. He reigned for nineteen years, but by 1384 power was effectively in the hands of his son John, who also took the name Robert. Scottish victories at Lochmaben in 1384 and (enshrined in ballad and story) Otterburn in 1388 kept the balance of the power on the Border. Robert III's (r. 1390–1406) younger brother, Alexander Stewart, Earl of Buchan and Lord of Badenoch created trouble in the north by abusing his position as Justiciar. Known as the Wolf of Badenoch in a comment on his derogation of duty to the people of his lordship, he went so far as to burn Elgin Cathedral in June 1390. Married to the Countess of Ross and with Mariette Nighean Eachainn as a mistress and John, Lord of the Isles as a brother-in-law, his family and exploits alike show the lack of a division between the great families of Highland and Lowland Scotland, though his actions no doubt helped to reinforce the idea of one.

The idea of such a divide, absent in the earlier period, seems first to appear in John of Fordoun's writing in the

1380s, though Fordoun does say that the Highlands are 'faithful and obedient to their king and country, and easily made to submit to law, if properly governed'. The recognition of the division seems to be linked not only to the activities of the Wolf of Badenoch, but also to the breakdown of the succession in northern magnate families, such as the Earls of Ross and Moray; indeed, Alexander Stewart took advantage of a 'power vacuum' in the latter province. Unsettled and violent conflict led to a raid by caterans (raiders and freebooters) into Angus in 1392. This was combined with the growth of the Anglic vernacular, by the early fifteenth century beginning to be called Scots, a word which gave the language the associations of a national tongue. Moreover, Scots began to replace Latin as an administrative language (Aberdeen's burgh records were in Scots from 1441, for example), thus by implication granting it an official status higher than that of Gaelic, although perhaps half of the population spoke the latter tongue as late as 1500. The lords themselves gradually changed from speaking in French to each other and Gaelic or Scots to servants, to speaking one language to all.[52]

In 1400, Henry IV (r. 1399–1413) once again attempted to use the argument that England was the 'lord superior' of Scotland. This time, in order to get round the Treaty of Edinburgh-Northampton, he produced 'forgeries purporting to record Robert II's submission', thus indicating that a post-1328 Scottish king had renewed his country's recognition of English overlordship. In August 1400, he invaded Scotland in a damp squib of a campaign, retreating 'within a fortnight, declaring himself satisfied with a Scottish promise to think about his claims'. The Scots, increasingly confident with a new archery force and better imported armour, attacked

English shipping in 1402, putting 'heavy pressure on Henry IV', who was also facing opposition from the Percys and Owain Glyn Dŵr. As so often however, the Scots overreached themselves, and were defeated by the Earl of March at Homildon Hill near Wooler in 1402.

In 1406, Robert III died in Bute, shortly after hearing that his son James had been captured by the English at sea. Naturally Henry IV and his successor Henry V (r. 1413–22) could not overlook such a powerful bargaining tool, and attempts to restore James in 1416 foundered on renewed claims for English overlordship. However, Henry, like Edward III, had wars to fight in France. The difficulty for Scotland was that, as was displayed at Agincourt in 1415, Henry V seemed too powerful an adversary for both countries. At this juncture, the Scots, under the leadership of Robert, Duke of Albany, younger son of Robert II, sent military support to France. In 1419 an expeditionary force of around 10,000 men arrived under the Earl of Buchan. In 1421 they secured victory at Baugé against the English army under the Duke of Clarence, the king's brother, thus saving central France from English control. Pope Martin V is alleged to have remarked 'Verily the Scots are the antidote to the English' on hearing the result of the battle. Henry's view was different; in 1421–2 he forbade quarter to the Scots, and remarked: 'that is a cursed nation – Wherever I go, I find them in my beard'. Moves to negotiate to release James nonetheless accelerated in response to military pressure, with Henry requiring 'in exchange . . . a heavy ransom, substantial hostages, and the withdrawal of Scottish troops from France'. Eventually, in April 1424, James returned to Scotland for 50,000 merks, twenty-seven hostages, a truce and his wife Joan Beaufort, 'granddaughter of John of Gaunt'.

Some Scots remained in France; their last major action came in defeat at Verneuil that August.[53]

James I's rule in Scotland ushered in a more central role for the country in European politics. A much broader range of diplomatic contacts was sought throughout Europe, and even the Auld Alliance with France was tempered by playing off England, France and Burgundy against each other. This was an era where the Scottish king took in marriage not only the daughters of the King of England and great European magnates, but the daughters of European monarchs. In 1427, James felt strong enough to stop paying his ransom, although he maintained an Anglo-Scottish truce until 1436, even while betrothing his eldest daughter to the Dauphin and promising 6,000 men for France – who were not sent. As it was, there were still some Scots in France fighting with St Jeanne d'Arc (d. 1431), whose victories began to turn the Hundred Years' War against the English. In 1436, James offered troops to France following an English raid in Berwickshire, but by then they were no longer required.

James also set himself the task of limiting the power of the nobility, beginning in 1425 with the house of Albany. His motivations were perhaps as much short-term and financial as anything else. Such innovations were unpopular, and James was murdered in February 1437 in Perth by a group of political dissidents 'led by Robert Graham of Kinpunt and Robert Stewart of Atholl, grandson of the earl of Atholl . . . who completely misjudged the attitude of the political community'. The king's assassins were caught and brutally put to death, Stewart being forced to wear a red-hot iron crown while being flogged for three days; the Earl of Atholl was beheaded. James's murder was, as Alexander Grant points out, the first murder of a Scottish king since the eleventh century, and the response to it was equally unusual. Between 1341 and 1469, forty-six English and only ten Scottish magnates were executed, although Scotland's aristocracy was 'much the same size' as England's, being closer to the Continental norm than the unusually small band of the titled south of the border. Grant argues that there is 'absolutely no evidence to support the idea of a continuous crown–nobility power struggle', whatever conflicts might from time to time occur (such as that between James II and the 8th Earl of Douglas, which led to Douglas's murder in Stirling Castle in February 1452 and the defeat of the Douglases at Arkinholm three years later). In 1455, James II (r. 1437–60) moved to annex many Douglas lordships to the Crown. Five years later, after an opportunistic attack on English-held Roxburgh during the Wars of the Roses, James died when a cannon he was standing close to at the siege exploded.[54]

James III (r. 1460–88), son of James II and Marie, daughter of the Duc de Gueldres, faced early difficulties following the victory of Edward IV of York (r. 1461–70; 1471–83) over Henry VI of Lancaster (r. 1422–61; 1470–71) in the Wars of the Roses in England in 1461. He had already received Berwick back from the Lancastrian Queen Margaret, who took refuge in Scotland with Henry VI, before using it as a base for her diplomatic offensive with Louis XI. Meanwhile, Marie de Gueldres negotiated with York. Playing off one English claimant against another proved beneficial, for a Douglas–Lord of the Isles axis was still seeking to restore their position by undermining the Scottish polity. In February 1462, by the Treaty of Ardtornish, the Lords of the Isles, 'bound themselves and their subjects and followers to become vassals of England', and this worrying spectre of a fifth column was only resolved by vigorous action at home (which in the long run finally broke the Lords of the Isles) and a switch in England to clear-cut support for Edward IV, easier after his final victories in 1464.[55]

In 1468, James married Christian I of Denmark's daughter Margaret. Her dowry was to be the ending of the small annual payment to Norway, in theoretical force since the Treaty of Perth in 1266, and the sum of 60,000 florins, for which Denmark mortgaged Orkney and (later) Shetland: the dowry was not paid, and Scotland kept both islands from 1472 to the present day. James's treatment of the islands 'as *de facto* part of Scotland' was a sign of his claim for the status of the Scottish crown, and formed part of his energetic foreign policy. In 1472, 'he master-minded the treaty' between Denmark and France, while during 1471–3, James 'proposed three campaigns', including a plan 'to annex part of Brittany'. He also pushed forward an English alliance, suggesting that his son should marry Edward IV's daughter Cecilia, but 'counter-pressure from Louis XI' led to a re-ratification of the Auld Alliance in 1479. England naturally responded to this, renewing claims to suzerainty in 1482, the year when Alexander, Duke of Albany, the king's brother, 'promised to do homage' to Edward IV, and to surrender southern Scotland to him. Edward invaded, while the Scots lords leading James's army quarreled among themselves. In this attack Berwick was taken, and it ever afterwards remained a part of England. In 1483, a grant by Edward IV of land in Cumberland with the right to conquer in Scotland to his brother the Duke of Gloucester raised the spectre of a 'palatinate in south west Scotland', but Gloucester had bigger fish to fry, usurping the Crown in the summer after Edward's death on 9 April as Richard III (r. 1483–5). Edward's death also put paid to Albany's hopes. James's reign meanwhile slipped into crisis, and an alienation from his own son which finally led to the collapse of his rule in 1488.[56]

After James III's murder following his defeat at Sauchieburn (1488) by a coalition of rebel lords headed by his own son, James IV (r. 1488–1513) came to the throne. He pursued much the same ambitious path as his father, and in his case also it ended in disaster. James IV, however, was more circumspect in any rapprochement with England, spending the early years of his reign in morale-boosting but lightweight military posturings, including the threat of his grandfather's giant cannon Mons Meg, a gift from the Duke of Burgundy in 1457, which weighed 6 tonnes, and fired a 150 kg shot over 3 km. In the 1490s, he supported the pretender to the English throne Perkin Warbeck, but from the 'Treaty of Perpetual Peace' in 1502 he pursued an English alliance, apparently cemented by his marriage to Henry VII's (r. 1485–1509) daughter Margaret in 1503. By the 1502 Holy League he became committed with Aragon, Venice and England to an attack on France. James then allied with France in breach of the treaty, and was excommunicated. In 1513, when Henry VIII (r. 1509–47) attacked France, James's magnificent army, perhaps 20,000 men with 29 guns and 370 draught animals, led by 15 earls (nine of whom were killed together with the king), marched south and, after taking Norham, was obliterated at Flodden by the Earl of Surrey, in the worst defeat ever suffered by a Scottish army, to which James's own chivalry and headstrong desire to charge with his own troops contributed in no small degree. James's arms race, which had in the *Margaret* and *Great Michael* produced the ships which Henry VIII had responded to by launching the *Mary Rose* and *Great Harry*, had come to nothing: European military, diplomatic and cultural ambitions annihilated in the mud of a grotesquely grandiose Border raid gone awry.[57]

Henry had already been promoting a pro-English party, one of the distinctive features of his Scottish policy, and his resentment of James's sea power had already led to an attack on the Scots captain Andrew Barton 'as a pirate'. In 1512, the English king renewed his claim to suzerainty and in France, on the eve of Flodden, told James's Lyon Herald that 'I am the very owner of Scotland'. Such an aggressive stance did not bode well for Scotland after such a defeat. The infant James V (r. 1513–42) was only a year old, and effective government was in the hands of John, Duke of Albany, James III's nephew.

Albany confined the Queen (who fled in 1516 to marry the Earl of Angus) and attempted to prevent the development of a pro-English party. In 1517–21 he was in France, returning with strengthened promises of alliance, but Henry VIII continued to press with both military threats and diplomatic initiatives. Albany left for France once more after an unsuccessful raid on England in 1524, and it was then proposed that James should marry Mary, King Henry's daughter and heir.[58]

The power of the increasingly centralised and sophisticated Tudor state apparatus was beginning to press on Scotland, but the Reformation in England offered James the hope of respite, and he took advantage of it to gain significant financial support from the Church and to increase his own rights 'to nominate rather than recommend' ecclesiastical appointments. Not only was Mary no longer Henry's heir; there was also now likely to be renewed Continental interest in a Catholic Scotland as a strategic ally in the Counter-Reformation. War between France and England allowed James V to marry the French king's daughter Madeleine in January 1537, and in the next month Paul III presented him with 'a consecrated cap and sword' and exhorted him 'to set an example for Christian kings as an opponent of heresy'. Financial benefits followed. During the Catholic protests of the Pilgrimage of Grace in 1536–7, when Henry's throne looked briefly insecure, it was rumoured 'that northern Catholics were calling upon James and his French allies to invade'. After his queen died in July 1537, James showed his enhanced European status once again by beating Henry VIII to the hand of Marie de Guise, and compounded his alienation of the arrogant English king by failing to turn up to meet him at York in 1541, a fault for which Henry apparently forgave James while in fact planning for war. Henry feared that the Scots king might intervene in Ireland with Continental backing.[59]

In 1542, an incursion of English troops was attacked and defeated by the Scots at Hadden Rig. Henry, already making military preparations, took this as his pretext, demanding that 'the Scots were to free all English prisoners, to give up claim to the "Debateable Lands" in the Cheviots and north of Carlisle, and to provide bishops and earls as hostages in pledge'. Henry, who was also seeking war with France, wanted to pin James down, and effectively destroyed him as an opponent when 3,000 English defeated 18,000 Scots at Solway Moss on 24 November. A broken man, James died within three weeks, and Henry appeared content to rely on the pro-English party in Scotland to neutralise further opposition – at Solway Moss, he had captured 23 Scottish lords, of whom 'ten agreed' to become 'Assured' in the English interest. The Papacy offered James's administration 60 per cent 'of the fruits of the church in Scotland for two years' to fight Henry. In his turn, Henry demanded the end of the French alliance, the surrender of six main Scottish castles, and the surrender of Queen Mary (r. 1542–67), James's infant daughter, to be brought up in England. The Scots refused, and in 1543 at Greenwich two treaties were agreed, one declaring peace; the other proposing the betrothal of Mary to Edward, Prince of Wales, Henry's son, and stating that after marriage, they should live in England, with any offspring inheriting both kingdoms.

Henry had his supporters in Scotland, but the history of English attempts on the kingdom's integrity suggested to many a different course of action. The Earl of Arran (1516–75), James III's great-nephew, had been appointed regent by Parliament in March 1543. Initially favourable to the English match, he changed his mind. On 26 July, Marie de Guise removed her daughter Mary from Linlithgow to Stirling, escorted by an army. Henry VIII tried to bribe Arran by offering Elizabeth (the future queen) as a wife for his son: after wavering, Arran turned it down. On 9 September 1543, Mary was crowned.

Henry was determined to get his way, and what followed passed down into history as the 'Rough Wooing'. In May 1544, the Earl of Hertford, the Prince of Wales's uncle, invaded Scotland, sacking the Borders and Edinburgh. Marie de Guise sent Queen Mary from Stirling to Dunkeld for safety. Hertford withdrew, leaving his loyal lieutenants and their

'Assured Scots' allies, of whom the Earl of Lennox was the most prominent, to secure southern Scotland. As in the Wars of Independence, 'the Scots were declared to be rebels', and hence not entitled to equal treatment. Patriotic feeling in Scotland increased, and in 1545 action was taken by government in respect of the 'Assured Scots'. Popular resentment no doubt helped the Earl of Angus to change sides, and his army defeated the English at Ancrum Moor on 27 February 1545. Hertford returned, and that autumn he and the Earl of Lennox laid waste southern Scotland.

Henry 'clearly saw that identity of religion would promote the union of the realms' and helped to foment Scottish Protestant resentment of Cardinal Beaton (c. 1494–1546), Archbishop of St Andrews and Chancellor of Scotland, who was one of the English king's chief opponents. Meanwhile, Scotland was further isolated on the Continent when Charles V, the Holy Roman Emperor, declared war following Scottish attacks on English Low Countries trade, which damaged Scotland economically. A more serious crisis was to follow. In May 1546, Scottish Protestant insurgents murdered the Cardinal at St Andrews, hanging his body on the wall and defiling it by urinating in its mouth. They appealed to England for help. Henry sent none, and he died the following January. Two months later, so did François I of France. Henri II, who succeeded him, was advised concerning the situation by the Guises, and a French fleet came to relieve Marie de Guise and bombarded the St Andrews Protestants into surrender on 31 July.

Hertford (now Duke of Somerset and Protector of England in the minority of Edward VI (r. 1547–53)) invaded Scotland again that summer, defeating Arran's 25,000 strong army at

Pinkie on 10 September. Mary was taken from Dunkeld to Inchmahome Priory on the Lake of Menteith, before being returned to Stirling as Somerset returned south. In November 1547, the Scottish Privy Council appealed for French aid, and in February 1548 the Estates agreed to betroth Mary to the Dauphin in return for French troops, an agreement sealed by the Treaty of Haddington in July. The Earl of Arran received the dukedom of Chatelherault so that Mary could go to France; some Scots castles also were to be passed into French hands. England again invaded and on 21 February, the Queen was moved to Dumbarton Castle. By 13 August, she was in France.

Somerset published pro-Union propaganda such as *An Exhortacion to the Scottes* (1547) and set up an English Pale in the south-west, called 'the King's Lordship of Scotland'. In it, 'Assured Scots' might find protection. Somerset also argued for an 'Empire of Great Britain' in Protestant unity (under Edward, of course) in preference to the Scots' alliance with France. The *Exhortacion* appealed to the notion of 'Britons'.

For the present, the Auld Alliance held. French troops arrived in force on 16 June 1548. By mid-1549, English soldiers were confined to their fortifications in southern Scotland, while English-held Boulogne in France was attacked by Henri II. In September, the English withdrew, making peace with first Scotland then France in 1550–1. By this time, Somerset was imprisoned, his expensive and ruinous war policy having collapsed. In January 1552, he was executed. Mary married the Dauphin in April 1558; in July 1559, he was king; on 5 December 1560 he died, shortly after Marie de Guise had died in Scotland. Parliament invited Queen Mary home, and she returned: but to a country changed for ever from that which she had left.[60]

THE REFORMATION

REFORMING SCOTLAND

Far more than was the case with its English equivalent under Henry VIII, Edward VI (r. 1547–53) and Elizabeth (r. 1558–1603), the Scottish Reformation represented a radical point of departure, a rewriting of the history, culture, religious and political relationships of the Scottish nation. In England, the Reformation was imposed by the Crown, or at least by the Crown acting in conjunction with a political elite (as in the 1559 settlement). In Scotland, it was gained in opposition to the Crown.

In the long run the Reformation undermined Scotland's Continental diplomatic alliances and other links on a number of levels. On the most obvious level, it had been clear from the hostilities of 1544–51 that Scotland was going to find it hard going resisting Tudor state power without French aid, and the Reformers' attack on the Guise regime in Scotland was accordingly the beginning of the end for the Auld Alliance. But there were many other cultural links. Many of Scotland's priests had been educated abroad; now, although in time to come ministers might train at Basle or at Utrecht in Protestant Europe, the major connection with the great power of France (which included many distinguished Scots working in its universities) was under threat. In its place came 'the democratic intellect, and a new sense of nationhood expressed in terms of the covenanted nation', a nation which had become 'Britain' by the time of the Solemn League and Covenant of 1643. The 'national liturgy' of the patriot Catholic Church where 'more than seventy Scottish saints, drawn from every district . . . all provided with historical lessons and their own feast days' were celebrated, was replaced by an exceptionalist yet often pro-British Protestantism. Catholic culture went into a rapid retreat. By the end of the sixteenth century, the pre-1560 traditions of drama and church music were either destroyed or badly damaged.[1]

On the threshold of Reformation, there was little sign of what was to come. Though it has been argued that the incidence of heresy in late medieval Scotland has been underestimated, 'evidence of actual hostility towards parochial incumbents is hard to come by'. As has been clear in chapters 2 and 3, Scotland was a country rich in religious houses – arguably too rich for its resources. In 1540, the country had over 1,000 parish kirks, 13 cathedrals, 40 collegiate kirks, over 50 abbeys and priories and the same number of friaries, and 12 nunneries. There were 'well over one hundred hospitals, founded in connection with the medieval church' which 'provided social services, catering for the needs of the sick, pilgrims, lepers, poor, aged and infirm of all kinds'. The religious, although resistant to secular interference, at the same time depended heavily on revenues from the secular clergy's charges to maintain their lavish provision: even an abbot such as Ninian Winyet could admit 'that there were too many monasteries' in Scotland. In order to replace this provision, the new Reformed Kirk depended on the 1574 Poor Law, itself modelled on English legislation of two years earlier, which laid stress on relief within each parish available only to the disabled and sick of that parish; in the successor Act of 1579 (which reiterated and expanded on that of 1535), 'beggars were actually to be licensed to beg their way back to their own parishes'. Although a combination of poor economic conditions and the nobility's power over Church lands meant that the Reformed Kirk 'never had the wealth of its Catholic predecessor', the nourishment and support of community action and parish responsibility were notable features of the early stages of the Protestant Reformation.[2]

These perhaps were already present to some extent in Scotland. Although the Catholic Church was intensely hierarchical, there were also some intriguing elements of democracy in its organisation. In Inverurie in 1536, the parish clerk was elected, and elected by both men and women: a similar event occurred at Daviot. Popular pilgrimages, although less common in the sixteenth century, still economically sustained the settings of the major shrines. When the Reformers destroyed the Scottish Church (rather than largely adopting it (bereft of monasticism) as happened in England), they inflicted not merely external, but deep-seated internal systemic damage, to Scottish society. Both the cultural and the economic fabric of life in the country were damaged, and the economic balance of parish revenues shifted between church and state, with the Protestant ministers of 1562 having to make do with 'only a third of the income from benefices of the Catholic clergy': and even this reduced portion had to be shared with the Crown.[3]

Reformation ideas began to arrive in east coast Scotland from Lutheran Germany in the 1520s: printing helped both their dissemination, and the spread of anti-Catholic propaganda. In 1525, an Act against heresy was passed, and in 1528 Patrick Hamilton became the first Scot to be executed for Lutheranism by the authorities, with the usual public barbarity which many found repulsive. Compared with the situation south of the border (and still more that in the Low Countries), however, repressive activity on behalf of the religious authorities was limited, fewer than 20 people being executed for heresy in the next 15 years. Protestantism was hardly a threat until the end of the 1530s, although this may be in part due to the fact that many Protestants could find refuge in exile in England during that decade. Dundee in particular 'became early a stronghold of Lutheran doctrines and it became the port of entry and departure for many religious idealists and refugees'. Evidence of reform feeling can be found even in the court culture of Scotland, in particular in Sir David Lyndsay's *Satyre of the Thrie Estatis* (1540), although his and similar views may well have been reconcilable with internal Church reform. Three provincial councils of the Catholic Church pursued a reform agenda in the 1540s and '50s.[4]

The execution of George Wishart, a Protestant seen (possibly rightly) as a pro-English agent by Cardinal Beaton, led to the Cardinal's own murder in 1546. Although Wishart had 'flirted with the radical ideas of Anabaptism', which most Reformers found heretical, his 'eloquent appeal to scripture alone discomfited the prosecution' at his trial. Whatever Wishart's differences with the mainstream Reformers who merely seemed to want a vernacular Bible (gained to some extent in 1543), Gospel preaching and 'communion under both kinds', the 'devout Biblical Christianity' of his personal faith was in tune with the shape of theirs. Wishart's death was the catalyst for the murder of the Primate of Scotland, and to some extent can be seen as marking the threshold of the Reformation.[5]

Marie de Guise became Regent of Scotland in April 1554. Already, in the mid-1550s, there were signs of Protestant leanings in the Estates. In 1557, following defeat by an Anglo-Spanish coalition (England was at this time being returned to Catholicism under Mary Tudor (r. 1553–8), who was married to Philip II of Spain), France made moves to secure Scotland. Mary and François were married in April 1558 'under a treaty providing for a union of the two crowns, François becoming King of Scots and the eldest son of the marriage being destined to reign in both realms'. This was in itself a momentous political event, which could have rewritten the history of Europe, but the Scottish commissioners were perhaps ignorant (it has been argued that the protocol was in fact well-known) of a secret protocol to the agreement, whereby in the event of the marriage being childless, Scotland was to be handed over to the King of France, to whom Mary also assigned her right to the English throne; she moreover 'mortgaged' Scotland to the French crown until her debts for 'education and . . . French military aid' were paid, and undertook to reject any 'agreement' made by the Estates 'which might contradict the terms of the protocol'.[6]

But by this time the situation in Scotland was changing rapidly. At the end of 1557, several leaders of the Reformed party, including the Earls of Argyll, Glencairn and Morton, 'signed the "Common Band", binding themselves to maintain and forward, with all their might, the most blessed word of God and His Congregation and to forsake and renounce the

Congregation of Satan'. These men and their allies became known as the 'Lords of the Congregation', and their 'Band' was the first religious association with this name; it provided a model for many subsequent examples. On the same day, 3 December, Lord James Stewart wrote to John Knox (c. 1512/14–72), intermittently in exile since Cardinal Beaton's murder eleven years earlier (in which he had no direct part, and was not impressed with the piety of the murderers), asking him to return to Scotland. On 28 April 1558, in the same month as the royal marriage, the burning of the Protestant schoolmaster Walter Myln served to harden opinion. Political and religious anxiety conjoined: Scotland was now viewed as a potential French satellite, and the visible repressiveness of the Scottish Guise regime against the new minority religion made people uneasy. The Lords of the Congegation and their clerical allies took advantage of these concerns. Just as Tertullian had once claimed the blood of the martyrs to be the seed of the Church ('the blood of the Christians is the seed' – *Apologeticus*), so Knox thought that from Myln's ashes 'there sprang "thousands of his opinion and religion in Scotland"'. More important perhaps was the death of England's Queen Mary on 17 November 1558, and the accession of Elizabeth, which suggested that a final Protestant settlement south of the Border might be imminent.

Knox finally returned to Scotland in May 1559. Within hardly more than a week of his return, after he preached a sermon against idolatry in Perth, a riot ensued in which the 'town's religious houses' were sacked. On 31 May, the Congregation signed a Second Band. The Lords of the Congregation now included a larger cross-section of the Scottish elite (down to burgesses), and they 'purged' a number of towns in Fife and central Scotland with their troops, then entered Edinburgh, where on 7 July, Knox became Scotland's first Protestant clergyman. The Congregation's linkage 'of largely unspecified religious reform and a patriotic political platform' brought them success, but at the price of a loose coalition which showed signs of dissolving as soon as it took the capital. Indeed, they had to evacuate Edinburgh, for although Marie de Guise faced deposition from her Regency in October 1559, the Congregation's position was precarious in the face of the French troops who came to reinforce her. But after François and Mary became monarchs of France and Scotland in July, 'their armorial quarterings announced their intention of adding England too (Mary also used the title Queen of Ireland, an additional threat), so that the defeat of French influence in Scotland became vital to Elizabeth', who, by the Treaty of Berwick in February 1560, allied England to the Congregation, whose 'provisional government' was 'still protesting its loyalty to Mary and Francis'.

In April 1560, English troops entered Scotland and besieged Leith; on 11 June, Marie de Guise died, and by the Treaty of Edinburgh between England and France of 6 July, the Lords of the Congregation won their Reformation in return for dependence on English power. France undermined its own claims by acknowledging Elizabeth as Queen of England, and withdrew its troops. English diplomacy was skilled. By the Treaty, Sir William Cecil 'ensured the elimination of French political and military influence in Scotland'. For such a triumph, military assistance to the Lords of the Congregation was a small price to pay. In 1559, England had finally rejected the Catholic faith and ensured a Protestant settlement – indeed, overly Protestant for the new Queen's liking. This settlement had, however, been threatened to an extent difficult to comprehend today. To the north lay a still (just) Catholic Scotland, under Marie de Guise, its formidable Regent; to the south lay France, with a Catholic king and a Scots Catholic queen, one whom moreover many believed had a better right to the throne than Elizabeth herself. France and Scotland were in effect a united kingdom: and indeed the iconography of François and Mary was already manifesting this. One year later, in December 1560, François was dead and Scotland was Protestant: and, in the latter case, all for a token outlay of English power.[7]

On 17–24 August 1560, the Reformation parliament of the Estates accepted the Knox-inspired *Confession of Faith*, which 'abolished the Pope's authority in Scotland and forbade the celebration of the Latin Mass', but did not approve the Reform programme, known as the *First Book of Discipline*; instead this was 'presented to a thinly attended convention of nobility and lairds' (only 30 or so) in December. The *First Book* promoted an ambitious programme of 'social expenditure on kirks, hospitals and schools' which the Reformed Kirk did not have the resources to pay for; its separation of Kirk and State interests was a sign of things to come. The religious programme of the Congregation had gained a notable victory; and the ground was laid for political changes which were to be just as great. The Reformation helped to increase pro-Englishness in Scotland, and support for 'security, profit and stable government' in place of the set attitudes of the 1540s, when one English envoy reported that if the Scots were threatened with subjection to England, 'there is not so little a boy but he will hurl stones against it, and the wives will handle their distaffs, and the commons universally will rather die'. The idea of a Protestant polity, and the concept of international Protestant solidarity, began very slowly to prepare the ground among many (though by no means all) Scots for a change in their country's future relationship with England. As early as James VI's christening (under Catholic rites) at Stirling in 1566, the 'young Protestant minister, Patrick Adamson' looked forward in his 'celebratory poem' to the day when 'the Britons, having finished with war, will learn at last to unite in one kingdom'.[8]

Events continued to move in the Reformers' direction. In December 1560, François died, and Mary, as merely queen dowager, became markedly more isolated and less powerful. In August 1561, she returned to Scotland, the first Stuart ruler, abandoning the 'w' which was not used in French. She received strong advice to let the Reformation be, even though Protestants were still a small minority in Edinburgh and many other places; and she declined the Earl of Huntly's offer to raise the north and use its military power to reduce Scotland to the Catholic faith. Huntly invited Mary to Mass, was declared a rebel in consequence, and died of a stroke after his defeat and capture at Corrichie by royal forces in 1562, the year in which the *Book of Common Order* began to be used by the new kirk. Mary, meanwhile, benefited from the church revenues of her newly-Protestant administration. Her government was run by James V's illegitimate son, the strongly pro-Reform Lord James Stewart (1531–70) (later Earl of Moray) and by the more conservative Sir Richard Maitland of Lethington (1496–1586); Mary herself accepted the Reformation parliament, but continued to offer hope to her co-religionists, a situation completely unacceptable to Knox, who tormented the queen in a number of interviews, and whose power over her demonstrated her isolation in the early 1560s, though by 1565 the situation was shifting slightly. Mary's own sympathy for the rights of conscience gave her a greater tolerance of the Reformers than some leading Catholics thought desirable, and her position was weakened thereby, as it was by her lack of a powerful husband in a divided realm.

Unmarried, Mary was vulnerable. In 1562, she may have considered converting to Anglicanism 'on Guise orders . . . to consolidate her claim to the English throne': and after a number of proposed husbands (including Don Carlos, son of the King of Spain and Elizabeth's favourite Lord Robert Dudley) were discussed, settled disastrously on Henry Stewart, Lord Darnley (1546–67), the English-born great-grandson of Henry VII via Margaret Tudor's second marriage to the Earl of Angus. Darnley was vain, ineffective and vicious, causing divisions in Mary's administration, including a minor rebellion and further problems when the new king consort returned publicly to Catholicism, and shortly afterwards murdered the queen's Italian secretary, David Rizzio, in March 1566 in the presence of his wife, who was six months pregnant. Her son, James, was born on 19 June, and 'baptised Charles James in the Chapel Royal at Stirling Castle on 17 December 1566, according to full Catholic rites'. Mary was now increasingly running a mixed Catholic and Protestant administration in Scotland. She restored the Archbishop of St Andrews to his see, and in December 1566, Knox went to England for a time. The Bishop of Galloway, who had accepted Reform, had already 'entered into negotiations with Rome' in 1565.

Then within a matter of weeks, this policy was shipwrecked. Divorce from Darnley had been in the air, but instead he was murdered while recovering from illness at Kirk o' Field (roughly where Bannerman's Bar in the Cowgate in Edinburgh now stands) in February 1567. James Hepburn, 4th Earl of Bothwell was widely suspected of being one of his murderers, and he stood high in the queen's favour. He was acquitted in a charade of a trial on 12 April, and after he abducted her on the 24th, Mary married him on 15 May by 'Protestant rites', having on the 12th created him 'Duke of Orkney and Lord of Shetland'. In April, she had promised to defend the reformed church against ' any interference from overseas', but time was running out. She was becoming isolated both within and outside Scotland: Pius V declined to continue to communicate with her after her marriage, until 'he shall see some better signs of her life and religion'.[9]

The Bothwell marriage destroyed Mary. The Reformers and their followers could identify the reference in Revelation 14 to the great harlot Babylon as applicable to Rome and the Catholic faith: now here was such a harlot, bearing the name Mary, but, like Babylon in Revelation, the antithesis of the purity of the Mother of God. Hence for the English poet Edmund Spenser (1552–99), Mary was to become 'Duessa', the double one, bearing the Virgin Mary's name but not her nature (the virginal Elizabeth was contrastingly Mary by nature but not by name). She appeared now a sign of the impurities of Catholicism to many Protestants, and the (probably faked) Casket Letters, purporting to show Mary's complicity with Bothwell in adultery and vice, were produced to swing public opinion against her. On 15 June 1567, she surrendered at Carberry Hill to the Confederate

Lords, and to avoid a trial resigned the throne to her infant
son James on 24 July. Although in its early years many
opposed this move, James was nonetheless crowned five
days later, the infant having 'to listen to a sermon from
Knox'. A limited Catholic revival directed from the capital
was now out of the question; indeed, 'the work of
Reformation could begin afresh': Moray, out of office since
1565, returned to power. Imprisoned at Lochleven Castle,
Mary escaped in 1568 only to meet fresh defeat at Langside
in May, and then fled across the Border. The Earl of Moray
became Regent, but was murdered in 1570, and succeeded
by the Earl of Lennox, Elizabeth's candidate, then by the
earls of Mar (1571–2) and Morton (1572–80). Mary's
'crimes' were investigated by Elizabeth, but with an
inconclusive result, which nonetheless left the shadow of
suspicion looming over her. Pius V's bill excommunicating
and deposing Elizabeth led to the possibility of Mary's
return in 1571, but, by the Treaty of Blois in April 1572,
Elizabeth was able to create an Anglo-French *rapprochement*
which excluded Scotland, although the St Bartholomew's
Day massacre of Paris Protestants on 24 August, in which
the figure of de Guise loomed large, did nothing for English
public opinion. Meanwhile, Mary's supporters, the 'Queen's
Men', who had continued to resist since 1567–8, were now
finally subdued. English artillery was brought in to bring
about the surrender of Edinburgh Castle, the last major
stronghold held for the queen, on 28 May 1573. In the
same year, a statute was passed decreeing that clergy must
give assent to 'the Confession of Faith, on pain of
deprivation'. The last vestiges of Mary's reign in Scotland
had disappeared.[10]

THE EFFECTS OF THE REFORMATION

Already, before the Treaty of Edinburgh, extensive damage had begun in the areas controlled by the Reformers, in what was to be 'the wholesale destruction . . . of medieval works of religious art . . . unparalleled in Christendom'. In 1498, the Spanish ambassador had termed the 'abbeys . . . very magnificent, the buildings fine and the revenues great', while a French commentator noted that Scotland's religious houses were 'highly ornamented'. Four hundred years later, 'so thoroughgoing has this [the Reformation's] destruction of liturgical accessories been that it is more difficult to find illustrative material showing the religious ideas and habits prevalent in Scotland five hundred years ago than to illustrate, from material evidence, the customs of ancient Egyptians or Babylonians'. As early as the 1530s, there had been cases of malicious damage; by 1580, 'we find almost all of the larger churches and (especially in the east-central lowlands) a proportion of parish churches in complete or partial ruin'. Many of the Border abbeys and other houses had been damaged in the English invasions of the 1540s, and now the process was taken more than one stage further. Melrose Abbey began to be dismantled in 1559; the choirs of Aberdeen and Brechin cathedrals were reduced to ruin, and in general that part of any cathedral not wanted for a parish kirk was ruined or left to rot. St Andrews Cathedral was 'scheduled for demolition under the Privy Council ordinance of 1561'. Glasgow Cathedral lost its roof, but regained it in 1583; the cathedral at Elgin was stripped of lead; at Fortrose, a grant was made of the cathedral roof lead to William, Lord Ruthven; the cathedral at Lismore fell into disrepair, while

Iona was 'denuded' and in decay, Scone Abbey was burnt, and so was (in a local conflict) Dornoch Cathedral. In 1570, Cambuskenneth's abbey buildings were 'demolished to provide material for the Earl of Mar's new palace in Stirling', itself never completed. There is only one nunnery in Scotland 'of which any substantial fabric remains'.

The burgh councils deepened the damage caused by this ideological destruction, taking stonework for their own use. Even the churches scheduled to serve as parish kirks were damaged, in an orgy of destruction frequently abetted by disorderly mobs bent on loot: theological and economic motives being very mixed throughout. The bishops' and abbots' tombs were violated or destroyed; stained glass, woodwork, reliquaries, eucharistic vessels, tabernacles, altarpieces, archives, manuscripts, printed books and libraries barely remain in fragments, and 'not a single royal tomb has survived the reformation attack, not even the elaborate monument which patriotic gratitude had once brought, at great expense, from Paris to Dunfermline, to house the mortal remains of Bruce'.

The pattern of destruction varied in different areas. Religious houses of all kinds suffered 'iconoclastic violence' at the heart of Reformation activity, subsiding 'as we move from the centre of the turmoil into the remoter provinces'. Orders to cast down churches led to the destruction of their contents, looting, breaking of doors and windows, seizure of the lead and damaging the fabric. Subsequent regret for this by the Episcopalian regime (the rebuilding of St Andrews Cathedral was considered in 1634, for example) was itself nullified by the renewed ferocity of the wars of 1638–51. In the 1650s, Cromwellian soldiers raided Fortrose and the religious houses at Beauly and Kinloss for stonework, and on a broader front 'in the north, the Cromwellian occupation was the principal period for the demolition of the actual fabric of churches'.

The Reformation was in a key sense a revolutionary Year Zero. To contrast the Church of England's adoption, even usurpation, of the Catholic past with the iconoclasm of Scotland is to see the beginnings of Enlightenment attitudes towards Scotland as barbarous and backward. Leading Anglicans from William Laud (1573–1645) to Samuel Johnson (1709–84) commented on the barbarism and destructiveness of the Scottish Reformation. When, in the eighteenth century, the Episcopalians and Catholics who provided the last military resistance to the end of the Scottish polity were defeated, their defeat made possible the Enlightenment historians' liberal codifying of the Presbyterian interpretation, which passed into the general stream of British Whig history. But much of Scotland's own destruction of, and later indifference to, both its own high culture and medieval past, has arguably left a lasting legacy of cultural inferiorism to other countries, notably England. The tourist in the south can see much of medieval and Renaissance England entire, despite some ruined abbeys and monasteries; in Scotland, much of what remains is only a skeleton, the bare bones of cathedrals standing like beached whales in more than one coastal city.[11]

Despite the extent of material destruction, the Reformation was largely bloodless as far as the Catholic clergy was concerned. A small number of priests and bishops were put to death, but for most the Reformation Parliament offered compensation to clerics who had received 'harm either in person or goods'; on the other hand, 'ecclesiastical property generally was regarded as being at the disposal of anyone who cared to resort to force', and those who failed to abandon their faith were quickly brought to book. The August 1560 'Reformation Parliament' in accordance with the *Confession of Faith*, passed strict laws against saying, hearing or being present at Mass, with confiscation, banishment and death for a third offence. These laws were applied, at least to some degree: in May 1563 for example, 'John Hamilton, subchantor of Glasgow, was tried for assisting at mass along with forty-seven others, at Kirkoswald, Maybole and Paisley'. In 1569, four priests were sentenced to death at Dunblane, and although this sentence was commuted, priests were hanged at Leith and Glasgow soon afterwards. James VI's (r. 1567–1625) influence tended towards the mitigation of anti-Catholic legislation: when Catholics 'came into the king's will, the sentence demanded by the letter of the penal laws was usually modified'.

Three bishops or bishops-elect in the north and west (Caithness, Galloway and Orkney) defected to Protestantism, rather uncertainly in the last case, but there was no *en masse* redefinition of the hierarchy's role as state servants rather than apostolic representatives, as in England in the 1530s. The role of these bishops has been seen by some scholars as presaging the development of the Episcopalian party in the Church of Scotland, and certainly the situation in Scotland in the 1560s was fluid. The Reformers 'thought of England as "of the same religion"', and based their early vernacular New Testament on that of the medieval English anticlericalist, Wyclif. The Superintendents appointed as provincial leaders in the Scottish dioceses were similar to bishops, if less overtly apostolic and sacramentalist. Many among the Reformers, Knox himself included, did not oppose the office of bishop. On the other hand, although the Reformers intended to abolish the dioceses and reform the administration of the church into districts, this did not consistently take place as intended, and the Superintendents functioned within a version of the old diocesan pattern, restored completely in 1572–6, then suspended again. It was intended that the Superintendents be elected, but in the end there were only five, and the Assembly appointed nine commissioners as well, among them the three bishops. To complicate matters, the General Assembly of the Church of Scotland in 1576 recognised 'five offices exercising oversight: archbishops, bishops, superintendents, commissioners and visitors'; yet in 1571, Erskine of Dun, one of the Superintendents, stated that 'I understand a bishop or a superintendent to be but one office'. Further confusion could derive from the fact that in 1576 there was still a pre-Reformation bishop in office! The Assembly set about reforming the diocesan pattern once again, and the development of presbyteries was agreed in 1581, whereby 'clusters of neighbouring churches' would 'form a common eldership'. This once again gave way to a more Episcopalian settlement in 1584. Among all this confusion, one thing is clear. The administrative spirit of the Reformation was by no means unequivocally Presbyterian.[12]

Presbyterian attitudes began to be in the ascendant in the 1570s, when Andrew Melville (1545–1622) brought in the idea of parity of esteem in the ministry (the subject of the *Second Book of Discipline* (1578)), and also argued for the separation of Church and State, as 'twa Kings and twa Kingdoms', an idea which arguably did much to foment the religious wars of the next century. During the 1580s, with the development of a Puritan party in the Church of England, the Scottish Church found itself attacked for the first time by the Anglican establishment. By that stage, James VI's 'Black Acts' of 1584 had been passed to assert 'episcopal authority' at a time when the Presbyterian party 'were in the ascendant', but a church–state struggle over the privileges of the Kirk continued into the 1590s and beyond. 'Banding', or the assembly of like-minded groups for politico-religious ends (as in the case of the Lords of the Congregation) became increasingly a 'theological concept', and in 1596 the term 'covenant' was used for the first time in this context. In the century that followed, it would form the basis of a crucial concept for the Scottish religious polity.[13]

Presbyterianism's 'impressive refusal to compromise' remained a 'tremendous source of strength': 'its combination of doctrinal certainty, discipline, and effective organisation offered, more than anything else in Scotland, the hope of stability'. The other side of this, however, was the growing parochialism and 'introspection' argued for by Ian Cowan, who notes that the 'Negative Confession of 1581' states that 'true Christian fayth' is 'defended by manie and sindrie notable kyrkis . . . but chiefly by the Kyrk of Scotland', while 'Refutation of error' could come about 'by the worde of God and Kirk of Scotland', as if this reformed church was closer to Scripture than all others. Scottish exceptionalism was teetering on the verge of provincial self-congratulation, and this was arguably to be even clearer in the century that followed when the leaders of the Covenant seriously overestimated both their military power and ability to convert England to Presbyterianism.[14]

Few Reformers came from further north than Angus or the Mearns, and Aberdeen, in particular the Aulton around King's College and St Machar's Cathedral, was the city where outright Protestantism arguably had least success. In December 1559, the Principal of King's College had defended the college buildings (including the chapel, which contains the only surviving medieval woodwork in the country) from an invading mob from Angus, who threw the statue of Our Lady of Good Succour in the river Dee, robbed and despoiled the Cathedral, and tore the lead from its roof, while one of the monks in the city was killed. St Machars was only saved 'from utter ruine' by the Earl of Huntly. In January 1561, the Sub-principal of King's College debated with Knox and his supporters, and in 1569 King's was purged. The year before an Edinburgh burgess had led the stripping of the roof of St Machar's and the removal of its bells, with 'the Aberdonians refusing to take part in its desecration'. The Aulton had no Protestant minister until 1569, and Aberdeen was able to hang on to its Catholic bishop until 1577, thanks to the protection of the Earl of Huntly. In King's College, Aberdeen, the students continued to write against Protestantism in both Scots and Latin. A powerful group of Catholic burgesses, centring on the Menzies of Pitfodels, retained a strong interest in the city. In 1574 'the privy council had to remind the provost, bailies and town council that only those who adhered to the protestant faith could hold office in the burgh', where the continued holding of Sunday markets bore witness to a resistance to Sabbatarianism. The Aberdeen Kirk Session Minutes of 27 June 1577 contained an imprecation to the fishing skippers to cease selling fish on Sunday and to 'forbeir superstitious dayis'; the inhabitants of the fishing village of Futtie were still causing trouble by being absent from communion in 1603, and in 1608 the salmon fishers had to be convened to ask them not to fish on Sunday. The Sang Schuill (Song School) also survived in Aberdeen, producing a number of distinguished musicians and composers until its closure in 1755, while elsewhere Church music was under pressure.[15]

There was more general opposition to the Reformation, particularly in its more extreme manifestations. Among its intellectual leaders was Ninian Winyet (1519–92), 'schoolmaster of Linlithgow and later abbot of St James in Ratisbon', who complained of the preference for the English over the Scots tongue among the Reformers. There was also some attempt to support the aims of the Counter-Reformation. In 1584, James Beaton, the exiled Archbishop of Glasgow, asked Gregory XIII 'to persuade the general of the Jesuits to send priests of Scottish birth into Scotland'. Few were sent, although Jesuits were reported moving freely in the two Aberdeen burghs in 1587–8. The Scottish Church now needed to be preserved abroad, and Mary supported the infant Scots College of Douai, which finally settled there in 1612: there were also Scots Colleges in Paris (founded by the Bishop of Moray in 1326), and later Rome (1600) and Madrid (1613).[16]

At home, Catholic nobility could resist the plantation of a Protestant ministry: the Earl of Erroll, for example, was 'accused of withholding stipends' and 'in March 1592/3 no fewer than twenty-seven influential persons in the north-east . . . were obliged by the privy council to give surety not to aid the Jesuits'. In 1596, there were 'public bandings against the popish lords' which evince the importance of lay activity and enthusiasm for the Reformation, even though the full 'participation of the laity in the organisation of the church' was compromised by rights of 'patronage' over ministerial livings, an issue which was to remain a thorn in Presbyterianism's internal disputes for centuries.

Even by the beginning of the seventeenth century, Catholicism prevailed in whole counties: Dumfries, Kirkcudbright and Banff among them. Although many parochial clergy had accepted the Reformation, the western Highlands and Islands often did not receive ministers until the early seventeenth century, and Islay was reported Catholic in 1615, while 'over much of the rest of Scotland . . . the success of the reformed church was to rest on determined missionary activity'. There was countervailing 'aggressive' Catholic activity in Paisley in 1597, and open Catholicism in Caithness, Sutherland and Aberdeenshire. Although 'determined and persistent recusancy was limited' outside Catholic strongholds, there is plenty of (still often unexamined) evidence of 'Church Papists', Catholics who conformed at least intermittently in the face of 'exhortation' and pressure. They numbered some distinguished names among them, notably that of Alexander Seton, Earl of Dunfermline and Chancellor of Scotland from 1605. Later, many of these may have provided the not insignificant 'apostasy to Popery' found in the seventeenth-century north-east. Architectural and design features with Catholic overtones continued to be used in domestic buildings 'even as late as the 18th century'.[17]

THE REFORMATION AND CULTURE

There is much to be said for the common and enduring caricature that life in Reformed Scotland was much stricter than what had preceded it. Public pageants and merrymaking were banned (there was in fact some sign of this before 1560); there were 'penalties for *not* working on Christmas Day'. Plays, at first accepted by Knox and other Reformers, went into decline by the 1580s, and drama did not recover until the mid-eighteenth century. People who continued to frequent sacred wells were supposed to be reported by their presbytery; idolatry was punishable by death for a second offence. Those who promised marriage were to be forced to marry; adultery would result in public humiliation in church, but the Kirk Session of Aberdeen observed that 'the dew punishment of the law of God is deth'. Witches were burnt or otherwise put to death, but action against them came in fits and starts, and there were counter-complaints for slander against accusers. Catholics who persisted in their faith were not to be talked to by their families. Children, however, were the same as always, if one Kirk Session minute of 20 October 1616 is to be relied on:

> That young bairnis, quha are not at the schoole, and ar not of sic aige and dispositioun as they can take thame selffis to ane seatt quhen they cum to the kirk, bot vaig [stray] throw the same heir and their in tyme of sermoun, and mak perturbatioun and disordour, be not sufferit to cum to the kirk in tyme of sermone, bot kepit at hame, for eschewing of clamour and disorder in the kirk.

The perceived resistance to Presbyterian church practice in the north of Scotland deepened antipathy to Gaelic, an attempt to abolish which was made in 1616. Little effort was made to speak it by those appointed by the Reformed government: in 1563, Robert Pont was 'appointed

Commissioner of Murray [Moray], Inverness and Bamf . . . but could do litle for want of the Irish [sic] tongue'. On the other hand, there was a contribution to learning in some areas, as with the minister Timothy Pont's (c. 1565–1614) maps, which provided an invaluable survey of the land and burghs of early modern Scotland.[18]

There was undoubtedly a sense of Protestant solidarity. Appeals were made in particular to raise money for those in the hands of the Ottoman Turks or the privateering Barbary states of North Africa, while at home the devolution of poor relief to the parish in the 1570s supported the close involvement of the Kirk both in the relief and enquiry into the morals of beggars. In 1592 ministers, elders and deacons were to elect 'justices and commissioners' for the 'enforcement of the poor law'. By the end of the sixteenth century, a lot of this responsibility was in the hands of kirk sessions. In Edinburgh, kirk taxation was levied in 1575, but 'voluntary contributions and fines . . . became the normal means' of paying for the upkeep of the kirk and its responsibilities. A sense of social care is clearly present from an early date. The 'vast majority of pecuniary penalties imposed upon those who appeared before the session accused of some moral lapse were devoted to the poor', and the idea of social Christianity, first clear in the thought of the Enlightenment Moderates of the Kirk, perhaps had its origins in this intensely localised sense of responsibility, operating within an environment of parochial equality.[19]

The Reformers inherited an already successful education system, but one which was closely tied to the Church, with appointments to grammar schools 'subject to the diocesan chancellor' or the archdeacon. John Knox proposed a school in every parish, and in 1567, rights over teachers' qualifications were given to the new Superintendents. The *First Book of Discipline* (1560–1), which laid out plans for the church, education and poor relief, proposed that 'in country parishes the minister or reader was to provide elementary education for the children'; that in towns there would be at least a rudimentary grammar school, and in the seats of Superintendents/bishops a '"college" with masters qualified to teach "Logic and Rhetoric and the Tongues"'. The kirk's lack of financial clout rendered this ambitious programme ineffective. However, schooling was developing, sometimes in response to 'community action', as at Monifieth in 1599; and by 1616, the Privy Council could propose for the first time 'a parochial system of schools'; further pieces of legislation followed throughout the century. In both schools and universities, standards were high. In the early 1600s, a university student at King's College, Aberdeen, who might be only at the beginning of adolescence, would get up at 6, read for two hours, register, have two hours of classes and an hour's discussion before lunch, and then four more hours study including three hours' classes before bed at 9 p.m.[20]

Seventeenth-century Episcopalian Scotland was certainly more friendly towards high culture than the other Reformed administrations of the country. The bishop's court at a place like Aberdeen was a cultural centre in the early 1600s, part of that 'castle culture' which survived the removal of the court in 1603. Its broader cultural base arguably helped nourish the theologians known as the 'Aberdeen Doctors', whom Presbyterians denounced 'as believers in "popish" ceremonies and suspect theological ideas'. Certainly, a number of Episcopalian thinkers, both in Aberdeen and elsewhere, believed that many Catholic practices were scriptural, and made extensive use of pre-Reformation theological and devotional writing. Episcopalian bishops such as Patrick Forbes of Aberdeen, John Spottiswoode of Glasgow and later St Andrews, William Forbes of Edinburgh and Robert Leighton of Dunblane and later Glasgow, regretted the excesses of the Reformation and showed themselves sympathetic to the inherited traditions and culture of medieval and Renaissance Scotland. The Episcopal party was however, like its Anglican brethren south of the Border, associated with the status of being principally servants of the Crown. In the seventeenth century the long-standing faultline between the interests of the Crown and the development of the Scottish Reformation was to erupt in a running sore of civil war, which persisted off and on for fifty years, and led in the end to the ruin of the Episcopal party and the legend of a solely Presbyterian Reformation.[21]

FIVE

A NATION DIVIDED, 1560–1746

SCOTLAND, BRITAIN AND THE REFORMATION

The Reformation of 1560, coupled with the death of François I, were events which for the first time presaged the possibility of a united Great Britain. This must be a highly provisional claim: one of the weaknesses of the new British History is its marked tendency towards colligation and emplotment. Colligation is 'the process of explaining an event by bringing together a set of seemingly separate and unconnected events under a general description or principle', while emplotment constructs a pattern through time of what is colligated across it. Like the Whig historians of an earlier generation, explaining Britain as it came to exist (and still exists) is often the goal of these processes, which all too often pay inadequate attention to the separateness of national histories, or model British state development on English norms, seeing in Scotland not a small state like many others on the Continent, but rather an England which failed to centralise and modernise adequately.

On the other hand, separate histories of Scotland after 1707 can all too often fail to do justice to the British dimension in Scottish consciousness, and present as nationally distinctive developments which were part of a provincial pattern: for example, particularist histories of heavy industry in Scotland sometimes do not pay enough attention to Liverpool and Newcastle as industrial comparators. By contrast, the demonstrably separate elements in Scotland after 1707 can be ignored or treated as marginal or with geographic vagueness: one of the worst elements of this is the conflation of the whole country north of the Forth with the Gaidhealtachd, an issue addressed in a Jacobite context by the present author in *The Myth of the Jacobite Clans* (1995, 99). The reason for this may be the presence of a continuing (albeit now secularised) Presbyterian and Central Belt bias in modern Scottish history. British history which gives weight to Scotland can readily be written from such a perspective; but a separate Scottish history is much more difficult to construct on such terms, because a national history which locates its core area of value as post-Reformation risks parochialism if it omits the British and international dimensions of post-1560 Scottish history, and if it includes them risks writing a history which is no longer national at all.

From the beginning, the Reformers had strong tendencies towards common British goals which contrasted markedly with the patriotism of the Scottish clergy of an earlier era. The vernacular Bible they chose was that of the English of William Tyndale; Catholic writers complained of their neglect of Scots, and from 1560 to 1610 the proportion of English forms in books printed in Scotland rose from the negligible to 80 per cent. The Treaty of Edinburgh, the willing acceptance of English military aid against the French in Scottish quarrels, the early presence of interest in and acceptance of a future united Britain among the Reformers, and the plans for such a country developed by the Covenanters in the 1640s, are all portions of the extensive evidence which links the Reformation to a sea-change in Scottish politics.

Against this must be set the battle-hardened view which places the National Covenant of 1638 as a patriotic rebellion against an Anglican king, who sought to impose alien ecclesiastical practices on the Scots, and the more arguable defence of pointing out the Kirk's early tendency to Scottish exceptionalism. What these kinds of interpretations tend to underestimate is first, the presence of a native tradition sympathetic to Episcopacy, which paradoxically often defended Scottish cultural difference while seeking ecclesiastical conformity; and secondly, the extent to which Presbyterian sentiments were shared by those among the English Puritans who cheered Covenanting successes in the Bishops' Wars of 1638–41. The Scottish exceptionalism of a 'true Protestant reformation' was itself very largely compatible with a British one. From the National Covenant via Burns to Red Clydeside, a mythos of Scottish identity as democratic, plain-talking and proletarian in contrast to an English identity which is snobbish, pretentious and upper class has had a powerful hold on the Scottish psyche. It means that court and high culture in Scotland have tended in the past to be neglected; and critically, it ignores the common Britishness of Yorkshire Puritan and Scottish Presbyterian; the extent to which the National Covenant did not herald an Anglo-Scottish war, but was part of a British pattern of events found also in Scotland. In 1644 at Marston Moor, Scottish troops helped English Parliamentary forces defeat the army of a Scots-born king. This pattern of events was new; and it was British. Undoubtedly it was reinforced and accelerated by James VI's accession to the English throne and the rule of the Kingdom of Ireland in 1603; but that itself might well have been inconceivable without war had James been a Catholic. As it was, the English political nation rebelled against a High Anglican monarchy in the 1640s just as effectively as its Scots counterpart; while in 1688–9, when the first openly Catholic Stuart since Mary was deposed (as Mary herself had been), the Bill of Rights in London was followed by the Claim of Right in Scotland. In both British kingdoms, Catholicism (and indeed to many sacramentalist high Anglicanism) had become unacceptable.

The historiographical presentation of this distinctively Presbyterian self-image of Scotland arguably mattered little when it took place in the framework of imperial localism: the expression of Scotland's distinct cultural identity within Great Britain and the British Empire. But when it survives into the post-1960 period, when Scottish exceptionalism is becoming more common in historical studies, it is less justifiable. Scottish Presbyterian culture is not a provincial chapter in the history of British Nonconformity; but elements of it are. There were many Scottish patriot Presbyterians, just as there had been many of other religious sympathies who could not be described in such terms; but structurally, 1560 marks a major shift. It is too deterministic to present it as the beginning of a British history which unfolded from it; but as long as England had reformed and Scotland had not, it is hard to see how such a history could have unfolded. Irish Britishness has tended to be underestimated by historians writing after 1922: but it was strongly associated with the Reformed community in Ireland, if not by the nineteenth century exclusively so. The 'Old English' who remained Catholic certainly became less distinguishable from the Gaeltacht after 1690, and the basis for personal status and access to power was in Ireland (as elsewhere in Britain) conformity to the Protestant establishment, with degrees of lenity extended to many non-conforming Protestants, but to no-one else. Although the present writer has disagreed with aspects of Linda Colley's *Britons* (1992) in the past, it is certainly the case that Protestantism underlay many of the possibilities of British unity not only after, but also before 1707. As Allan Macinnes puts it, 'from a Scottish perspective, the pursuit of British union was but the first . . . step towards universal reform'.[1]

JAMES VI AND CHARLES I

The reign of James VI (1567–1625) was the longest of any monarch crowned in Scotland. It saw the transformation of Scotland from a state struggling with civil conflict to one which was a component in a much larger multi-kingdom polity: the kingdoms of England, Scotland and Ireland united for the first time under a single crown.

James, whose tutor was the distinguished Latinist George Buchanan (1506–82), was brought up under the shadow of civil war between the Queen's and King's parties in Scotland, which in its turn was succeeded by the continuation of pro- and anti-Reform intrigue by other means. In 1571, the Ridolfi plot against Elizabeth in England helped turn the balance against Mary's party north of the Border. In the same year, John Hamilton, last Catholic Archbishop of St Andrews, was hanged, following the murder of the Earl of Moray by a relative. In 1573, English troops and artillery helped dislodge the last important supporter of Mary, Kirkcaldy of Grange, from Edinburgh Castle.

Grange's execution, and the defeat of Mary's cause, did not end tension and intrigue in the realm. In 1581, Esme Stewart, the 1st Duke of Lennox, Darnley's cousin, intrigued with Spain, and to forestall growing Catholic influence, the Kirk designed the Negative Confession, which was later incorporated in the National Covenant of 1638. Fearing the king would be seduced to the Catholic party, a group of Protestant nobles led by the Earl of Gowrie kidnapped him in August 1582 in the so-called Ruthven Raid, and kept him in Ruthven Castle till the following spring. The king, who persuaded his captors to allow him to go to St Andrews Castle, where he took refuge from them, emerged from this ordeal more his own man; but the Catholic party was defeated, although intrigues with Spain continued. In November 1585, a defensive league was concluded with England, while at home John Maitland, Lord Thirlestane, James's chancellor, attempted to modernise the government of the kingdom. In 1587, most ecclesiastical lordships were annexed to the crown, and later converted to temporal lordships: a further increase in royal power.[2]

In 1586–7, it was clear that time had finally run out for Mary in England. Already implicated in the Ridolfi plot of 1571, the Throckmorton Plot of 1583 and the Parry Plot of 1585, in 1586, Anthony Babington's plot against Elizabeth's life sealed Mary's fate. In all these cases (save the last) there was little evidence against Mary; but the revelation of her name by tortured Catholics and Francis Walsingham's (the head of the Elizabethan secret service) *agents provocateurs* helped to create a climate of deep distrust. Mary failed to condemn Babington's plot, and implicitly approved it in her confinement and desperation. She was arrested and tried at

Fotheringhay Castle in October: such a proceeding was unconstitutional, and Elizabeth's recourse to it was to foreshadow the use of doubtful legal process against Mary's grandson, Charles I, in 1648. Realising the implications of executing a Queen, Elizabeth wished to have Mary secretly murdered, but failing in this purpose, signed Mary's death warrant on 1 February 1587; a week later, Mary was beheaded, claiming that she spent her blood in defence of the Catholic faith. James's advisers recommended that he should take a strong line on his mother's situation; but her abandoned, neglected, manipulated and wary son declined to do so, merely making a token threat towards the possibility of severing diplomatic relations with England, while tamely appearing to accept Elizabeth's assurances that his mother's death had been 'a terrible mistake'. James was in a quandary: too strong a protest would associate him with Mary's own 'guilt' in the Babington plot, and his prospects of succession would be endangered; too weak, and Scottish public opinion would be disgusted. James did the minimum, and sixteen years later he got his reward. On his accession to the English throne in 1603, James gave his mother a splendid tomb.

The king could also address other constitutional issues in terms of 'show': in 1587, penalties for 'absentee members . . . heralds, macers and trumpeters' were intended to make the Estates look more impressive, and the king also stipulated that each estate 'sal have thair severall apparrell in semelie fassioun'. This policy reached an apogee in the 'crimson and scarlet silks . . . velvet, ermine, and furs' of the 'dazzling "Riding of Parliament" in 1606'.[3]

Domestically, Scotland had economic problems to match the disruption caused by the Reformation. Between 1565 and

1601, the exchange rate of the pound Scots dropped from six to twelve to the pound sterling, the government profiting considerably by the depreciation: nonetheless, 'inflation helped to make Scotland a client state of England'. The number of coins which circulated in Scotland from different countries, particularly in the coastal ports, made a fluctuating exchange rate complex to manage, as a list of no fewer than 28 European coins and their Scottish exchange value set at Edinburgh in 1598 makes clear. Nonetheless, the suspension of war with her southern neighbour brought a 'sudden increase in wealth and comfort' which astonished the English ambassador in 1574; from 1585, much of this was paid for by an annual subsidy of £35,000 sterling from Elizabeth. Even so, central finances were unstable and deteriorated markedly in the 1590s. Famine and plague outbreaks also began to manifest themselves: between 1550 and 1600 there were '24 years of dearth'.[4]

Scotland, now a state in long-term economic decline, was moving closer into England's orbit. However, even in the climate of Protestant *rapprochement* between the two countries, James adopted a different position from Elizabeth, both before and after acceding to the English throne in 1603, seeking 'to limit the results of the Reformation' and appeared to make several moves towards an attempt to reunite western Christendom. His wife, Anne of Denmark, whom he married in 1590, 'eventually became a Catholic'. There were those among the surviving Catholic community who expected a great deal from the king on this issue: but James was slippery, and the disappointment felt by many Catholics in 1603–4 led to the fanatical terrorism of the Gunpowder Plot, which of course made the lot of Catholics worse than ever on both sides of the Border. Jesuits in particular were loathed and pursued, and the executions of 1605–6 were succeeded by the martyrdom of St John Ogilvie at Glasgow Cross in 1615. James was keen that such executions should not be seen as being for faith alone (how could anyone who professed to wish to reunite western Christendom admit that?), but the assertions of treason which often accompanied the priests' deaths were usually unconvincing, although St Pius V's 1570 excommunication and purported deposition of Elizabeth had contributed to an atmosphere where Catholics could all too readily be seen as the agents of a foreign power.[5]

James's court in Edinburgh witnessed a revival in Scottish high culture, with the king promoting the threatened art of music as well as setting himself to write an important work of literary criticism in Scots, *Reulis and Cautelis* (1584). During the 1580s, the king surrounded himself with what has been identified as a 'Castalian Band' of 'an inner group of poets at the Scottish court', whose 'major poetic aim' was to emphasise 'Scotland's readiness to make its unique contribution to the Renaissance'. This was important because of the greater marginalising of Scotland from Catholic Continental influences in the decades after the Reformation. Some of the poets associated with this group wrote poetry in anticipation of James's succession to the English throne, such as John Stewart of Baldynneis' 'propyne' of 1584, although Alexander Montgomerie's *The Cherrie and the Slae*, which was perhaps the greatest of this group's poetic productions, was rather a pro-Catholic lament for Reformation. Montgomerie wrote in Scots; sometimes, as in 'The Flyting of Montgomerie and Polwarth' in quite dense Scots, but there was a steady drift towards English, rationalised by some poets such as Sir

William Alexander and Alexander Craig. The balladic tradition was marginalised in Scottish high culture, not to be revivified until after the Union. It is interesting to note in this context that it was strongest in the conservative north-east, where a distinctively Scottish high culture arguably survived longest. Although the drift towards the English language was opposed by Catholic apologists, the trend continued. It is important, nonetheless, to note that writing in English did not necessarily indicate pro-Union or pro-English politics on the part of the writer.[6]

In the last years of James's reign in Scotland, concern began to grow because Elizabeth had not yet nominated a successor. There was no equivocation among the Scottish elite as to whom it should be: in 1600, it was proposed in the Estates that a tax should be levied 'to raise an army to make good James's claim to the English throne by force if need be'. Taxes were by now very much part of James's armoury. In the 1590s, James's deteriorating finances had led to the establishment of the 'Octavians', the eight-man commission of 1596, with wide-ranging powers to increase taxes. After the commission was disbanded in 1597, James continued to survive precariously on a mixture of 'unprecedented, regular taxation and massive credit'. Deficit financing was very much part of his administration. A suspicion even hangs over the 1600 Gowrie Conspiracy against James's life to the effect that the king set up the Gowries to evade the large debts he owed them.[7]

The departure of James's court from Edinburgh to London in 1603 was assuredly a blow to Scottish high culture, but one which has been exaggerated, for, as Keith Brown points out, 'baronial or country house culture sustained a great body of Gaelic bards, family historians, architects, craftsmen, musicians and painters that has been overlooked'. The nobility 'formed an enormous reservoir of patronage that was collectively wealthier than the crown', and many noblemen either remained in Scotland or returned there. The Latin poetry of seventeenth-century Scotland, the art of the portraitist George Jamesone (1588–1644) and those of his family who followed him, the Aberdeen school of theology, the music of the great houses and the development of Renaissance architecture at places such as Heriot's Hospital in Edinburgh, built in the years from 1628, all testify to the continuation and development of Scottish high culture. Nonetheless, a note of anxiety tending towards lamentation can be found in Scottish poetry as the seventeenth century progresses, with poets such as Thomas Craig and William Drummond feminising their country in the person of a neglected lover, a literary trope found also in Ireland, where the feminine principle is representative of national sovereignty.[8]

In London, James moved towards extending the Union of the Crowns into a more complete constitutional union, but his attempts met with limited success. The images of unity and imperium in royal iconography were so strong that it was even rumoured that the king 'intended to change his name to Arthur', and the new Great Seal 'conjoined not only the English and Scottish arms but also those of Cadwallader and Edward the Confessor, respectively the last undisputed kings of Celtic Britain and Anglo-Saxon England'. Various royal titles were suggested, including 'King of Britain, France and Ireland', 'King of Britain' and 'King of the British Isles and France': all three of these titles were put forward by Sir Henry Savile, and neatly indicate the ambivalent position of Ireland within Britain. From October 1604, James used the title 'King of Great Britain, France and Ireland', but the concept of a united crown as well as united kingdoms did not survive. Various designs for a new Union flag were mooted, ranging from those which gave parity to Scotland's Saltire to those on which it barely appeared. The final design, which presaged our own Union Flag, could be used only conditionally, being 'only . . . flown in conjunction with one or other of the two national flags'. After James's death in 1625, it began to fall out of use. In 1634, the Union flag was reserved for the King's service, with English or Scottish ships carrying their own national flags.

On the broader constitutional front, James 'could not force the English Parliament to proceed with the Instrument of Union against their will. An act for the repeal of mutually hostile legislation' was 'the sole clause of the Instrument to reach the English statute book' in 1607. James's appointment of Scots to English Court offices did little to reconcile the southern elite to further moves towards union. On the other hand, the king's administration could effect much in the way of development towards a closer union, and 'three civilizing projects were designed to bring order throughout his exclusive British empire – namely, the cross-Border policing of the Middle Shires, the plantation of Ulster and the military and legislative offensive directed against the clans on the western seaboard of Scottish Gaeldom'. James even toyed with making York his seat of government. From 1607, the Campbell house of Argyll was using the term 'North British' to describe Scotland; in 1634, England was described as 'South Britain' in a Royal Proclamation. The nobility in particular began to move gradually towards a more united Britishness, with a loss of easy intimacy and greater aloofness among some of the Scottish aristocracy noted by Patrick Gordon of Ruthven in the 1640s. The Scottish Convention of Royal Burghs, established in the 1550s, added a lobbyist in London to their Edinburgh representative by 1613, and there is some evidence that Scots working in England took more care to modify their speech than they had done hitherto, for in 1617 'interpreters were declared no longer necessary at the port of London'. On the other hand, there was also suspicion in Scotland of the country's drift into England's orbit. In 1610, the Privy Council of Scotland requested that copies of treaties should be supplied to both countries. In discussing union, the Scottish Parliament feared it might turn the country into 'a conquered and slavish province'.[9]

The infamous Bond and Statutes of Iona of 1609 represented an attempt to include the West Highlands more closely in this increasingly Anglocentric polity. It was in this area of Scotland that traditional links with Ireland remained strongest after the Reformation: indeed West Highlanders had fought against England in the recent Irish wars, which had ended in 1604. Attempts to colonise the west had already begun, and in the year of the Statutes of Iona, the plantation of Ulster also commenced. In Scotland, from 1598, attempts 'to colonise Lewis' had been made by the 'Fife Adventurers', and the idea was also floated that Huntly should occupy Uist and other islands: this fact does not prevent the Marquess of Huntly's being cast as a 'Highlander' in the Jacobite period. Such ventures amounted to little, and in fact met with repeated failure, but the Statutes were a more focused attempt to bring the post-Reformation west into the orbit of Protestant Britain. Promoted by Andrew Knox (1559–1633), Bishop of the Isles, the Statutes thus used the royal servant status of Episcopal bishops to promote the king's will. Nine leading chiefs came to Edinburgh, and were forced to attend a conference on Iona where they had to agree the Statutes. There were nine clauses in the Statutes: revealingly, the first dealt with the arrival of parish ministers. There were also to be inns throughout the Western Isles, a diminution of the military resources of the region, and sorning (the extraction of maintenance by the threat of violence from one's fighting tail) was to be abolished. There was to be control on the importation of wine and whisky; chief's sons were to be educated in the Lowlands; firearms and Gaelic bards were to be alike suppressed, and chiefs were to hand over offenders. Overwhelmingly, 'Gaelic culture was to be discouraged and the English language promoted'.[10]

By no means all of these measures were effective, but they marked the beginning of a process of painful integration for the west Highlands into an Anglo-British body politic, which was to be neither as flexible nor as hybrid as its Scottish predecessor had been. The wars of 1638–51, which involved both the west Highlands and Ulster in the civil wars of Britain for the first time, and that to an unprecedented degree, were the beginning of the end of this process, which culminated in Scotland in the abolition of heritable jurisdictions in 1747, which both dispossessed the Chiefs of the Name of legal power, and undermined the relationship between them and the noble *fine*. In the 1640s, Catholic Highlanders did not necessarily share the brutal fate meted out by the Covenanters to their Irish co-religionists, but they nonetheless witnessed it, and with it the alienation of Irish from Scottish identity to a degree hitherto unfamiliar. To the Gaelic-speaking Catholic, Ireland was part of the same cultural realm, as it had been to Robert the Bruce, but this was no longer the case for Lowland Presbyterians.[11]

If there were signs of internal colonisation in the promotion of closer shared interests between England and Scotland through the further erosion of the Scots-Irish link, there was also the possibility of Scottish colonisation abroad, now that a Scottish king sat in London. After some early moves in this direction, the poet Sir William Alexander of Menstrie (*c.* 1567–1640), later Earl of Stirling, was granted seisin of Nova Scotia ('the entire territories between New England and Newfoundland') at Edinburgh Castle in 1621 (he gained further grants of land in North America in 1628), and in turn seisin was also granted to those prepared to contribute to the colonisation of this province, who became baronets (a new rank of hereditary knighthood introduced by James) of Nova Scotia. In 1629, Sir William organised a small colony, but the territory was in French hands by 1632, where it remained until the Treaty of Utrecht in 1713. In 1634, a 'short-lived Scottish Guinea Company' emerged. In 1626, James Hay the Earl of Carlisle was made Proprietor of Barbados, and a Scots West Indies trade began to develop, and later in the century a Scots colony was considered in the West Indies, but nothing came of it. By this time, both the Cromwellian administration and the Restoration Scottish Privy Council had been involved in transporting dissidents and undesirables to the islands from Scotland.

James returned to Scotland briefly in 1617, but despite the considerable if somewhat anxious welcome he received, this was to be the only occasion. He planned to impose Episcopacy on a firmer basis than before, and the 'Five Articles of Perth' which endorsed this were finally passed the next year, following an initial rejection by the General Assembly at St Andrews. The Articles enjoined 'private baptism, private communion, confirmation by bishops, observance of holy days and kneeling at communion'. James's version of Episcopacy was modelled on the 'royal servant' school of Anglicanism, which was begun by Archbishop Cranmer and became the tool of Henry VIII's ecclesiastical policy and the figleaf of its respectability; Cranmer's theological belief in the royal will as the arbiter of ecclesial order eventually destroyed him in an era of conflicting royal wills. Just as Cranmer and later Archbishop Laud (1573–1645) tried to impose the royal version of the Church of England on their diverse Protestant and Catholic flocks, so James's bishops were to be instruments of royal policy in Scotland. In a country which had reformed in the face of the Crown, this was a risky policy, especially south of the Tay. When it was intensified under Charles I, disaster followed.[12]

If the Scottish Presbyterian kirk appeared to be in danger of losing domestic influence, Scottish foreign policy was critically undermined by the personal union of 1603. Scotland ceased to send its own ambassadors abroad, and frequently found itself compromised by English policy in the century that followed, being implicated in English wars against erstwhile allies and trading partners from France to the Netherlands. England's three wars with the United Provinces from 1652–74 'sabotaged the growing Dutch trade'. In the 1620s, Scotland was dragged into England's war with Spain. Internally, the English administration sometimes acted as if there were no Scottish government – the Scottish Privy Council objected to Charles I's establishment of a British

Fisheries Company in London amid other suppressions of the identity of Scotland, 'confounding the same under the name of Great Britain, although there is no Union as yet with England'. In 1635, Charles set up the 'Letter Office of England and Scotland'.[13]

Not only was Scotland both colonising abroad and involved in England's foreign wars; it was also exporting military expertise. Figures such as General Sir Thomas Dalziel (1599–1685), General Patrick Gordon of Auchleuchries (1635–99), his son-in-law Lieutenant General Alexander Gordon of Auchintoul (1669–1751) and nephew Admiral Thomas Gordon (1658–1714) rose to the highest ranks in the Russian service. Other professional Scots could also be found throughout Protestant and Orthodox Europe. Most important for the civil wars which were to follow was the experience of Scottish soldiers in the Swedish service from the 1560s, and especially in the 1630s, when Gustavus Adolphus had 34 Scottish colonels and 50 lieutenant colonels in his service. The new tactics developed in his wars were brought home by Field Marshal Alexander Leslie (c. 1580–1661), later 1st Earl of Leven, who returned from Sweden and commanded the Covenanting armies in 1638–41. The presence of large bodies of Scots troops in support of English Parliamentarians at critical battles such as Marston Moor (1644) presaged the growing integration of Scottish troops into the British army under Charles II (r. 1649/60–85) and William II and III (r. 1689–1702). The Scots Guards (1661) and Royal Scots Greys (founded by General Dalziel in 1681) both date their foundation to this period, as do the Royal Scots (1678), the first Scottish regiment to be used in British colonial service at Tangier in 1680.[14]

In 1625, James died and was succeeded by Charles, his second son, who married Henrietta Maria, daughter of the king of France, on 1 May following. Henrietta was a Catholic queen, not by conversion but by birth: she was the first such to marry an English or Scottish king since the Reformation. Charles's interest in art and high culture, particularly painting and the masque, brought him close in temper to the great Catholic courts of Europe. Although he remained strongly attached to the Church of England, the very presence of his wife at court, and the limited rights of Catholic worship enjoyed by her circle, meant that suspicion attached to the motives of the king's advisers, especially after the high churchman William Laud was elevated to the See of Canterbury in 1628. The Catholic Church apparently thought it worth its while to offer Laud a cardinal's hat; and the archbishop himself was prey to anxious dreams about returning to Catholicism. Charles's policy of extending the secular power of bishops led some south of the Border to believe that he was prepared to undo some of the Reformation landgrab in the Church's interest. The English Act of Revocation of 1625, which enabled the king 'to claw back all the awards of Church lands and tithes since the Reformation, ostensibly to return the revenues to the Church', provided a strong premise for such doubts. In England, bishops reached state office for the first time since the Reformation. In Scotland, their numbers on the Privy Council increased, and a new generation of strongly anti-presbyterian clergy began to rise to prominence.[15]

In the 1630s, Charles I and Laud sought in their policy of 'thorough' an Episcopal conformity throughout the British Isles, one which closely adhered to a high church model, with strong overtones of caesarosacramentalism (the conflation of royal with sacred authority) and (at times) pre-Reformation Christianity. The Code of Canons in 1636 helped to extend Laudian practices to Scotland, invoked the Anglican doctrine of the Royal Supremacy, and marginalised the democratic structures of the Kirk. In Scotland, such measures were anathema to the Presbyterians, for whom 1560 was a revolutionary Year of Righteousness; and they were repugnant also, no doubt, to some on the more moderate wing of the Episcopal party in the Kirk of Scotland. But it is important to note that although these changes implied the final steps towards control of the church in Scotland and England by a class of royal servant bishops, whose domestic, if not theological, function would be similar to the statesmen ecclesiastics of Catholic France, absolute uniformity with the Church of England was not required. Scotland would have its own Prayer Book, which would commemorate its own saints, as well as those of the English church. This in itself was a problem: by restoring the feasts of the saints (for example, that of St Drostan, restored on 14 October 1637), Charles I was re-emphasising the sacral character of Scotland's monarchy, which had proved so important in its national history. His order to the Scottish bishops to keep the feasts of 'Catholick saints' in Scotland, 'especially those which were of the Royal blood, and some of the most holy bishops', turned the clock back before 1560, to 'ane kingdom' rather than 'twa', and to the sacral power of the Scottish crown and bishops. But many in Scotland believed in Melville's 'twa' kingdoms and their division of sovereignty. As Jesus observed, a kingdom divided against itself cannot stand, and this was to be Scotland's case long after the attempt to restore St Drostan's feast.

Riots greeted the Scottish Prayer Book in 1637, and the Privy Council 'received petitions from many parts of the country' against it. Four committees, the 'Tables', were set up to represent the views and interests of Lords, barons, burgesses and ministers. In December, they petitioned the king to withdraw the liturgy and remove 'bishops from the Privy Council'. Charles refused. The Tables protested, and a far more formal, potent and evocative document followed: the National Covenant.[16]

The National Covenant of 1638 was an attempt to provide a written constitution 'that prioritized parliamentary sovereignty within the fundamental context of a religious and constitutional compact between God, king and people'. As the latest expression of a long radical tradition, it echoed earlier political thought in distinguishing between 'the office of the monarch and the person of the king', and reserved the right of rebellion against an uncovenanted king by a spectrum of the leadership of Scottish society: 'the corporate embodiment of the national interest'. The Covenant's title and format were returned to repeatedly in later years, most recently in the Home Rule Covenant of 1950–2 and the Scottish Constitutional Convention of 1988–97.[17]

The Covenant 'was in three parts', which respectively upheld the Negative Confession of 1581, enumerated the acts of the Estates and the statutes which guaranteed the establishment of the Presbyterian Kirk, and requested 'free . . . parliaments and assemblies' while pledging to defend the Reformed faith against all comers. The Covenant was signed throughout the country, though Aberdeen refused it on 16 July, receiving approval for having done so from the king's 'sacred maiestie'.[18]

Charles I issued 'various royal proclamations' against the Covenanters; the Marquess of Hamilton, his Lord High Commissioner, attempted 'to dissolve the meeting of the General Assembly' at which episcopacy and Charles's other measures were annulled or abolished. In 1639–40, Charles's forces twice failed to impose their will on the Army of the Covenant under Alexander Leslie. The first Bishop's War ended in a truce at Berwick on 18 June 1639; the second, in which the Scots took Newcastle, at Ripon on 26 October 1640. Neither settlement was in Charles's favour. He owed the Scots reparations, to obtain which he recalled Parliament in London. The Puritan leaders John Pym and John Hampden saw their chance, and two of the king's leading supporters, the Earl of Strafford and Archbishop Laud himself were impeached. The king was forced to sign Strafford's death-warrant, and when rebellion broke out in Ireland in October 1641, Charles was forced to rely on Covenanting troops to suppress it. The Catholic rising in Ireland suggested to many that there was truth in the rumour that Charles intended to bring over an Irish Catholic army to subdue his Protestant subjects. In November 1641, radicals in London passed the Grand Remonstrance against the king in Parliament, which had by now paid Scotland some reparations. After an unsuccessful attempt to arrest the opposition ringleaders, Charles withdrew from London and raised his standard at Nottingham on 22 August 1642. The battle of Edgehill followed in October. By December, both king and parliament were seeking the intervention of Scotland's forces on their side.[19]

By this time Covenanting activity had already attained an international dimension, with the attempt to create a 'tripartite confederation' between England, Scotland and the

United Provinces. This was unsuccessful, but a confederal league with the English Parliamentarians was agreed, which evolved into the new Covenant of 1643, which 'represented a British endeavour to achieve common spiritual and material aims while maintaining distinctive national structures in Church and State'. On 17 August that year, the Solemn League and Covenant promised Scottish aid to Parliament in return for the establishment of Presbyterianism in England, Scotland and Ireland and a closer Anglo-Scottish Union; the English parliament accepted it on 25 September, and the following July saw Scottish troops play a central part at the critical battle of Marston Moor. That same year, the 'Committee for Both Kingdoms' represented the beginnings of a confederal or federal executive; Scottish attempts to promote its authority were resisted by the English Parliament.[20]

The Marquess of Montrose (previously a supporter of the National Covenant) and Alasdair MacColla's series of magnificent victories against the Covenanters within Scotland, which led briefly to Royalist control over most of the country in 1644–5, in the end proved little more than a rearguard action against the king's defeat. As the English parliament began to look less and less likely to fulfil the terms of the Solemn League and Covenant, pro-Stuart feeling increased in Scotland, but when the captured king would not agree to it either, the Scottish Covenanters sold him to the parliamentarians for £200,000 English. The sublime spiritual disinterestedness of this act unaccountably increased the unpopularity of the radical Covenanters, and led to the moderate Engagement of December 1647, by which Scottish troops would fight for the king in conjunction with English Royalists, provided that Charles established

Presbyterianism 'for a trial period of three years' in England, and allowed Scots 'full participation in the commercial privileges of his English subjects', including 'a complete union of the kingdoms' along the lines planned by James VI. In 1648 the Scots 'undertook to invade England' by the terms of the Engagement, which allowed all those 'willing to fight for king and country' to do so: Royalist and Covenanter could thus unite. The Estates supported the Engagement, but the General Assembly did not, and, after the Engagers were defeated at Preston, reasserted control. The Whiggamore Raid of autumn 1648, when 2,000 radicals marched on Edinburgh, effectively seized authority for the extremist wing of the Covenanters, as well as giving the political term 'Whig' to the anti-Stuart left.

Charles I was executed on 30 January 1649, and in March a republic was proclaimed in England, by which time the king's son had already been declared his successor in Scotland. Further war was now inevitable. Charles II had to agree to the terms of the Solemn League and Covenant before he could be crowned, an event which took place, with great deference to Scottish tradition, on the Moot Hill at Scone on 1 January 1651. His new kingdom was already in turmoil. A last raid by Montrose had led to his capture and execution in May 1650, in which Charles had 'disowned' his strongest supporter for the political necessity of retaining Scottish government support. On 17 October, the 'Remonstrance', with support in the radical south-west, opposed the admission of former Royalist 'Malignants' into the army. Although the General Assembly did not support this move, the radical Covenanting wing had shown the strength and intransigence of its view, derived from Melville's 'twa kings' dictum whereby

Christ 'was head of the state as well as the church, and the ministers, as interpreters of the will of God, could instruct the king and the civil authority generally how to do their duty'. On 3 September 1650, Cromwell smashed a Scottish army at Dunbar; on 3 September 1651, Charles II's invading Scottish forces met the same fate at Worcester.[21]

The creation of a united Commonwealth of England, Scotland and Ireland from 1654, which only briefly enjoyed 'formal parliamentary warrant' from 1657–9, deliberately eschewed the term 'Britain' and the ideas of commonality of purpose from the previous decade. In 1649, Cromwell had withdrawn the Union flag, as it was associated with the personal union of the Crowns, and not with any underlying political linkage. On 9 September 1651, six days after Charles II's Scottish army had been beaten at Worcester, a committee of the Rump Parliament asserted 'the right of England to Scotland', and thereafter Scotland's public records were again plundered, as they had been under Edward I, although Cromwell's attempt to seize the Honours of Scotland (the crown jewels) from Dunottar Castle in 1651–2 was foiled by their being smuggled out to Kinneff, 15 km away. In February 1652 a 'tender of Union' was imposed on a reluctant country, but it had little underlying constitutional infrastructure. The 'dismissal' of the Rump Parliament in 1653 caused a legislative log-jam which was only resolved in Scotland's case by the issue of an Ordinance of Union from the Council of State in 1654. Both this and the statutory provision of 1657 were rather *ad hoc* arrangements: in both cases, England was the core state and there was little sign of 'Britain'. Scotland lost its judicial and administrative systems, and returned a mere thirty MPs to London, whose role was 'merely to rubber-stamp policies for Scotland over which they had no control', which did, however, include greater access to English trade and a greater Anglicisation of Scottish society. English garrisons held down the north; the Kirk's authority was compromised by a toleration of all Reformed ministry (short of Anglicanism). Relatively heavy taxation compounded the misery of a country which had already suffered badly from both the wars and the severe plague in the east coast ports in 1645. As Michael Lynch observes, 'the crisis which affected most east-coast burghs between Edinburgh and Aberdeen was as severe as any since the Wars of Independence'.[22]

CHARLES II AND JAMES VII

This situation changed in early 1660 when General George Monck (1608–70), the Cromwellian commander in Scotland, marched south in the aftermath of the collapse of Richard Cromwell's administration to secure parliamentary agreement to the king's return. Charles II's restoration in England on 29 May 1660 inaugurated a 'centrifugal reflex' to the centripetal policies of the Commonwealth in Scotland, and both the Anglocentric Cromwellian regime and Covenanting notions of Britain were for the time abandoned. It was indeed 'deliberate royal policy to keep the settlement of the three kingdoms apart from each other', and, as Keith Brown notes, 'the republican experiment of the 1650s left no-one with any enthusiasm for Britain in Scotland or England'. Charles II was, for his part, conscious of the value of potential centres of loyalty outside the English core, for in the War of the Three Kingdoms it was the south-east of England which had proved most hostile to the Crown.[23]

In the Act Rescissory of 1661, all the 1639–51 Covenanting legislation was annulled. Episcopacy was re-established in Scotland in 1661–2, but dissatisfaction with the settlement was rife among the Covenanters, particularly in the south-west, where most of the 274 ministers who were dispossessed by the Restoration regime lost their livings. A western rebellion was defeated at Rullion Green on the Pentland Hills in 1666, and limited toleration for Presbyterianism followed, which was scorned by the radicals. The murder of the Episcopal primate, James Sharp, Archbishop of St Andrews, at Magus Muir near the city in 1679, was followed by a minor victory for Covenanting forces at Drumclog in the west. The Duke of Monmouth came north to head the Crown's response, and victory was gained over the insurgents at Bothwell Brig. Repression followed, notably the harrying of disaffected areas by the so-called 'Highland Host' (many of whom were in fact northern Lowland militia) in 1679–80. The Host was intended by government to extract 'bonds of surety' from 'recalcitrant . . . landlords', but in the end many of those involved exceeded their brief.[24]

Although the Scottish royal palaces of Holyrood, Stirling and Falkland had been upgraded for James VI's visit in 1617, on the whole the Stuart administration after 1603 had paid relatively little attention to the palaces of its northern realm. Charles and his brother made more concentrated attempts to develop the status of Edinburgh as a royal capital, and thus perhaps an alternative powerbase should anti-Stuart feeling once again rear its head in the south. When elements in the parliament in London were pressing for James's exclusion from the crown on account of his Catholicism, Edinburgh became precisely an alternative capital of this kind, where

James, as Duke of Albany and York, encouraged artistic and professional life. The foundation of institutions such as the Advocates' Library (1682) (later to evolve into the National Library of Scotland) and the Royal College of Physicians (1681), combined with the Stuart emphasis on Scotland as the 2000-year-old source of their dynasty, boosted James's popularity.

At the same time, James preferred to see Covenanters transported rather than being 'martyred'. Overseas colonies were founded by the Covenanters in New Jersey (1682) and off the South Carolina coast in 1684. On the other hand, the equivocation of many Covenanters when asked to abjure the Archbishop's murder or express their loyalty to the Crown helped to underpin the repressive Test Act of 1681, which 'required every office-holder to swear an oath of loyalty to the king, accepting royal supremacy in all spiritual and temporal matters, and abjuring all political or religious reforms'. The radical Covenanters, called Cameronians after Richard Cameron and his rebellious Sanquhar Declaration of 1680, now became increasingly troublesome, and parts of Scottish society polarised. What followed became known (from the pen of Robert Wodrow (1679–1734)) as the 'Killing Times', when (often armed) radical Covenanters were intercepted and killed or captured for torture and hanging in police operations throughout southern Scotland. Terrorist assassinations were met with intensified violent repression, and the injustices which always occur in such situations were amplified by the dignity of the Covenanters into a myth which bears little relation to the relatively small-scale civil disorder of the 1680s. Far fewer died in 'the Killing Times', for example, than in 'the Troubles' in Northern Ireland in the 1970s and '80s.

Nevertheless they represent what Michael Lynch has called 'a serious fissure in the culture of Scottish Protestantism', which nonetheless has been mythologised into a unitary tradition whose legacy was one which until recently Presbyterians of all sorts were anxious to claim. In fact, the Covenanters were a sign of a divided society, not just a repressed one, while the extremism of the Cameronians, and their willingness to kill for their right to impose their brand of religion on anyone else, are less evidence of a struggle for liberty than a late flourishing of the most fanatical practices of the Reformation. Like the Quakers, inner spirit and inner light meant much to the Covenanters: two kinds of personal religious experience, one devoted to tolerance and peace, the other too often to its opposite. Both were oppressed by the Restoration regime: the different spirits in which Covenanting and Quaker history record that period of repression are in themselves interesting manifestations of their ethos during it.[25]

Commercial confederation between Scotland and England was discussed between 1664 and 1668 and again in 1674, while John Maitland, Earl (later Duke) of Lauderdale, Secretary of State for Scotland from 1661–80, put forward a scheme for a fuller union in 1670. The Navigation Acts of the 1660s 'prevented Scottish ships from carrying goods to and from English colonial ports', and thus intensified the pressures operating on the Scottish economy. Scottish economic interests were being frustrated by the lack of common economic policies between the two kingdoms, and in the 1670s Lauderdale chose colonial expansion as a route out of this *impasse*, gaining authorisation for Scottish colonisation in Georgia, Florida and the West Indies. In 1681, the Council of Trade report to James, Duke of Albany expressed Scotland's continuing economic dilemma in stating 'that the only effective way to cope with mercantilism and growing dependence on English trade was either to seek commercial union or to develop overseas colonies'. James 'chose the latter option, warranting Scottish colonies in South Carolina (1682) and East New Jersey (1685)'. At home, he aimed to consolidate his support in Scotland, and the 'Commission for Securing the Peace of the Highlands' of 1682–4 was designed to involve cooperation 'with the chiefs and leading gentry'. After James VII came to the throne in 1685, this policy was somewhat less in evidence; hardly surprising, given that the Earl of Argyll, the mightiest among Highland magnates, rebelled against the king.[26]

On his accession to the throne, James faced an early challenge from a Protestant rebellion by James Scott, the Duke of Monmouth and Buccleuch in the West Country, which was supported by the Earl of Argyll in Scotland. The rebellions were easily defeated, but the king's popularity began to diminish as he promoted a policy of toleration towards both Catholics and Dissenters. In England, this undermined the special status of the Church of England, and a number of Anglican bishops refused to support it. It also seemed to some to presage an attempt to restore Catholicism; this was especially true in Scotland and Ireland. In 1686, the Scottish Estates were offered 'free trade with England in return for relieving Roman Catholics of the penal laws against them'. James's 'Proclamation for the Universal Liberty of Conscience' was issued in Edinburgh on 17 February 1687. It offended Episcopalians, whose establishment was owed to the Stuarts, less than their Anglican brethren; but south of the Tay those of Presbyterian sympathies were dominant, and anti-Catholic rioting in Edinburgh occurred when William, Prince of Orange, James's son-in-law and nephew, entered England with a force of 15,000 men in November 1688, five months after concerns regarding James's regime had intensified following the birth of a son on 10 June. Although William was already making plans to invade, the invitation he received from a group of Whig magnates concerned at the prospect of a Catholic heir was undoubtedly a boost to his cause; he aimed to forestall any Catholic alliance between James and Louis XIV of France, and (probably) to have himself crowned king into the bargain.[27]

When it was known that James's kingdoms were under threat, the Scottish Privy Council ordered two divisions of the Scottish army south to support the king, but their commander, Major-General John Graham, Viscount Dundee was unable to persuade James either to stay in London or make a stand in Scotland. The king, who had already tried to flee unsuccessfully, finally left for France on 23 December 1688. The English Parliament declared William and his wife, James's Protestant daughter Mary, joint sovereigns; Dundee, who had remained with the Scottish forces first at Watford, then at Abingdon, withdrew to Scotland, where the Estates met in convention on 14 March. Armed Presbyterian bands roamed the capital, and the high-handed letter sent to the Estates by the Earl of Melfort, James's Secretary of State, did nothing for the king's cause. James had, in fact, already landed at Kinsale with French forces. On 18 March, seeing that the Convention would endorse William and Mary, Dundee withdrew, hoping to set up an alternative convention at Stirling hosted by the Earl of Mar. Mar sat on his hands, and on 11 April William and Mary were proclaimed at Edinburgh, with the Castle still in the hands of the Duke of

Gordon, loyal to James VII. Five days later, Dundee raised King James's standard on Dundee Law, thus beginning a campaign which ended for him in his death at the victory of Killiecrankie on 27 July, and for his army when James allowed them to submit in December 1691. By this time, three years of vicious war in Scotland and Ireland had confirmed William and Mary on their thrones, the Presbyterian Kirk's establishment, the beginning of the centralisation of the British state, the beginning of the illimitable doctrine of Parliamentary sovereignty and the beginning of the end for both the Stuarts and Scottish independence. The Massacre of Glencoe on 13 February 1692, authorised by William and the Williamite Scottish government in order to make an example of a Jacobite clan, was a presage of the destruction of the Highlands after Culloden in 1746, the end of the end for both the Stuarts and Scottish independence.[28]

THE REVOLUTION, THE JACOBITES AND UNION

In exile, the Stuarts were associated with a variety of symbols, historic or iconic figures. In classical guise, the exiled king was represented as Aeneas, the exiled Trojan hero who founded Rome and whose descendant Brut had, according to Geoffrey of Monmouth, founded 'Britain'. Aeneas was perhaps first identified with the Stuarts under James VI, whose destiny was to become the first king of Britain, while the exile of Charles II may have reinforced the identification. Poets such as John Dryden (1631–1700) emphasised this link, while Dryden also produced a coded version of the *Aeneid* in the 1690s which favoured the cause of the exiled James; nor was Dryden the first to do this. The *Aeneid* was also associated with Catholicism.[29]

On a popular level, the king was the lost lover of the feminised land, a trope which endured powerfully in Scottish literature. After Lieutenant General Paul Menzies, younger brother of Montrose's standard-bearer, prevailed on Pope Clement to 'sanction a service to commemorate St Margaret', Catholics and some Episcopalians renewed the veneration of the holy queen, whose feast was placed on 10 June from 1693, the birthday of the exiled Prince of Wales: it only changed to 16 November in 1903. The ancient sacramental links of Scottish nationality were returned to for the last time by the Jacobite patriots of 1689–1746.[30]

Despite his Calvinism, the unruly history of Scotland under Presbyterian domination and its tendency to oppose the Crown, meant that William II and III was ready to confirm an Episcopalian establishment in the country; but after the Episcopal bishop of Edinburgh had given William an equivocal answer in respect of his loyalty, the way lay open for the Presbyterians. The General Assembly of 1690 which established Presbyterianism was solely constituted of those from south of the Tay. As Michael Lynch argues, 'in effect, it was a partition church of southern Scotland which claimed the right to deprive all ministers who fell short of its ideal of full-blown presbyterianism'. Its divisiveness meant that it was more than twenty years before the last official Episcopalian clergy were evicted, and it helped to confirm the Episcopalian areas of Scotland in their Jacobitism for more than half a century. Episcopal 'refusal to abjure the House of Stuart led them to reject an accommodation with the Presbyterian establishment in 1695 and toleration from the British government in 1712', they therefore 'no less than the Catholic community, were subject to the penal laws', although the Kirk preferred to 'discriminate . . . discreetly' rather than 'fulminate . . . publicly' in deference to the pro-Episcopal feelings of many in the Church of England.

An attempt to impose Presbyterianism by the 'Committee of the General Assembly for the North' in 1694 failed, and Presbyterian intrusion was long resisted by landowners and the local population – as late as 1710 there were still 113 Episcopal incumbents north of Tay. Some Episcopal areas drew closer to Catholicism, and many Episcopalians, also suffering discrimination 'did what they could apparently to obstruct the inquiries of Presbyteries as to the movements and actions of the "trafficking priests"'. Episcopalian religious practice, particularly in the north-east, was given to sympathies with Catholic doctrines, mysticism and high church practices in general: anathema to Presbyterians. Episcopalians also, like Catholics, refused to see 1560 as a national revolution after which nothing could be the same, and 'made use of the rich medieval, religious heritage of Gaeldom to spread its gospel message'. The two confessions were thus often seen in similar terms. The Presbytery of Caithness described its Jacobite Episcopalians as inclining 'more to Popery than presbytery' and the Presbytery of Meigle described them as 'much akin to Popery', while the Presbytery of Fordyce suggested that conversion to Catholicism had come about through the suppression of Episcopalians. To complicate matters further, conforming Catholics can be found as late as 1777. Limited toleration was granted to Episcopalians in 1712 on the basis of loyalty to the Crown; but this was not usually forthcoming, and after the 1745 Jacobite Rising an attempt was made to suppress Scottish Episcopalianism completely, and to serve the taste for such worship from chapels staffed by Anglican clergy from England or Ireland, or ordained by English or Irish bishops.[31]

William's government in England was financially innovative, developing many of the structures (such as government bonds and the National Debt) through which British ascendancy in the world would be funded in the century that followed. Despite the wars of 1689–91 and Jacobite scares in 1692 and 1696, his throne (Mary died in 1694) remained relatively secure. Peace with France in 1697 was followed by constitutional measures to exclude James VII and II's son, also James, from the throne, especially once it was clear that there was no chance of his becoming an Anglican. After James VII died in 1701, the Act of Settlement (see below) excluded Catholic heirs from the English throne, while on 7 March 1702, the Act of Abjuration required formal renunciation of allegiance to James III, widely recognised as such on the Continent. If Anne, James VII's other daughter and William's nominated successor, died without heirs, the crown would pass to Sophia of Hanover, the senior Protestant heir, though there were more than fifty Catholics closer in blood than she. This succession did not extend to Scotland, although the English Parliament no doubt thought that their northern neighbour would follow suit, as in 1688–9. This was not, however, to be the case.

In the 1690s, Scotland's capacity for enterprise exceeded her economic potential as an independent state. As an innovator, the country was ahead of major European powers such as France. Scotland rapidly developed a working paper currency, and by 1707 there was nationwide bank lending south of the Great Glen. William Paterson (1658–1719), who founded the Bank of England in 1694, involved himself in the development of The Company of Scotland Trading to Africa and the Indies in 1695, the year in which the Bank of Scotland was also founded. As early as 1634 the Scottish Guinea Company had tried to 'break into the African trade'; now it seemed that the financial structure existed to place the whole country's resources at the disposal of colonial development. This was the era of mighty schemes and projects aimed at transforming the private and public economies of Europe – the dotcom boom of early modern history. But whereas John Law's Mississippi Scheme in France and England's South Sea Bubble could both be absorbed by their major and broad-based economies, Scotland's frail finances were ruined by Darien.

The Company of Scotland was designed both to finance and to found new colonies for Scotland, and in 1698 it projected and funded an expedition to found a colony at Darien, close to what is today the Panama Canal. It was a brilliant identification of a key commercial area, but Scotland could not fund a successful colonisation there. The financier William Paterson's vision of trade as a bloodless route to empire was frustrated, for English government figures saw that Scottish success might outflank them. King William forbade 'his English subjects' to give the Company of Scotland 'any aid or comfort, let alone commerce', and the 50 per cent of initial capital to be raised south of the Border was lost. Attempts to raise the money from Dutch and German sources were also frustrated, Scotland's lack of an independent foreign policy leaving the country vulnerable to the machinations of English diplomacy. The project was isolated internationally, the climate was difficult, and Spanish hostility did the rest. At first successful, a second and a third expedition ran into greater and greater difficulties. By the time Darien had collapsed, it had absorbed perhaps 25 per cent of the working capital available in Scotland. Moreover, this working capital was itself constrained by the European diaspora (100,000 Scots emigrated in 1600–50 alone) and the internal British political economy. As Chris Whatley observes, 'transatlantic colonial ventures . . . were constrained by the lack of resources – human and financial – available to the Scots, owing to high levels of emigration to Europe and the credit-stretching cost of settlement in Ulster'. A weakened Scotland was stretched in different directions at once, trying to become a major modern state and yet unable to do so. The disaster of Darien came in the wake of the multiple failed harvests of the 1690s, 'King William's ill years', which had killed many (up to 20 per cent in some areas) and forced others to leave Scotland. The Episcopal clergy claimed that they represented a judgement on Scotland for abandoning the Stuarts; whatever the case was, Scotland was facing something not far from 'an economic armageddon'.[32]

Scotland's economy, already in long-term decline, had been seriously damaged by fifty years of intermittent religious and dynastic war. The country's export strengths were in linen (in particular), wool, sheepskin, cattle and herrings (though Scotland could not match the Netherlands as a fishing nation); developing business areas such as coal and salt were threatened by English competition, while established ones such as hides and fish faced deteriorating market conditions. At the same time, 'virtually all manufactured goods were imported, including iron and copper . . . as were luxuries'. In 1707, around half Scotland's exports, 'in the shape of black cattle and linen', went to England. Although the merchants of

Glasgow had begun a tobacco trade with England's North American colonies, this was 'illicit' without a proper trade agreement, such as had been discussed in the 1660s and which would be included in the Union negotiations. Scotland's close trading links with 'Scandinavia and the Baltic' no doubt had their development hindered by the very underdevelopment of those areas. Combined with the casualties of war and the plague's depradations in the east coast burghs in the 1640s, the famines of the 1690s meant that Scotland's population barely budged in the century from 1638.

Scotland's armed forces were also in a weak state. The country's available army was small, and her navy amounted to three ships in 1696, and even these had their 'hulls borrowed from England'. Militarily weaker than ever before, the country was also isolated diplomatically. Scotland's foreign policy had atrophied during the seventeenth century, and was frequently bound up with English interests: William pressed 1,000 Scottish seamen to resist an expected French invasion. The Estates protested, but the act summed up the intensity of Scottish isolation: not only was the country without allies, but allies against England were even more difficult to find because of a century's involvement with English foreign policy.[33]

Scottish petitioning of William for Union in the early part of his reign was largely in response to the Jacobite military threat, and the power of Louis XIV ensured that it remained a live option in royal policy, though the House of Commons rejected it in 1700. By this time the Darien Scheme, Scotland's last independent major colonial venture, had failed, and to the non-Jacobite elite, the negotiation of union of some kind became a more urgent possibility. An initial attempt to appoint commissioners failed in 1702–3 over Scottish insistence on compensation for Darien.

When it finally occurred, the key motivation for the Union was the succession to the Crown. The heir presumptive, Princess Anne's son and heir, the Duke of Gloucester, had died on 30 July 1700, leaving no Stuart heir in the Protestant line. When James VII and II died in 1701 with the prospect of a line of Catholic heirs to succeed him beginning with his son, the twelve-year-old Prince of Wales, the need for parliamentary action became urgent: few now believed that James VIII and III had been illegitimate, as had been pretended by Williamite propaganda. By the Act of Settlement of 1701, the English Parliament excluded all Catholics from succession to the Crown, settling it on Sophia, Electress of Hanover and her issue, as the nearest Protestant heirs. In doing so, they had excluded the exiled Scottish dynasty, the Stuarts, from the throne, as well as fifty other Catholics who were closer by blood than Sophia. After William died in February 1702, Anne became queen, and the situation became yet more urgent. Scotland still did not follow England's suit. The Scottish Parliament passed the Act Anent Peace and War (1703) which reserved an independent foreign policy to Scotland, the Wine Act which maintained Scoto-French links and the Act of Security (1704), which reserved to Scotland the right to alter the Hanoverian Succession. Although it made provision for the heir to be a Protestant (which might mean the Duke of Hamilton, as direct descendant of James II), the Act could be seen as a threat to restore the Stuarts. There was unwillingness to have Queen Anne assent to the Act; the Scottish Parliament threatened to withhold supply, and in retaliation Westminster passed the Alien Act (1705), designed to rob Scots of the right to settle and trade in England. Scottish fury spilled over into the courts, where Thomas Green, an English East India captain, was condemned to death 'with two of his officers' for 'piracy' against Scottish shipping: Green was probably not guilty. It was against this background that pressure was brought to bear for Union as the only solution to the impasse over the succession and Scottish national rights; and it was for this reason among others that the Stuarts in exile continued to vigorously oppose the Union, as one of the key reasons for it had been to secure their exclusion.

The Treaty of Union between England and Scotland, which created the United Kingdom of Great Britain, was the product of negotiation between English and Scottish Commissioners between April and July 1706. Support for a federal or more limited commercial confederal Union was marginalised by the royal appointment of the commissioners, itself sought by James Douglas, 4th Duke of Hamilton (1658–1712), who notwithstanding continued to play the patriot card with an astonishing degree of plausibility. At the last Union was negotiated with little difficulty: once both sets of commissioners had been appointed by the queen, 'the only reported discourse of substance between the commissioners was over the size of Scottish representation in the United Kingdom parliament'. Activity elsewhere told a different story: many counties and towns from Galloway to Peterhead petitioned against Union, with few addresses in favour and 'even supporters of the Union admitted that more than three-quarters of the Scottish people disliked it'. Many saw it as the end of the Scottish nation, with its defensive patriotic tradition of valour and resistance, and 'some of the western parishes added the inconsistency of the Union with the National and Solemn, League and Covenants'. The Union articles were burnt at Dumfries, and both popular protest and patriotic rhetoric in the Estates appealed to the Tacitean tradition of Scotland's heroic valour in the face of mighty odds. Even Hamilton talked of 'those worthy patriots who defended the liberty of their country against all invaders', and twenty-six burghs signed a remonstrance in favour of 'Privileges . . . maintain'd by our Heroick ancestors'. Defensive patriotism was widely voiced: but what would the Scots be defending? The Stuarts? a confederal or federal republic? the Covenants? The forces opposing Union were divided, and small bands of troops and rumours swilled about the country to no end.

The pro-Union Duke of Queensberry requested that English troops be brought to the Border, and other English forces entered the Scottish plantation in Northern Ireland. The threat of English military action and the adroit use of patronage helped to provide the focused result required by the elite who sought or were prepared to accept Union from a variety of motives, ranging from jobbery and disappointment through to principle. The political theorist Andrew Fletcher of Saltoun (1653–1716) was by far the measure's most sophisticated opponent, and he appealed to subsequent tastes partly on account of this and partly on account of his isolation and ineffectiveness. However, the Jacobites were incomparably the most powerful party to object to Union, and it was they who helped almost to overthrow it in the years that followed. In 1707, Jacobite support for federalism as a compromise position was undercut by the Squadrone Volante of floating MPs' decision to support Union. Attempts to suspend proceedings to take account of widespread public hostility foundered on 'Hamilton's insistence that any address to the Crown must acknowledge the Hanoverian succession', a thing that Jacobites could not do. The first article was passed with a vote of 116–83 with 36 abstentions on 4 November 1706; ratification on 16 January 1707 saw the majority rise to 110–69 with 46 abstentions. Of the three estates, only the nobility mustered an absolute majority for Union on either vote: a sign perhaps of the supremacy of political jobbery over economic far-sightedness among the politicians who had made a decision opposed by their people.[34]

Approved by both Parliaments, the Union received the Royal Assent in England on 6 March, and came into effect on 1 May 1707. Under the terms of the Treaty forty-five Scottish MPs would sit in Westminster, and 16 representative peers would sit in the Lords: the small number chosen made considerable patronage control possible, as did the smaller proportionate size of the franchised electorate north of the Border. Scotland's population, at that time about one-fifth of England's, was underrepresented, though of course, at a time when there were fewer than 200 electors per constituency and there were no voters in Shetland at all, the concept of 'representation' differs considerably from its status today.

The Union brought into permanent being a single flag, the Union Jack, and uniformity of taxation, duties and coin throughout the United Kingdom, with a number of Scottish exemptions and a special compensation, the 'Equivalent' (Clause XV), in recognition of Scotland's share of what was now a British, and not merely English, National Debt. After

Union, Scotland was to gain free trade with England and overseas colonies; the availability of the Irish market and the Royal Navy's protection of overseas trade were particularly useful measures. The 'Equivalent' was to be used for paying the debt of the Company of Scotland (who had financed Darien), the debts of the Scottish Crown, to compensate those who lost out through standardising the coinage, and to encourage and support certain manufactures. Scotland was to keep her legal system (recently defined in standard works such as Viscount Stair's *Institutions* (1681) and Sir George Mackenzie's *Laws and Customs of Scotland on Matters Criminal* (1684)), her burgh rights and her Court of Exchequer together with her heritable jurisdictions of barony and regality. The Scottish Mint survived until 1836, although its last coin was struck in 1709. The Commissioners were forbidden to treat of ecclesiastical matters, and no mention of these were made in the Union. Instead, the two parliaments passed separate acts, which preserved the establishment of the Presbyterian Church of Scotland and the country's universities. The establishment of the Church of Scotland within the Union worked well, but the issue of lay patronage of ministerial livings endorsed by the Patronage Act of 1712 (which breached the separation of lay and clerical into 'twa kingdoms') remained unresolved. The patronage question and related questions (such as the secular law's demands on the religious beliefs of burgh office-holders) caused major secessions from the Kirk in the eighteenth century, and eventually contributed to the Disruption of 1843, and the secession of the Free Kirk, most of whom rejoined after 1921 when Parliamentary and lay powers over the Kirk were modified or removed.[35]

The Union remained unpopular, and the exclusion of the Stuarts and introduction of the Malt Tax and other unpopular measures helped to keep it so. By 1712, 'it appeared that Scotland had become a victim of exploitation by English traders whose merchandise was permitted to invade the north at cheap prices to the prejudice of the Scottish market', while even limited Episcopalian toleration in this year provoked a nationalist upsurge. In 1713, an attempt to repeal the Union in response to the introduction of the Malt Tax narrowly failed. Though the vote in the Lords may have been, as Michael Lynch observes, 'only a parliamentary gesture, part of the Westminster game of charades', it rattled the Crown. When the tax was fully introduced in 1725, there were riots. Likewise, excise duty politicised smuggling as a crime, thus lending an implicitly anti-Union dimension to the Porteous Riots at Edinburgh in 1736. As in the Cromwellian period, taxation tended to increase: Chris Whatley estimates it as rising 'approximately five-fold overall' after 1707, and it was this that helped the Jacobites argue for what one historian has called 'an end to Union and tax cuts'. National identity was bound up as much with the suffering economy as with the exiled king. It should also be noted in this context, that the Union's effects were very gradual in operation, with Scottish measures and Scottish currency surviving both in use and as a measure of account, while the whole country was under a semi-autonomous administration. In this sense, little changed: Charles II's Lauderdale was succeeded by George II's Argyll and George III's Dundas.[36]

Jacobite activity had been going on in Scotland before the Union was passed, with Colonel Nathaniel Hooke leading the exiled court's efforts. Shortly after the Union had occurred, a Jacobite memorial was circulated calling for restoration of King James VIII in Scotland, and was signed by or on behalf of the Duke of Atholl, the Marquess of Drummond, the Earls of Galloway, Home, Linlithgow, Nithsdale, Strathmore, Traquair and Wigton, as well as a number of other barons and lords of parliament. The plan was to bring in French troops, to waste the country south of Forth–Clyde to deter a British invasion, and to occupy the Tyne-Tees coalfield, cutting off London's fuel and forcing the government to negotiate James's return, possibly as King of Scots alone.

In March 1708, a small French fleet reached the Fife coast with the exiled James VIII, but the French admiral, Comte de Forbin, was shadowed by the Royal Navy. Unable to put troops ashore, and unwilling to take the risk of landing James alone, he returned to France. Such Jacobites as were waiting for their king quietly disbanded and went home. Jacobites could not readily be convicted by Scottish courts, and the neighbours of Jacobite gentry sought to protect rather than inform on them. It was to be a feature of Jacobite activity in Scottish society that endured throughout the first half of the eighteenth century. Men who in England were regarded as traitors were seen in Scotland, even by their foes, as patriots who had made the wrong choice, or at least kin or countrymen whose lives, families and estates ought to be protected from the savage justice of British retribution. Only in the Gaidhealtachd did this fellow-feeling not always hold good.[37]

In the 1710 General Election, about sixteen of the forty-five Scottish members returned could be identified as Jacobites, and the pressure towards toleration for loyal Episcopalians and for a repeal of the Union was fed by this group. Scottish civic society was also full of those with similar sympathies. The scale of the government purge in connection with the first major Rising of 1715 demonstrates this. In August and September 1715, almost one in five Scottish JPs were dismissed for Jacobite sympathies, but this did not solve the problem for the government, for 'after the Rising, 77 per cent of the JPs in Kincardine were dismissed, 54 per cent of those in Forfarshire, a half of those in Inverness-shire, and three in ten of those in Aberdeenshire'. Half of Scotland's population lived north of the Tay, and in this part of the country there was massive opposition to the Hanoverians and the Union. There were also significant numbers of Jacobites in the capital. James's birthday was celebrated in Edinburgh and Leith in 1712–13, and institutions of Edinburgh society (such as the Faculty of Advocates and Company of Archers) maintained Jacobite loyalties. After 1715, 'universities, town councils, schools and the clergy, even Presbyterian clergy' would all be purged, and Scottish society's professional Jacobite elite would be badly damaged.[38]

The Rising of 1715 aimed, in James VIII's words, to 'restore the Kingdom [of Scotland] to its ancient free and independent state' with 'a free and independent Scots Parliament'. The erstwhile Unionist Earl of Mar, still Secretary of State at the time of Anne's death in 1714, lost his office under George I, switched sides, and headed the Rising. There was to be a Jacobite rising in England as well, but Mar acted at least in part unilaterally in raising the king's standard at Braemar on 6 September 1715. Two marquesses and eight earls joined almost at once, and recruits poured in until Mar had nearly 20,000 men (over 50 battalions). An understrength brigade under Mackintosh of Borlum moved south to link with the northern English Jacobites (those in the south had been outmanoeuvred by the government), but General Forster, the English Jacobite commander, was as incompetent a general as Mar, and the English Rising was defeated at Preston, while Mar wasted a massive advantage in numbers in fighting out a losing draw at Sheriffmuir. By the time James (who had not authorised the beginning of the Rising) landed at Peterhead on 22 December, the Jacobites were in retreat, finally moving north of Perthshire in early February. Shortly afterwards, James and Mar sailed from Montrose for France.[39]

Although many Presbyterian Scots appear to have supported the Jacobite Rising of 1715, the Episcopalians remained the overwhelming source of strength for the Jacobite movement, and this became relatively truer as the century wore on. High Church thinking was important in some Episcopalian ecclesiology: they were 'the Catholic remnant of the ancient Church of Scotland', and it was in these terms that they signed their 'Concordat Bond of Union' with the American Episcopalian Church, which became a daughter Church of the Scottish Episcopalians in 1783. Scottish Episcopal orders had been banned in 1748, and during the War of Independence the Americans in solidarity declined to accept 'schismaticall intruders' in English or Irish Anglican orders. The Episcopal Church in America thus became the daughter church of the Nonjuring Episcopalians of Scotland, who finally officially renounced their Jacobitism in 1788, though Stuart sympathies (and even the odd Jacobite clergyman) continued in evidence for much longer.[40]

In 1715, 'dissatisfaction with the Union had been a highly effective recruiting agent' for the Jacobites, but, despite continuing problems over taxation, the Scottish economy started to improve in the 1720s. The linen trade was developing, and the increase in Bank of Scotland lending between 1722 and 1726 indicated growing economic vibrancy. Even the hostility to the Malt Tax could be partially defused by the decision taken with Walpole's support 'to divert any surplus from the malt tax' to promote Scottish industry, while the use of the Equivalent to stimulate economic development in the 1720s also improved conditions in the country.

However some economic improvement was controversial, particularly that which affected landholding, as greater efficiency in land use tended both to diminish runrig (where the land was farmed in alternate strips for mutual protection, so that A's land might lie either side of B's, and both in turn could be enveloped by C's divided property), smallholdings and the holding of land in common. In 1661, the General Enclosure Act and in 1695 the 'Act anent lands lying run-rig' had allowed consolidation of land, while in 1723 a 'Society for Improving in the Knowledge of Agriculture' was founded in Edinburgh. Enclosure led to riots in Galloway and elsewhere, while the improving Grants of Monymusk faced legal resistance to their measures. 'Land reclamation' was also developing, especially on ground 'near big urban markets': in the course of the century it would drain the ground near Stirling which had for so long marked the impenetrability of the Forth–Clyde line. The enclosure of common land drove out the cottars, that class of poor peasant smallholders who depended on its free resource for their maintenance, and whose idealisation by Burns in 'The Cottar's Saturday Night' may thus be a political act.

'Covert confrontation' to economic change was widespread, and so was more direct action: 'the Lowlands of Scotland was a specific area to which men from Britain's standing army of between ten and fifteen thousand were sent' on occasion. In 1707, English and Scottish fishermen fought in the borders. In 1725, the Shawfield riots against the Malt Tax led to twenty-six casualties when soldiers opened fire, with the mob subsequently forcing the troops to flee to Dumbarton. General Wade had to move in with 'seven troops of dragoons' to restore order. Discontent was still widespread. The loss of national symbols such as the currency 'and the appearance of large numbers of tax officials' helped to create a 'flammable' atmosphere, and the removal of the Scottish Privy Council in 1708 meant that political control was unduly vested in London. This point was brought home both by the treason trials of the Jacobites of 1715 (when, as in 1745, the British authorities refused to let cases be heard in Scottish courts from (justified) fear of an acquittal) and the removal of the separate Scottish customs board in 1723 – both measures were in breach of the Union. The patronage and management of the Argyll family in Scotland ameliorated the situation, but there were definite indications of the intrusion of English power. London would not permit even Hanoverian loyalist Scots to form their own militia in 1715, evincing a fear of Scottish disloyalty which was to persist for over half a century. The Disarming Act of 1716 'banned the carrying of weapons in public'; in 1717, the Highland Companies were disbanded. An 'English commission' sought to dispose of estates forfeited by the Jacobites; blocked by a combination of kinship interests and legal proceedings the government attempted to sell the estates to a company (the York Buildings Company) which it had itself set up to buy them. If this too proved unsuccessful in the face of Scottish social solidarity with deprived Jacobites, it was nonetheless evidence of a trend.[41]

In 1725, the government responded to Lord Lovat's self-serving 1724 'Memoir on the State of the Highlands' by adopting a programme of improvement which may have owed as much to a desire to put troops in a disaffected country as anything else. General Wade's soldiers dealt with Malt Tax riots in Glasgow, and then Wade embarked on a sixteen-year programme to improve roads and communications in the Highlands, to develop Independent Companies of Highlanders to police the area, and to emplace an upgraded cadre of local law officers. Wade's roads proved advantageous to the Jacobites in 1745, while the Highland Companies proved little more than an irritant, even if their loyalty to the Hanoverians was unshakeable, which was not always the case.

In the east coast towns in particular, the 'ubiquitous fiddlers' and the pipers helped to spread the Jacobite airs which fed on popular discontent. Another rising in 1719 was confined to the Highlands, but intermittent Jacobite and Jacobite-related disorder continued. In 1731, Aberdeen town council banned 'Andrew Ferguson, a piper' from playing at night, as he raised 'mobs and tumults in the streets', and this was dangerous in a town with many Jacobite supporters. In 1734, King's Birthday celebrations saw clashes between Jacobites and Hanoverians 'in both Kinghorn and Stirling'.[42]

After a French attempt to invade England in 1744 was undermined by British intelligence, Charles Edward Stuart (1720–88), the Jacobite Prince of Wales, raised the money to set out for Scotland himself to raise his father's standard. Most of his military equipment and the Irish regulars donated by Lord Clare were forced to return to France after a Royal Navy attack, but Charles successfully made landfall in Eriskay on 23 July 1745 with a few supporters, and reached the mainland two weeks later. At first, he was told to go home, to which he responded 'I am come home'. When Charles persuaded Cameron of Lochiel, who had a fighting tail of a thousand, to join the Rising, it became possible to raise the standard at Glenfinnan at the head of Loch Shiel on 19 August. The army of 'King James the Eight . . . prosperity to Scotland and no Union' marched south, outmanoeuvring General Cope's army in Scotland, and taking Edinburgh, possibly by collusion. Few Scots showed themselves prepared to fight for Hanover, and Cope's force was defeated at Prestonpans on 21 September.

After holding court and gathering reinforcements in the capital, Charles swept south, narrowly carrying a vote to do so, for many of the Jacobite leadership thought that they could hole up in Scotland, underestimating the blockading power of the Royal Navy. Lack of English support and a failure of the explicit French commitment Charles had promised led to a vote among the commanders to retreat from Derby on 5 December, by which time a Franco-Scottish force had landed in Scotland under Lord John Drummond to join the Jacobite army of occupation. The loss of momentum foredoomed the risky rising to defeat, for the longer the British state had to defend itself, the more were the human and financial resources on which it could call. Victory for Charles's forces at Falkirk in January only delayed the inevitable. The French invasion (which was planned) had been called off, and the trickle of Irish soldiers sent by Louis XV which beat the naval blockade could no longer get through at all after the Jacobites withdrew from the east coast ports in late February. Inverness was the last burgh of any size in Jacobite hands, and defending it on poor ground after a failed night attack, Charles's army was defeated at Culloden on 16 April 1746 by a British force almost twice its size under the Duke of Cumberland. The last major battle on Scottish soil was fought in the shade of mountains, and to the north of Strathnairn: but neither the mountain nor the flood was put to any good use as the Jacobite army surged forward over flat, rough and boggy ground into the killing field of front and flank musket fire which, together with the canister shot of the artillery, produced 200 casualties a minute. A *sauve qui peut* order greeted the remnants of the army at Ruthven in Badenoch, and after many well-documented adventures, Charles escaped to France, together with many of his officers. The government, however, determined to break Jacobitism in Scotland for ever ('I tremble to think that this accursed spot may still be the ruin of my family' said the Duke of Cumberland at Culloden), followed a policy of brutal repression combined with occupation and the creation of a huge white elephant, Fort George near Inverness, which was finally completed when the Jacobite threat had disappeared altogether.[43]

Culloden effectively ended the Jacobite challenge, and the threat to the Union. It was not a Highland or Gaelic rising, though it was demonised as such by English propaganda which characterised all Scots in such terms, and later by Lowland Scots who wanted to distance themselves from a failed cause in which many of their relatives (and perhaps even themselves) had been involved. In order to stress the patriot quality of his army, Charles had uniformed them all (even the English Manchester Regiment and some French officers) in a version of Highland dress, the badge of old, patriotic Scotland. Yet his recruits were men from north of Forth–Clyde and especially north of Tay, rather than Gaelic-speaking Highlanders. The 11–14,000 men (half the country's effective maximum levy) who fought with Charles were divided into up to 31 battalions and 10 troops of horse. Of these, 4–5 battalions came from Perthshire, *c.* 11 from the central and west Highlands, 7–8 from Aberdeenshire, Banffshire and the Mearns, 2 from Forfarshire, 1 from the Black Isle and Inverness, 1–2 from Edinburgh and environs; and of the horse 2 troops from Perthshire and Angus, 2 from the north-east and 4 from Edinburgh and the east coast. One infantry battalion came from the Scots, and one from the Irish in France, formed out of picquets from different regiments; there was in addition one squadron (the troops) of Irish horse.[44]

Charles's army was thus not a Highland army; but the government attacked the Highlands as the core area of the Rising, and, more significantly, the area whose outlook and mores was most alien to British opinion. In the same way, fifty years later the Irish Catholics were to be blamed for the Rising of 1798 more than their Protestant northern radical allies. As Allan Macinnes has argued:

The immediate aftermath of the 'Forty-Five was marked by systematic state terrorism, characterised by a genocidal intent that verged on ethnic cleansing; by banditry as a form of social protest; and by cultural alienation as chiefs and leading gentry abandoned their traditional obligations as protectors and patrons in pursuit of their commercial aspirations as proprietors.

Macinnes identifies three stages: the wholesale slaughter by Cumberland; the selective terror of the Duke of Albemarle, his successor; and the constructive starvation of Jacobite districts 'through the wilful destruction of crops, livestock and property with the stated intention to effect either clearance or death'. A fourth stage can also be identified: the recruitment of Highland regiments into the British army, who alone were allowed to wear the tartan banned at home: 'the avowed objective was to transport potential Jacobites to foreign battlefields where they could be slaughtered fighting the French, rather than leave them to plot subversion at home'. The military prowess of these Scots helped to secure the restoration of the remaining forfeited Jacobite estates in 1784, but it cost them (or rather, those they commanded) dearly. In the Seven Years' War of 1756–63 alone, the Scots' casualty rate in five major engagements was 32 per cent to the Anglo-American 9 per cent.[45]

It is, however, important to note that despite the strength of Jacobitism up to 1750, increasing numbers of Scots began to conform to the expectations of British society, to which they contributed in no small degree. The quintessentially English image of John Bull himself can perhaps be traced back to the Scot Dr John Arbuthnot's *The famous History of John Bull* from 1712, while James Thomson (1700–48) wrote the anthem 'Rule Britannia'. Arbuthnot had supported the Union, although his use of Britishness was rather instrumental and his confidence in the stability of a single Scottish interest over-optimistic in the light of the variety of opportunities the new British state could offer. However, his view that Scottish independence was unsustainable ('undeniable in law, as well as justifiable from history, yet, at present, it is in effect precarious, imaginary, and fantastical') was held by many Whigs, for although Jacobites might praise the Auld Alliance and hold out nostalgia for the regnal union with France of the 1550s, only a Catholic/Episcopal Scotland could begin to subscribe to such views. For the Protestants who dominated Forth–Clyde and south Scotland, they were anathema. However much they hated the Union (and some did hate it), in the long run they had no alternative to a Protestant Britain. That was the logic of 1560, finally come home to roost.[46]

Because of the lack of alternatives short of Jacobitism, many more adopted Arbuthnot's outlook as the century progressed. By 1745, Britishness was growing among the settled Whig commercial and professional elites of southern Scotland, and elsewhere also it was gaining strength. Many Scots might grumble about the Union in their cups and resent English presumption, but equally and paralysingly they saw their own country as increasingly provincial and inadequate: a childhood home from which the British Empire let them escape. This combination of love for Scotland as a home identity, combined with despising its 'provincialism' as a place of limited opportunity can be seen in the careers of many Scots, and is beautifully summed up in the Journals of James Boswell (1740–95). By 1745, the elite (and the above was mainly true only of that elite) were beginning to move their children's education away from Scotland to English schools. Lord George Murray, lieutenant general in Charles Edward's army in 1745, had attended Perth Grammar School, but his son went to Eton. Although the distinctiveness of Scottish education was preserved in part because the middle classes did not follow this gentry example, a unified British aristocracy was in the making, and at least in terms of the external show of fashion and consumer culture, features of unity in the middle classes were not far behind. Unlike Ireland, Scotland did not (vis-à-vis England) have a significantly disenfranchised elite after the fading of the Jacobites in the 1760s. It was to make an enormous difference to the future history of the two countries.

DID BRITAIN BENEFIT SCOTLAND?

Scotland was by no means badly underdeveloped as an urban society before the Union, being on a par with Ireland or Denmark. In 1700, Edinburgh had a population of around 54,000, including the surrounding area. It was the second largest city in mainland Britain. The 1696 Education Act had confirmed the Reformation aim of a school in every parish, and many of those parishes which did not endow a school had one founded for them by the Society in Scotland for Propagating Christian Knowledge, which 'opened 176 schools' in the fifty years after its foundation in 1709. 'Low cost' or 'free' education was already beginning to be a feature of Scottish society by the time of the Union.[47]

Agricultural and urban improvement certainly received more of the capital it required after the Union, for just as Scottish enterprise in the 1690s exceeded the capabilities of the Scottish state, so did ideas for improving Scottish society. Many areas remained untouched for a long time, enclosure and improvement only gradually affecting practices such as runrig. Originally intended to unite the community in defence of each other's property, by the eighteenth century this form of landholding was becoming increasingly redundant, as well as a drag on economic returns, already undermined by poor or non-existent roads and undrained land. Figures such as 'John Cockburn, William Cullen, Sir Archibald Grant of Monymusk and Alexander Murray . . . criticised overstocking, poor ploughing, insufficient manuring and run-rig farming with its interspersed strips of land'. 'Reafforestation, drainage and enclosures' all increased, although two 1695 Acts of the Scottish Parliament had already 'aided the process of consolidation of holdings and enclosure' before the Union. By 1750, the process of enclosure was 'well-advanced in the Lothians', and in this decade sheep-farming begins to appear in the Highlands. By the 1770s, cotton-spinning was developing at Penicuik and elsewhere.[48]

In the Highlands in particular, the 'prime tenants' of many estates were the so-called tacksmen, who held their tack of land from the chief and were often related to him by blood, in a system of landholding ultimately related to the gavelkind of joint inheritance, where land was partitioned between all sons equally, not simply granted to the eldest. Where the tack system was strongest, economic disruption of familial ties had severe social consequences. Many tacksmen were forced out in the 1760s and '70s, often 'taking . . . large numbers of their sub-tenants and other dependents' with them abroad, frequently to North America. The hybridity of Scottish society's dual kin and feudal landholding was more and more under attrition, and the end of heritable jurisdictions left the road open for Anglocentric patterns of landholding to triumph rapidly. Enclosure meant the loss 'without recompense' of 'age-old rights of free grazing on the moors and hillsides', and many were thus driven off the land by economic change, even before the beginning of mass forced clearance at the end of the century. Some emigrated; others began to populate 'the mills and slums of Glasgow and Dundee'. Population shift began in earnest. Although in 1750, over 50 per cent of Scotland's population still lived north of the Tay, a pattern was emerging where Lothian and Tweeddale, Glasgow, the south-west and the east coast up to the Mearns were growing rapidly, with other parts of the country hardly growing at all or in decline (up to 1 per cent a year in the southern uplands and some parts of Aberdeenshire).[49]

The verdict of many at the time, and of much conventional historiography since, was that many of these changes were the result of the beneficial effects of Union. The 'indefatigable improver' Sir Archibald Grant of Monymusk opined that 'all improvements of security, husbandry, manufactures, commerce, or police, are since 1707'. And, although the monies promised in the Union 'for the encouragement of fisheries and manufactures' were not 'put to the purpose for which they had been designed', the Equivalent was used to support bodies such as the Honourable Society of Improvers in the Knowledge of Agriculture (1723), the Board of Trustees for Fisheries and Manufactures (1727) and the Royal Bank of Scotland (1727). Colonial trade gradually began to flourish as Scots took advantage of the opportunities available in imperial markets. By 1722, the East India Company had a Scottish director; in 1769, Scotland reached a high point of 52 per cent of the UK tobacco trade. In the slave trade, Scots linen was used for slave clothing, although Scots such as the Quaker George Keith, who 'wrote . . . the first protest against slavery to be published in America' in 1693, were also beginning to oppose slavery.

Not only were the Scots trading, they were also working and settling. In 1750, around one-third of Indian appointments went to Scots, and by 1772 approximately 20 per cent of East India company employees were Scots, while in the latter part of the eighteenth century, half of the fourteen regiments for India were raised in Scotland, with over 30 per cent of officers in Bengal alone Scots in that year. In the 1690s, only about 5 per cent of the diplomatic service were Scots; by the reign of George III this proportion had virtually trebled. After 1760, the rewards offered by Hanoverian Britain were 'real enough to head off any serious discontent' in Scotland. Moreover, the more Scots who were appointed, the more advantage they could confer on their fellows, in what was still strongly a patronage and kin-based society. A Scottish mafia emerged, being identified by antipathetic London opinion as early as the 1760s, and more kindly satirised in John Galt's novel *The Member* (1832).[50]

Union was important in this process, but not for the ideas which underpinned it, which had often been developed in the seventeenth century. In the eighteenth, many of their most marked advocates were Jacobites, such as John Law (1671–1732) and Sir James Steuart. Brigadier Uílleam Dearg Mackintosh of Borlum (1662–1743) wished to establish a College of Agriculture in Scotland, and raise its study to the dignity of a science, while George Lockhart of Carnwath (1673–1732) was 'the first that attempted raising or feeding cattle to size'. Other improvers from this political tradition included the 3rd Earl of Cromartie. Jacobite entrepreneurs made major contributions to both the Scottish and overseas economies, and banking developed rapidly, with the Royal Bank of Scotland (1727) and the British Linen Bank (1750) being accompanied by 'nearly twenty important private banks in Edinburgh'.[51]

Scottish wages and living standards improved for the masses in the eighteenth century, albeit from a base rendered artificially low by many years of civil and religious conflict, which created conditions intensified by the economic depression of the 1690s. Skilled wages in Scotland had been similar to those in England in the seventeenth century, although unskilled labour was plentiful, and earned less; but by 1730, provincial English skilled wages were 50 per cent higher, a differential still evident fifty years later. Unskilled wages, however, 100 per cent higher in England in 1700 (except for the poorest northern counties), were back down to a differential of 55 per cent in the 1790s, though even this merely restored the situation which had existed at the beginning of the seventeenth century. It was only after the Industrial Revolution that Scottish wage rates improved to match or in some cases surpass English norms. Significantly for future discontents, the gap in prosperity between Scotland and Ireland widened in the former's favour as the eighteenth century wore on.[52]

The narrowing wage gap between skilled and unskilled workers was 'a telling indicator of relative economic growth'. The importance of 'show', with its emphasis on consumer goods and conspicuous consumption was fed by the developing press, heavy with advertisements (up to 50 per cent in some publications) which was contributing hugely to the evolution of more unified middle- and upper-class tastes and habits, where the signifiers of wealth and status were universally recognisable throughout the British realms. The influence of print also helped communication, and Scotland's 'semi-independent' position, with its own institutions and society, helped to create networking and lobbying on a scale both recognised and resented in England. The Convention of Royal Burghs made an important contribution to a unified economic policy, and this was especially evident in the case of urban improvement. In 1775, the Forth–Clyde canal was 'approved by Parliament', and by this time a major expansion of the capital to turn it into a suitable metropolis for North Britain was under way.[53]

Communication improved and towns developed. In 1720, there were still 'many wooden, mud, and thatched houses' within the gates of Edinburgh, Glasgow and Aberdeen. Although coaches first appeared in Inverness in 1725, even in 1740 it took Lord Lovat as much as 40 days to travel from Inverness to London. Scottish fortified houses were modernised, although some individuals, such as Lord Glenorchy, regretted that decision during the 'Forty-Five.[54]

Plans to expand Edinburgh were first put forward in the 1680s, 'with the encouragement of James VII' who had done much to support arts, science and culture in his stay there as Duke of Albany during the Exclusion Crisis. The Jacobite Earl of Mar too, had 'utopian architectural schemes', some of which he thought of realising through his patronage of James Gibbs (1682–1754), an Aberdeen-born architect and secret Catholic. In 1728, Mar proposed an early version of what was to become the Edinburgh New Town. If no longer a political capital in the fullest sense, Edinburgh was nonetheless the centre of the church, law and financial system in Scotland, and 'the leaders of the council almost always looked for a patron to represent the city's interests among the great at the centre of power', a kind of ambassadorial envoy on behalf of a government which no longer existed. The Duke of Argyll and Henry Dundas, later Viscount Melville, both played this role. Glasgow also prospered as an urban centre throughout the eighteenth century, developing the first Chamber of Commerce in Britain in 1783 'to press the commercial interests of the Glasgow district'.[55]

Intellectual life in urban Scotland foreshadowed the later development of the Scottish Enlightenment. The poet and bookseller Allan Ramsay (1684–1758) aimed to unite Scottish vernacular literature with the forms of high metropolitan culture in order to preserve a distinctly Scottish national literature, a project he reinforced by editing medieval texts and collecting songs. Ramsay founded the first circulating library in Britain in Edinburgh in 1728, and they spread rapidly. That of Angus & Son in the Castlegate in Aberdeen had 1,150 titles by 1765 and more than double that by the end of the 1770s. Scottish antiquarianism, and a celebration of the past was especially popular among Jacobites, and it was also revived in a new hybrid, literary Jacobite form, which promoted the Scottish vernacular in order to preserve and articulate Scottish difference. Even those who did not write using Scots, such as Tobias Smollett (1721–71) and (largely) Susan Ferrier (1782–1854), expressed the ideas and manners of a national tradition and national peculiarities in a manner which preserved the status of Scots as a national literature.

The ideas of the Enlightenment thus had strong native roots, and this was true not only in the arts but also in the sciences and the law. John Napier of Merchiston's (1550–1617) invention of logarithms was only the most famous innovation in a network of scientific participation which crossed Europe. Robert Sibbald (1641–1723) and Andrew Balfour (1630–94) co-founded what was to become the Royal Botanic Gardens in Edinburgh in 1670, while James Gregory (1638–75) provided a 'mathematical account of the reflecting telescope' and James Dalrymple, 1st Viscount Stair (1619–95), codified the 'philosophical base' of Scots Law in his still influential *Institutions of the Law of Scotland* (1681); while George Dalgarno (1626–87) pursued the project of a universal language; and in 1725–6, plans were laid for a new medical school at Edinburgh University. Nor were the social ideas of Enlightenment the children of the later eighteenth century alone. In 1642, Lady Rothiemay's mortification provided for a girls' school in Aberdeen and in 1796, Anderson's University in Glasgow (today the University of Strathclyde) made provision for both men and women to attend classes. Even before the 'Enlightenment' as such began, education for women was more widespread in Scotland and divorce procedures were more accessible.

Moreover, the democratic values of the Presbyterian Kirk arguably gave rise to the dimension of social Christianity in the Enlightenment, as well as the widespread opposition to slavery among Enlightenment thinkers. The mercantilism of Enlightenment Scotland was closely bound in with its educational values: almost a quarter of Glasgow's tobacco merchants had been students at the city's university. Above all, the importance of socialising through clubs and societies which lay at the heart of the Enlightenment was well established in Scotland by the age of Culloden. The Easy Club of Edinburgh (1709), the Aberdeen Musical Society (1748), Gordon's Mill Farming Club (1758) and even Thomas Reid's own Philosophical Club (1736) all foreshadowed the intensely social world of later Enlightenment discourse on every level.[56]

Did the Union benefit Scotland? In 1707, the arguments made for it were not good, and were often espoused reluctantly. The English government indubitably saw it as a takeover; pro-Union opinion in Scotland overestimated the continuing existence of the Scotland they knew and a national interest to be expressed by its representatives. As yet there were few integrationists, who wanted to see Scotland disappear completely as a separate entity, and the Union settlement reflected this. Scottish civil society remained intact, and the British government was content to run it by patronage (which indeed reinforced Scottish society's established networks) during the eighteenth century, much as Charles II had in the late seventeenth.

The Union had an ambivalent status. For most Scottish Unionists, it was and remained a founding constitutional document; in England, it was seen as subject to Parliamentary sovereignty in a country without a written constitution. For Scots, it was almost a sacred text; for the English, a convenient compromise to attach their northern neighbour to them and their interests on a permanent basis. It was abrogated several times before 1750, arguably more than it has been since, and although compromise with Scottish interests was possible, it rarely prevailed in critical matters. By mid-century, Scotland had lost its Privy Council, Customs Board, Secretary of State and heritable jurisdictions; it had had English treason law imposed on it more than once, had breaches in the law of Scotland tried in English courts, and had been refused parity of esteem in the right to raise its own militia. It was a country in suspicion, and in part under occupation. Ten years after Culloden, there were no fewer than 60 British army patrols and outposts in Scotland.[57]

Scotland advanced materially and intellectually in the eighteenth century, of that there can be no doubt. A greater degree of peace and broadening overseas opportunities helped many of the developing intellectual, cultural and commercial excellences of Scottish society to reach their potential, and magnificent thinkers developed the process still further. Would there have been peace without Union? Possibly, for the Jacobites would have been much weaker without the national issue, and would probably have been unable to mount the grandstand Risings of 1715 and 1745. What there would not have been were the wider markets and the capital means to exploit them. Scotland could have had these with a more limited free trade commercial union or confederation in the seventeenth-century style: and perhaps this would have been preferable for the political and cultural identity and well-being of the country. But it was unrealistic to expect England to agree to such advantages without exacting a price, and that price was control. The greatest advantages of the Union were economic ones – on that the 'bought and sold for English gold' Jacobite school and their Whig opponents could agree. In the century and a half after 1760, the Union would help a British Scotland to become one of the richest and most advanced countries in the world, while the British Empire would present many channels through which Scottish ideas could have a hitherto unimaginable international influence.

SIX

ENLIGHTENMENT AND VICTORIAN SCOTLAND

The Scottish Enlightenment was both a distinctly national phenomenon and a part of a Europe-wide intellectual movement, being particularly influenced by the thought of the French *savants* of the eighteenth century, in a kind of intellectual afterlife of the Auld Alliance. Indeed, while many of the eighteenth-century Enlightenment figures in Scotland opposed the French-sponsored Jacobite attempts to end the Union and restore the Stuarts, they at the same time proved receptive to the intellectual life of the country which was now their political enemy. The term 'Scottish Enlightenment' is customarily confined to the eighteenth century, but in this chapter I will argue that to do this is to misunderstand the scope of the Enlightenment project and its influence (particularly on technology and material development) which only became fully visible in the Victorian period.

The definition of the Scottish Enlightenment which best encapsulates both its distinctive and international qualities is that it consisted in the application of reason to knowledge in a context of material improvement. The use of reason to assess the corpus of what was known, asserting rationality's primacy over both authority and superstition, was a key element in the Enlightenment internationally. The identification of the importance of reason naturally involved speculation on the true essence of human nature. It also involved theorising knowledge in a systematic way, an extension of the principles of Newtonian physics into the realm of the humanities. In making the arts scientific, the Enlightenment gave birth to the social sciences; in systematising and codifying knowledge, it created modern historiography and the idea of the encyclopaedia, found in the French *Encyclopedie* (1751–76) and the Scottish *Encyclopaedia Britannica* (1768–71).

Although such intellectual developments were in any case friendly to further advances in science and technology, Scotland's focus on material improvement was particularly pronounced, and forms the basis for an evaluation of the Scottish Enlightenment in particularist terms, as specifically 'Scottish'. There were many reasons for this focus. Scotland was poorer than any other country which made a major contribution to the European Enlightenment, and its relative poverty was all the more obvious now that it was joined to England by Union. Thinkers in Scotland became interested in the question of the development of societies, and the forms and speed through and with which they evolved, because they wanted to catch up with England. Scotland's historic spirit of martial valour became gradually downgraded domestically (its role overseas in the emerging British Empire remained more highly valued). It was argued that it was peace and not war which brought riches and 'civility', the refinement of manners which was perceived as the (desirable) English norm, and which endemic conflict had held back in Scotland. Medieval and early modern Scotland was not a society in endemic conflict, of course, at least not until 1638, but the contrast between this immediately pre- and the post-Union era helped to underpin a profoundly influential historiography which argued that Scotland had been rescued from infighting and division by the Union. Meanwhile events such as the Wars of the Roses or the English Civil War could be set aside as atypical within the context of the general march to civility of an idealised southern polity.[1]

Adam Smith (1723–90) and William Robertson (1721–93) argued that human societies go through certain stages in their development, and that that development is towards a higher stage of society. Their teleological history helped to illustrate this concept, which also underlies the history of David Hume (1711–76), albeit to a lesser extent. Dugald Stewart (1753–1828) expanded the notion in his idea (borrowing from both Montesquieu (1689–1755) and Robertson) of 'conjectural history', whereby ancient practices in a more advanced society (such as England) can be viewed in the same terms as modern ones in a primitive society. This view informed early anthropology. For example, the Scottish anthropologist Sir James Frazer (1854–1941) thought that we could align ritual practices in ancient Rome (of which we may know little) with documented practices among African tribes, for at an early stage in their development all societies have fundamentally similar features, and visible differences derive from the differential pace of progress in different places. In *The Golden Bough* (1890–1915), Frazer saw human history as developing from magic through religion to science at different speeds in different nations. The greatness of Frazer's ideas partly inheres in the fact that, unlike some earlier Enlightenment figures, he left open the possibility that rational scientific thought itself was only a stage in, and not the ultimate goal of, human thought.

The classic period of the Enlightenment in the mid-eighteenth century was not without its sceptical voices in the question of historical progress. Adam Ferguson (1723–1816), arguably the founder of modern sociology, was more sceptical of progress than others, as was the historian Gilbert Stuart (1743–86), but many thinkers in large part accepted the notion of the staged development of society. In the eighteenth century, it was regarded by many among its intellectual elite as being Scotland's task to catch up. Where material progress was less at stake, this was arguably less of an issue. Scepticism was more usually found in the realm of philosophy than in that of history, as in Hume's *Treatise of Human Nature* (1739). Hume's scepticism was itself combated by Thomas Reid (1710–96), who developed some of the ideas of Scottish medieval philosophy, arguing in *An Inquiry into the Human Mind on the Principles of Common Sense* (1764) the 'Common Sense' position. This was to be very influential on both philosophical education in nineteenth-century France and 'the shapers of the American republic', in particular John Witherspoon (1723–94), who was in part responsible for the American Declaration of Independence. As early as 1740, the Ulster Scot Francis Hutcheson (1694–1746) had addressed himself to the question of American independence. Among the American republicans, John Adams and James Wilson read Hutcheson's *System of Moral Philosophy*, which probably also influenced Thomas Jefferson, while 'Hutcheson and Reid were certainly on the curriculum at Princeton', where Witherspoon was president. By 1790, there were some 260,000 people of Scots descent in the United States, of whom 'at least 150,000' had settled from Scotland before the Declaration of Independence.[2]

The emphasis on history as a process acting uniformly over time in stages or periods can also be found in the science of the Enlightenment. James Hutton (1726–97) in his *Theory of the Earth* (1785) developed some of the founding ideas of modern geology by arguing that the formation of the rocks was the result of a process acting uniformly over time. Charles Lyell (1767–1849) argued in *Principles of Geology* (1830) that the earth was several hundred million years old. By 1850, the idea of the periodisation of geological strata had begun to be developed. In the division of geological time into periods we can still see the faint echoes of stadial history, and it has taken the efforts of neo-Darwinists in the last years of the twentieth century to challenge in the popular mind the idea that evolution is some kind of ascent towards a teleological goal, just as figures such as Robertson and Smith argued human history was.

The theorisation of history as ascent, the teleology of civility, underlies the school of academic and popular history which is called Whig, and which was further developed by Thomas Babington Macaulay (1800–59) and others in nineteenth-century England. Although this Whig history was mocked as long ago as the 1930s in the classic *1066 and All That* and the more sophisticated though less funny Sir Herbert Butterfield's attack in *The Whig Interpretation of History* (1931), it continues to exercise a grip on popular historical portrayal, which presents Cromwell or the American Revolution (in its way, a quintessentially Enlightenment project) as progressive, in an argument which is supported by the premise that history has a general tendency to improve, and implies that material wealth is a sign of this improvement. This is a classic Scottish Enlightenment position. From the eighteenth century on it has made writing Scottish history, especially in a British context, very difficult, for all Scottish history in a British Whig context must deal with the political extinction of Scotland, which is assumed to be progressive. Today, it hinders Western understanding of the importance to human thought and society of religion in general and Islam in particular. The power of the Enlightenment model still routinely identifies Islamic society as 'medieval', because our model of modernity is civil, secular and pluralist. As in eighteenth-century imperialism, military action by the civil and enlightened against the backward and barbarous is permitted and even encouraged by the model. In Hume's *History of England* (1754–61) Scottish attacks on England throughout history are castigated, but English ones excused; the civilised have inbuilt rights over the barbarous in the teleology of civility. No level playing field is required, hence in the Seven Years' War Scots Highlanders suffered many times more casualties than English or American troops, for it was, as General Wolfe observed, small matter if they fell.

By the third quarter of the eighteenth century, the realities of economic growth and social change began to mirror the underlying values of the Enlightenment project. There was a greater willingness among many Scots to accept Union and make the best of it. After a still suspicious London government excluded Scotland from the provisions of the 1757 Militia Act, due to the fear that militia might be used for Jacobite purposes, Scottish protests tended to alienise the Jacobite phenomenon as purely 'Highland', arguing that a Scottish militia could have protected Edinburgh in 1745.

Many Scots with Jacobite connections or who knew the reality of Lowland Jacobitism, distanced themselves from it, instead looking 'forward to a degree of integration with and participation in the British state well beyond that taken for granted by their elderly leaders'. Although there was a good deal of resentment at the new generation of Scots on the make in 1760s London, they continued to be able to make full use of the opportunities open to them, at the same time as many erstwhile Jacobite clansmen were being killed in the battle for Canada in the Seven Years' War (1756–63). As the rewards for it became more visible, the Union began to bed down, although Scotland remained largely run by domestic elites who identified with their own nationality. Henry Dundas (1742–1811), who ran Scottish politics in the British interest and his own for a generation, 'was, and would avow himself, a Scot' and occasionally 'broke out into an invective against the English'. Even among their leaders, Scots remained ready to resent any slight.

Material improvement nonetheless of course delivers tangible benefits. The architecture of William (1689–1748) and Robert Adam (1728–92) developed the magnificence of the country houses of the Scottish gentry and nobility, and it was proposed in the New Town of Edinburgh to set up an equivalent space of elegant privacy for their town houses, although the New Town turned out in the end to be largely occupied by the professional classes. The tight, intimate living quarters of the huge lands (tenements) in the Old Town, where rich and poor lived cheek by jowl, gave way after the 1770s to what has been called 'the heavenly city of the Enlightenment philosophers', the geometrically planned (it was originally intended to contain a Union Flag design) and executed New Town, the largest single concentration of Georgian buildings anywhere in the British Isles. Edinburgh had already been dubbed 'the Athens of Great Britain' by Thomas Sheridan in 1761, before the New Town was built. Its building was to give North Britain a worthy metropolis to rival London. An ironic by-product of its creation was that it undermined the conditions of social intimacy in which some of the greatest thought of the Enlightenment was engendered.

If Edinburgh's classicism was recognisably domestic, owing more than a little to Bath, the role of Glasgow as imperial city in the nineteenth century was reflected in the oriental influences in the work of major architects such as William 'Greek' Thomson (1817–75) and Charles Rennie Mackintosh (1868–1928), both of whom developed new styles of living space for public buildings and upper middle-class clients, while in Edinburgh visionaries such as Sir Patrick Geddes (1854–1932) helped to create modern ideas concerning the use of urban space. Cultural space devoted to museums and libraries increased: King's College, Aberdeen founded a museum of natural history in 1754. Throughout Scotland from the 1820s, the growth of 'Scots baronial' in the architecture of both public and domestic buildings simultaneously displayed a celebration of the past and confidence in the present and future.[3]

Despite the greater privacy and distance from one's neighbours created by the New Town, Scotland's cities in the eighteenth century in general helped to grow and maintain the conditions in which clubs and societies, major bodies for the circulation of Enlightenment ideas, could flourish (see pp. 222–3). The Select Society of Edinburgh (1754) and other societies, dealt both with intellectual matters and suitable means of deploying them for material improvement. Not all these societies of civility abandoned native models, by any means, and in music there was a considerable struggle between the traditional song and classical influences: despite the presence of Scottish songs on concert programmes in Aberdeen (also reflected in Edinburgh and Glasgow), a protest was made 'by the members of the Aberdeen Musical Society that their national music was not being given an appropriate or timely position'. Eventually, the native tradition was itself adopted by and was influential on classical composers.

Together with innovation went a sense of the value of history, more prominent in some disciplines than others. The Society of Antiquaries (1780) was founded to celebrate Scotland's past, but it and the historical clubs which followed it in the wake of Scott's Waverley Novels, could prioritise the antiquarian anecdote over systematic history, and thus seldom posed a threat to the teleological account, although the Earl of Buchan, who founded the Society, was more politicised than most, and argued 'for an independent Scottish republic'. Although figures such as Alexander Law in 1826 and William Burns in 1874 opposed the fate of Scottish history in Whig teleology, it was an Englishman, J.A. Froude, who argued in 1876 that 'Scottish history should be an integral, if not a central, part of the new curriculum' in the universities. Needless to say it was not, and Scottish education long remained one of the main obstacles to a serious understanding of Scottish history among the country's population. Hume and Robertson's best-selling histories had a profound legacy.[4]

Religion was also affected by the dominance of the teleology of civility in the Enlightenment. The development of a 'Moderate' party within the Kirk of Scotland led to a diminution of the more severe forms of Presbyterianism, at least in the life of the capital, and the first ideas of what came to be known as social theology developed – the idea that the Kirk's role was to do good here and now with a positive social commitment, as much as it was to manifest and recommend the road to personal salvation. To some extent this concern for community had been part of the Kirk's character since the Reformation, and the Protestantism of the Moderates should not (as David Allan argues) be underestimated; but this position developed further in the eighteenth and nineteenth centuries as part of the climate of social improvement that was intimately linked to the Enlightenment. Moderatism became the established option, and between 1752 and 1805 39 of the 54 Moderators of the General Assembly could be classed as Moderates. Theirs was part of a wider pattern of social concern, for noteworthy also was the widespread opposition to slavery among Enlightenment thinkers such as Francis Hutcheson, Adam Smith, James Beattie (1735–1803), John Millar (1735–1801) and James Ramsay (1733–1789), supported by judgements from both the Court of Session and William Murray, Lord Mansfield (1705–93) the Scottish Lord Chief Justice of England. In 1784, Ramsay's *Essay on the Treatment and Conversion of African Slaves in the British Sugar Colonies* devoted 'a long chapter . . . to showing that the black race is equal to the white in ability'. Even in the colonies, there are signs that such attitudes prevailed; as Michael Fry points out, 'the widest survey of records left by Scots in the West Indies concludes that on the whole they disapproved of slavery'.[5]

Education prospered in Scotland. Although several schools (such as Fettes (1865–70), Merchiston Castle (1833), Loretto and Trinity College, Glenalmond (1847)) were set up to provide 'public schools' on the English model, the Scottish professional classes continued in large numbers to support the burgh grammar schools and their local universities. Some of these universities also attracted students internationally, even in an era of difficult travel and poor communication. In the early nineteenth century, some 70 per cent of Edinburgh's medical students were non-Scots, with 18 per cent being from the Continent or the colonies.

Within Scotland, theories of education were developing. David Fordyce (1711–51) was arguably the first to advocate student-centred learning; his *Dialogues Concerning Education* were influential on English dissenting academies. Curricular innovation continued: from the early eighteenth century schools in Scotland south of Aberdeen taught French as a foreign language, while the development of the discipline now known as English took shape in Scotland's universities, notably St Andrews and Edinburgh, where Hugh Blair, Regius Professor of Rhetoric and Belles Lettres from 1762, was arguably the first chair in the subject anywhere in the world. If education is to be judged by its provision at the lowest and highest levels, Scots were right to be proud of their educational standards. In 1872, Scotland shared with Germany, Netherlands, Switzerland and Scandinavia the lowest rates of adult illiteracy in Europe, while there were six times as many university students per capita in Scotland as in England. Women attended Anderson's University as early as 1796, and by the 1870s, they were students at the ancient universities. Social opportunity also extended into the working class; although there were few members of the professions from poor backgrounds, there was still an appreciable number who had benefited from the parochial school and local university system. In 1860, 19 per cent of students at Glasgow University had working-class backgrounds, 16 per cent in Scotland as a whole. The discipline of education as a professional subject also began to be developed. In 1836, David Stow (1793–1864) founded the first teacher training college in Scotland, while in 1847 the Educational Institute of Scotland was founded as a professional body for teachers.[6]

The Kirk supported many of these developments in their early stages. Professor Thomas Chalmers (1780–1847), minister and academic, developed the social Christianity of the Enlightenment Moderates in a manner which, while strongly stressing self-help, also stressed that 'the provision of parochial education would close the divisions of urban society through a mutual early experience in the republic of letters'. This policy, linked with others intended 'at most . . . to soften the painful processes of change' in Industrial Revolution Scotland, was tried in the parish of St John's in Glasgow from 1819. But the link between the Kirk and education weakened in the nineteenth century, despite fresh foundations in the early years of the Free Kirk following the Disruption of 1843. Chalmers was prominent in the Disruption, which divided the Free Kirk from the Kirk of Scotland, principally on the long-festering issue of lay patronage, which had led to the first post-Union fissures in the established Kirk after 1712, when Robert Harley's Tory administration introduced the Patronage Act. Splits had occurred over patronage in 1733 and 1761, and over the burgess oath, with its perceived implicit endorsement of the established Kirk, in 1745–7. The Disruption, in which a large minority of the Kirk eventually joined the seceding churches, further weakened the grip of the clerisy on a rapidly industrialising and urbanising society, and profoundly affected the structure of both education and the Poor Law. In 1845, poor relief was transferred from the Kirk to parochial boards, while in 1872 'elected school boards' under the London-based Scottish Education Department further secularised the education system, although it was not until 1905 that 'the Presbyterian churches finally relinquished their hold over the teachers' training colleges to the SED [Scottish Education Department]'.

Forty per cent of the Kirk's membership and 470 of its 1,200 ministers seceded in 1843, and the Free Kirk grew in strength in the Highlands in particular, where the established order was tainted by its sympathy with the landlord interest during the age of the Clearances, and in the colonies, where 'almost all missionaries' joined the Free Kirk. The Relief Kirk of 1761 and the Secessionist Burgher and anti-Burgher kirk parties united as the United Presbyterians in 1847, and UP membership gradually dissolved into the Free Kirk in 1852, 1876, 1893 and finally in 1900, with the successor United Free Kirk of this date absorbing all the Free Kirk save for the 'wee Free' Highland parishes which remained loyal to the 1843 Disruption Kirk. The Free Presbyterians seceded towards the end of the nineteenth century, while the Cameronian Reformed Presbyterians (most of whom joined the Free Kirk in 1876) and some of the continuing 1733/47 Secession kirk parties survived into the twentieth. The nineteenth century thus saw the minor secessions which had plagued the Kirk for 200 years turn into a world of shifting alliances and major rifts, where large and expensive rival churches for three Presbyterian denominations, perhaps indistinguishable to the uninterested English visitor, might be found in the same town – a costly means of diverting attention back to the minutiae of theology and ecclesiology from the challenges of Victorian society. This weakening in Presbyterianism was matched by a rehabilitation of Scotland's suppressed Christian confessions. Although Methodism made few inroads in Scotland, Baptists and Congregationalists (whose policy of congregational choice of minister was decisively anti-patronage) grew in numbers from the 1790s. The Episcopalians, who had had the last post-Jacobite penalties against them lifted in the early nineteenth century, built many new churches and in 1867 joined the Anglican Communion, while the Catholic Church restored its Hierarchy of territorial bishoprics in 1878, twenty-eight years later than in England.[7]

The Enlightenment's legacy was, however, to be as much technological as spiritual and intellectual. One of the errors in confining the term 'Scottish Enlightenment' to the eighteenth century is that the nineteenth saw massive scientific and technological developments which were in part the fruits of earlier concerns with material improvement. In 1764, Professor Joseph Black (1728–99) described the phenomenon of specific and latent heat at Glasgow University. The limitations in the working models designed to show this were the subject of a conversation between Professor John Anderson (1726–96), who at his death endowed Anderson's University, arguably 'the world's first institute of technology', and James Watt (1736–1819), instrument-maker to the University of Glasgow, on Glasgow

Green. Watt moved towards the development of a practical steam engine, and 'the application of steam power to mill spinning machinery, in the form of his invention of rotative motion, was crucial to the emergence of Glasgow as Scotland's leading industrial city'. The Glasgow industrialist James Beaumont Neilson (1792–1865) 'revolutionized iron manufacture', while Henry Bell's (1767–1830) *Comet*, built at Port Glasgow, 'was the second successful commercial steamship in the world' and the 'first . . . to be propelled by steam on a navigable river in Europe'. The situation had radically changed from that in 1770 when Scottish capitalism was still mercantilist, and the Carron iron works, established by an Englishman, was 'dependent . . . on war orders'. By 1830, heavy industry was beginning to dominate in Scotland; and Scotland was completely dominated by the Central Belt, and within that by the West, where by 1901 more than 40 per cent of the country's population lived.

These developments were important, not only in wealth creation, but in the reinforcement they provided to a local elite largely protected from professional competition from south of the border by the provisions attendant on Union, both those which protected Scottish institutions, and those which promoted domestic networking (e.g. a separate national educational system) where these were not the same. The Union had preserved a national professional class in Scotland: its lawyers, ministers, doctors and professors. As a consequence, the concentration of professional men might (especially in Edinburgh) vastly exceed both in number and proportion the provincial English upper middle class. In the 1770s and '80s, Edinburgh had a professional class of 734 in a population of 70,000 (81,000 in 1801); Manchester 228 from about 60,000 (95,000 in 1801); Birmingham, 197 (1801 population 71,000), Newcastle 67 from about 30,000 (42,000 in 1801) and Sheffield 70 (46,000 in 1801). Scotland's capital was an intellectual centre not by virtue of its great thinkers only, but also by virtue of its concentration of educated intellectuals, unique outside London. By 1841, 13 per cent of adult men in Edinburgh could be described as 'professional'; proportions in Glasgow, Dundee and Aberdeen ranged from 4½ to 6½ per cent, possibly still higher than in English provincial centres, judging by their proportionate inferiority to Edinburgh sixty years earlier. In addition, the Scottish professions began to export talent in significant numbers: between 1750 and 1800 Scotland's universities produced 90 per cent of British medical graduates. With Oxford and Cambridge only open to Anglicans until 1870, many colonials attended Scottish universities, and the university system was exported from Scotland rather than England to the British Empire, in particular North America, where 'there is not the slightest doubt that the Scottish imprint upon American collegiate training is the only imprint worth talking about'. Scottish societies set up overseas tended by their nature to be dominated by exported professionals, which further reinforced this effect.[8]

The confluence of a strong local elite, fresh monies coming in from Scotland's role in the empire and advanced banking and economic theory all helped to make Scotland a major contributor to both the practical and theoretical aspects of economics and finance. Scotland had long been a country where many currencies circulated, often with uncertain exchange rates; it was thus a society where many were familiar with the concept of arbitrage and were more flexible in their approach to issues such as convertibility, exchange and the dematerialisation of money into value implied by the complex exchange rate rulings issued by the burghs since medieval times. John Law (1671–1732), whose *Money and Trade Considered* was published in 1705, made the first attempt to introduce a paper money system in France in 1720, while Sir James Steuart (1713–80) in his *An Inquiry into the Principles of Political Oeconomy* (1767) and still more Adam Smith in *The Wealth of Nations* (1776) made major contributions to the development of modern economics, perhaps adapting the idea of the circulation of money from the mechanistic and physiological explanations of the world of human experience found in Harvey and Newton, which were so influential on the Scottish Enlightenment as a whole. At the same time, philosophers such as Francis Hutcheson and John Stuart Mill (1806–73) developed in utilitarianism a new philosophy for the public governance of the crystallising middle class, whose values were propagated by Samuel Smiles (1812–1904) and other writers.[9]

Both Anderson's endowment of his university in 1796 and the charter of the Royal Society of Edinburgh (founded in 1783) stressed the importance of 'useful learning'. This application of scientific discovery to technological advance became a key part of nineteenth-century Scottish intellectual life, among whose leading figures were Professor James Clerk Maxwell (1831–79), the Scots-Irish Professor Sir William Thomson, Lord Kelvin (1824–1907), Professor Sir William Ramsay (1852–1916), Professor Sir James Young Simpson (1811–70) who developed the use of modern medical anaesthetics and Professor James 'Paraffin' Young (1811–83), who received the chair of Technical Chemistry at John

Anderson's College for his work in extracting oil from shale, which led to 2 million tonnes of shale being dug annually. In 1840, the first chair of engineering in the world was founded at Glasgow University, where Lord Kelvin was making £5,000 per annum from his scientific patents, and where Professor Archibald Barr's (1855–1931) rangefinder enabled Japan to 'totally . . . destroy the Russian fleet' in 1904. The Englishman Joseph Lister (1827–1912) developed antiseptic surgery in Glasgow Royal Infirmary in the 1860s; thirty years later, William Macewen (1848–1924) put 'the world's doctors in white coats', while in 1896 at the Royal Infirmary, John Macintyre achieved the 'first X-ray cinematograph'. In 1876, Alexander Graham Bell (1847–1922) developed the first telephone, while in 1929, John Logie Baird (1888–1946) invented the first 'practicable' television.[10]

Scottish financial institutions and entrepreneurs developed many businesses and investments in the Empire and the US, such as P & O, the Scottish American Investment Company, the first investment trust, founded in Edinburgh in 1873 and the Dundee-based Alliance investment trusts. Scotland was already a leader in the Industrial Revolution, producing nearly 30 per cent of UK pig-iron by 1835. Between 1840 and 1865, the Govan shipyard engineered the entire Cunard fleet, and the famous tea trade clipper *Cutty Sark* was built at Dumbarton in 1870. The deepening of the Clyde meant that by the 1830s shipping from Scotland to London was as cheap as moving materials there from the Home Counties. From 1856, the advent of the limited liability company encouraged enterprise further, while infrastructure, including rail bridges over the Tay (the first of which collapsed tragically in 1879) and the Forth (1890) were built. By the late 1880s,

Scotland's tax revenues yielded a slight national surplus, and by 1900 Scotland had one of the highest average wages in the UK. On the threshold of the First World War, Scotland had world leadership in certain areas of industrial production, such as shipping, sugar and processing machinery (80 per cent of global output). In 1901, the second International Exhibition was held in Glasgow, attended by '11½ million, including the Tsar of Russia'. In 1913, Greater Glasgow produced half of UK marine horsepower and one-third of its railway engines, together with one-fifth of world shipping tonnage. 'No less than 80 per cent of the global thread-making capacity' was controlled from Paisley.[11]

Despite industrial success, progress in social conditions was slow. Health was bad, and many died young. In one Kincardineshire parish in 1792–3, smallpox accounted for 13 per cent of deaths, consumption 7 per cent and injuries 7–8 per cent. Life was hard and dangerous, and the major diseases claimed many victims. However, crop rotation and the gradual introduction of machinery as the nineteenth century progressed, brought positive changes to many in Scotland's farming counties. In the cities, it was otherwise: urban mortality was 57 per cent above its rural counterpart in the 1860s, while infant mortality in the (now highly urbanised) country as a whole was 20 per cent or more above English levels. In 1832, a cholera epidemic claimed the lives of thousands, and there were three further epidemics before 1870. Public health action was taken, including the 'triumph of civic endeavour' required in supplying Glasgow from Loch Katrine, 80 km distant, in a scheme opened by Queen Victoria in 1859. The 1860s saw the first round of slum clearance, yet as late as 1911 'nearly 50 per cent of the Scottish population lived in one or two roomed dwellings compared with just over 7 per cent in England'. By this time, however, improvements in public space, culture and infrastructure had all helped reduce the urban mortality rate, which now stood only 17 per cent higher than the rural one.[12]

SCOTTISH WRITING AND THE ARTS

The preservation of a distinctive national literature in post-Union Scotland can to some extent be attributed to the so-called Vernacular Revival, in which the poet Allan Ramsay (1684–1758) united the forms of English literary high culture (elegy, pastoral and so on) with the vigour of the popular and folk traditions of the Scots vernacular, helping to create a democratic literature of communitarian identity with a strong streak of Jacobitism and a special place for the Scottish song tradition. Ramsay's example was followed by Robert Fergusson (1750–74), who in 'The Gowdspink' (1773) wrote arguably the first Romantic ode, and was surpassed by Robert Burns (1759–96), who created a powerful fusion between the folk and traditional culture of Scotland and the highest literary subject-matter, often disguised by humour or bathos. In 'To a Mouse' for example, Burns criticises the Enlightenment idea of progress in favour of the common (and often miserable) experience of all creatures. The mouse is his 'fellow-mortal', part of a compact of sensibility and sympathy which itself depends on the ideas of Adam Smith's *Theory of Moral Sentiments* (1759) and the more general Enlightenment view that moral benevolence underpins the 'social union' of mankind. Burns was, however, conscious that this 'social union' was not being promoted by the adoption of 'progress', with its concomitant enclosure, emigration and pressure on the lower class of farmer, to which he belonged. Progress, as Burns repeatedly pointed out, benefited the great, not the benevolent. His stanza in 'To a Mouse', the Scots form termed 'Standard Habbie', was originally and frequently used for elegy, hence there is an additional comment by the form on the spirit of the content.[13]

What Ramsay and Burns did for the tradition in the Scots language and Scottish English, James Macpherson (1736/8–96) did for the Gaelic tradition, translating and adapting Gaelic heroic poetry and its subject matter into English in his Ossianic poems of 1759–63, chiefly *Fingal* (1761). Just as the Vernacular Revival helped to preserve a national literature by re-engaging with tradition rather than arguing for mental, moral and material improvement, so Macpherson's presentation of Scotland's Gaelic past in heroic quasi-Jacobite form revalued the 'primitive' in positive terms, giving Scotland a national epic, albeit one edited for eighteenth-century tastes. Ossian was a powerful influence throughout Europe on figures as diverse as Napoleon and Goethe. It helped to create Scotland as a Romantic nation, a land of bards, mountain, flood and heroes. The Highland Society of Scotland was formed in 1784, that of London in 1788, and Highland Games developed as a showpiece of the 'pre-industrial vigour and strength' of these domestic primitives, whose Gaelic voice was permitted only in the transmuted form of the Anglophone culture of Sensibility and Romanticism. The role of the Highlands became more prominent when 'the Napoleonic Wars . . . made Scotland virtually the only (even partly) foreign place to which English tourists could safely travel . . . aside from Gaelic Ireland'.[14]

Critical as he was of the authenticity of Macpherson's poems, this vision was systematised and completed in the work of Sir Walter Scott (1771–1832), who created an image of Scotland's past as a romance to enchant the onlooker, while conforming the plots of his novels to Enlightenment historiography, which sternly suppressed a romantic violent past in its welcome of a civil and united British future. In books such as *Waverley* (1814), *Old Mortality* (1816), *Rob Roy* (1817), *The Bride of Lammermoor* (1819), *The Fair Maid of Perth* (1828) and many others, Scott creates a towering historical fiction which both gives full rein to the romantic appeal of the Scottish past while also successfully stigmatising it as barbaric, violent and inevitably superseded. The Scottish past had a role in Scott's writing, however; it guaranteed the nation the separate identity of a *Kulturvolk* within Britain, while foreclosing any threat from that identity to the state. Its place as 'a source of visual and literary stimulus' rather than a tool of political and cultural analysis was well established, and by the time of Waterloo the concern over the political implications of Scottish history that had greeted the foundation of the Society of Antiquaries in 1780 seemed almost as far-fetched as French foreign policy's long-standing aim in the eighteenth century of detaching Scotland from England. Far from 'panting to throw off the English yoke', Scotland was prospering in the British Empire, and was even able to celebrate a muted version of its own national story, still believing itself 'a distinct people', defined behind Tweed and Solway.

Scott's efforts helped to crystallise modern Scottish history, with clubs such as the Bannatyne (1823), the Maitland (1829) and the Spalding (1840) founded to print primary texts, although it was to be long before Scottish history began to escape from the manacles of the Enlightenment account. The pinnacle of Scott's success in promoting the individuality of Scottish history within the common endeavour of a British present came in his stage-managed Royal Visit of 1822, when George IV was exposed to the full force of this kind of romanticism. Drawing on Jacobite sentiment and imagery, Scott presented an image of a loyal subsidiary nation with a glorious and defunct past, the spirit of which nonetheless survived in the military exploits of Scottish troops in the British Army. The tartan décor of Balmoral and the creation of Scotland as a distinct destination for the royal family during the Victorian period confirmed the long-term success of Scott's endeavour, though in his later work, such as *Redgauntlet* (1824), *The Letters of Malachi Malagrowther* (1826) and 'The Highland Widow' in *Chronicles of the Canongate* (1827), Scott shows some reservations about the nature of British progress in Scotland.

Nonetheless, due in no small part to his influence, in conjunction with the vast social changes which came from clearing the countryside for sheep and deer, Scottish nationality at home was cast as the *Gemeinschaft* of rural idyll, while industrial, professional and imperial Scotland performed a fully integrated role in the *Gesellschaft* of urban, cosmopolitan and impersonal Britain. Scotland existed as a nation in popular British consciousness, but one which tended to the national in proportion to its quaintness or history, and to the provincial in proportion to its dynamism and enterprise. The 'rural idyll' of Scotland the nation was for touristic consumption or military display; Scottish economy or government was arguably integrated into Britain more closely than ever before or since in the high Victorian period, although it is equally arguable that Britain then had a more international identity than it does now, as Sir John Seeley claimed in *The Expansion of England* (1883).[15]

If the eighteenth century saw the confirmation of a Scottish national literature through the rehabilitation of traditional forms and a revisitation of Scottish history, it also bore witness to a Scottish literature concerned with the Union and aspects of dual Scottish and British identity, as in the novels of Tobias Smollett (1721–71) or Susan Ferrier (1782–1854), or one which avoided dilemmas over Britishness by outsourcing the language and traditions of Scottish national struggle to Corsica, as did James Boswell (1740–95) or Greece, as in the case of George Gordon, 6th Lord Byron (1788–1824). Duality and division of internal as well as external kinds was also powerfully present in Scottish literature, as in the classic *Confessions of a Justified Sinner* (1824) by James Hogg (1770–1835) and the work of George MacDonald (1824–1905) and Robert Louis Stevenson (1850–94), notably in *Dr Jekyll and Mr Hyde* (1886). Anxiety and resentment about Empire was also present in important writers such as Sir Arthur Conan Doyle (1859–1930) and Sir James Barrie (1860–1937), whose *The Admirable Crichton* (1902) provides an allegory of an empire run by subaltern Scots abroad on behalf of an incompetent and effete English ruling class which dominates them at home.

In an age when Enlightenment and Empire dominated the external life of the country and its internal ideas and advances, the importance of history, the supernatural and anxious critiques of conscience, consciousness and mind show that many of the key figures of Scotland's national literature were more ambivalent about developments in the national life than were most of their intellectual contemporaries. In particular, writer after writer returned to explore the conflicts of the seventeenth and eighteenth centuries, particularly of the Jacobite period: Burns, Scott, Hogg, John Galt (1779–1839), Stevenson, Barrie, John Buchan, Viscount Tweedsmuir (1875–1940), Naomi Mitchison (1897–1998), Neil Gunn (1891–1973), Hugh MacDiarmid (1892–1978), Edwin Muir (1887–1959), Iain Crichton Smith (1928–99), Sydney Goodsir Smith (1915–75) and many others all revisit this central period of concern as a time when Scotland lost her way.[16]

The visual arts in Scotland continued to exemplify a distinct national culture, as well as vigorously participating in contemporary movements in English and Continental art. Allan Ramsay (1713–84), son of the poet, who trained at Rome, became court painter to George III, Sir Henry Raeburn (1756–1823) produced hundreds of images of Scottish gentry and public figures in a manner which both advertised their status to a wider audience while exemplifying in their portrayal a more private language of allusion which could be recognised by his countrymen, while Gavin Hamilton (1721–98) and Alexander Runciman (1736–85) promoted Primitivist themes. Alexander Nasmyth (1758–1840), who also experimented on steamboats, David Wilkie (1785–1841) and others continued the public portrayal of Scotland, while E.A. Hornel (1864–1933), S.J. Peploe (1871–1935), F.C.B Cadell (1883–1937) and others began to introduce influences from Continental art into a Scottish context.

A cultural infrastructure for all this developed in the eighteenth and nineteenth centuries, including the provision of public libraries, an expansion in the number of theatres, a greater awareness of the importance of urban recreation, ranging from football to public parks, and the opening of civic resources such as the 'Museum of Science and Art in Edinburgh' in 1861 (from 1904, the Royal Scottish Museum), Glasgow Museum (1870), Dundee Museum (1872) and Aberdeen Art Gallery (1885). The Victorian age saw Scotland, like the rest of Britain, take a powerful and simultaneous interest in local culture as a reflection both of parochial importance and international power: bringing the gains of Empire home to be controlled by the British localities.[17]

EMPIRE AND EXPLORATION

In the period from Culloden to the early nineteenth century, Scotland remained a largely separate society governed by local elites. Indeed, Henry Dundas, for more than a generation the dominant source of patronage and power in the country, was sufficiently like a monarch to be christened 'Harry the Ninth' by James Boswell. Dundas's political control of Scotland, which began with his early elevation to the dignities of Solicitor-General in 1766 and Lord Advocate in 1775, expanded when as President of the Board of Control for India after 1783, he was able to use 'Indian patronage . . . in binding together his domestic political empire'. By 1790, Dundas controlled thirty-four of the forty-one contested Scottish constituencies. Within India, East India Company servants profited from internal and east Asian trade; they brought these profits home. Graft and jobbery reached new heights in Scottish affairs as nabob wealth poured into the country, a process satirised by John Galt in *The Member* (1832). Pitt's India Bill, which 'established a joint regime of

Company and Crown' became law in 1784, and under it Scottish Indian wealth continued to flourish, and this remained true long after the East India Company's monopoly ceased in 1812. Companies and investors such as Jardine Matheson (founded by William Jardine (1784–1843) and Alexander Matheson (1796–1878)) continued to develop Scottish commercial interests in the East.[18]

Prominent as professionals and official servants in the Empire, Scots also supplied many of the military commanders for which Britain was distinguished: generals such as Sir Ralph Abercromby (1734–1801), Sir David Baird (1757–1829), Sir John Moore (1761–1809) and Sir Charles Stuart (1753–1801). At the same time, the rank and file suffered disproportionate casualties in Britain's wars: for most of the Scottish regiments, this appears to have been a matter of pride.[19]

In the United States, there had been extensive Scottish emigration since the middle of the seventeenth century, when almost 3,000 Scots had been sent by Cromwell to America after the defeats of Dunbar (1650) and Worcester (1651). Emigration (forced and otherwise – several hundred Jacobites were transported after 1745) continued, and by the end of the eighteenth century there was a significant Scottish minority in the United States. Gaelic was spoken in the US until 1850 and is still spoken in Canada. Much early emigration came from northern Scotland, although in the economic conditions of the 1920s, some 300,000 left southern Scotland for the United States. It has been argued that poor conditions at home made Scottish emigrants readier to risk the marginal environments of the colonial frontier than those from England; the long-standing Scottish mercantile, academic and military diaspora to northern Europe may also have played an important role in the manner in which Scots were acclimatised to emigration as a source of opportunity. Between 1871 and 1914 320,000 Scots emigrated to Canada alone.

Scottish emigration touched every continent of the Empire: between 1841 and 1931 2¾ million Scots left the country. Lower levels of transportation from Scotland than from England and Wales limited the number of Scottish criminals sent to Australia, but many other Scots emigrated there: Scottish societies developed, and golf was introduced. At the beginning of the reign of Queen Victoria (1837–1901), Scots began to settle in New Zealand, founding the city of Dunedin there in 1843. Eventually, 39 Edinburghs, 25 Glasgows and 19 Dundees together with 75 Hamiltons would find their way onto the face of the globe. In 1820, Thomas Pringle (1789–1834) led a group of emigrants to the Cape, before returning to Britain in 1826 to become 'Secretary of the Anti-Slavery Society' in which capacity he 'saw the emancipation of the slaves throughout the British Empire to a successful conclusion'. At the same time, ordinary Scots emigrants could display a racism just as ruthless as that of any Europeans of the time, as in the 1842 slaughter of the Aborigines at Warrigal Creek or Colonel John Neill's revoltingly indiscrimate humiliation and massacre after the Indian Mutiny, itself suppressed by Sir Colin Campbell, Lord Clyde (1792–1863), the son of a Glasgow joiner.

Scots were among those at the forefront in the field of exploration as well as that of emigration. In 1770, James Bruce of Kinnaird (1730–94) discovered the 'source of [the] Blue Nile'; in 1788 Alexander Mackenzie (c. 1755/63–1820) reached the '*Arctic Sea* along Mackenzie River'. Mungo Park (1771–1806), who extensively explored West Africa, was among the many doctors exported by Scotland to the Empire in the first phase of colonial expansion. But exploration did not stop at these frontiers. In 1818, Sir John Ross (1777–1856) began exploring the North-West Passage in the Arctic. David Livingstone (1813–73) helped open up knowledge of the interior of Africa, promoting 'Christianity and commerce' as the two key elements in developing the continent. One of his successors, Alexander Mackay (1849–90), 'compared the gospel in Africa to the cantilever principle of the Forth Road Bridge which was opened in the year of his death', thus indicating 'in no uncertain manner the intermingling of technology and social service from Scotland in Africa'. Many African students came to Scottish universities: probably the first was James Africanus Beale Horton (1835–83) from Sierra Leone, who graduated in medicine from Edinburgh in 1858.[20]

Scottish entrepreneurs were important both in Canada and New Zealand, while exiled Jacobites supported allied non-British imperial ventures by the European powers, such as Denmark's 'East Indian Asiatic Company'. In 1853, Dundee entrepreneurs set up factories in Calcutta to take advantage of cheaper labour rates in the production of jute. Scots abroad could frequently be astute to the point of 'ruthlessness', as in Victoria, Australia, where they were 'notorious'. By 1900, vast international business enterprises were being controlled from Scotland. The investment trust industry, strongly based on foreign investment, helped 'Scotland to export more capital per head than any other part of Britain'.[21]

Although Scots were implicated in the imperial project at every level, it would be wrong not to draw attention to their role in liberation movements, most notably in the United States, where Scottish Whiggery was profoundly influential, but also in Spanish colonies such as Chile and Venezuela, where Sir Gregor MacGregor led native Indian regiments in Highland dress to victory over the Spaniards. Thomas Cochrane, 10th Earl of Dundonald (1775–1860), 'placed on half-pay' for attacking naval abuses in 1806, went on to command in the Chilean, Brazilian and Greek fleets in the age of their national liberation. Scottish nationalism as such 'tended to be a vicarious matter: middle and working-class radicals identified with the aspirations of the oppressed nations and minorities of Europe'.[22]

EXILE AND INTERNAL COLONIALISM

The impulse towards material improvement in the eighteenth century naturally led to many of the clan leaders and great landowners seeking to raise the return from their estates; their increasing integration with the British state also played a part, as they now required funding to cut a dash in London as well as Edinburgh society. London was very expensive for a Scot: even a landowner such as James Boswell, 8th Baron Auchinleck, one of the half-dozen most influential estates in Ayrshire, found London life a financial strain in the 1780s, and this was merely the life of a gentleman, not the life of the Court.

The tacksmen who were the senior tenants on many estates in northern Scotland were no longer needed as company commanders in their leader's fighting tail. As they were also an economic burden, they began to be forced out in the 1760s and '70s, leaving for America and 'taking with them large numbers of their sub-tenants and other dependants'. This was not the Highland Clearances proper, but it was a shadow of what was to come. In a country where in 1878 'nearly half the land' was owned by 68 people, and 580 'owned three-quarters of it', relatively small shifts in outlook within one crucial group could affect the lives of tens of thousands. Towards the end of the eighteenth century, 'it is possible that a tenth of the population, or more, was lost by emigration'. Moreover there was substantial internal movement: by the 1790s for example, 'between 20 and 30 per cent of the population of Greenock was Highland-born'.[23]

The Chiefs of the Name, who had needed fighting men fifty years before, now found them much less necessary, while they themselves had greater need of wealth in order to join the British governing elite. Moreover, there was a general climate of agricultural and commercial improvement, and such improvement as was practicable on their estates required extensive use of them. Sheep-farming needed land, and if the land was occupied by large numbers of people, they had to be cleared: this was the situation from the 1790s, when a faster and more direct mode of clearance began. The economic crisis of the Napoleonic Wars resulted in the advocacy of 'wholesale clearance as the only solution'. In 1814–20, the largest and arguably most infamous Clearances occurred in Sutherland, when 15,000 were evicted and the Duchess appropriated over 3,000 square kilometres of clan land. In the years that followed, between one and two-thirds of the population of Caithness, Sutherland, Ross-shire and Inverness-shire were dispersed. There was resistance: 'in 1820 and 1821 clearances in Culrain, Ross-shire and Sutherland . . . were only effected with the use of guns and swords'. By

1811 there were 250,000 sheep in the Highlands; by the 1840s, close on a million.

On the whole, a good deal of mainstream opinion in Scotland favoured or at least accepted the process of clearing the land in order to economically improve it, however much the benefits of that improvement might flow narrowly into the landlord's interest. There were, however, voices early raised in opposition, including that of the Perthshire landowner Colonel David Stewart of Garth, who had cooperated with Scott in hosting the 1822 royal visit, and whose *Sketches of the Character, Manners and Present State of the Highlanders of Scotland* appeared in the same year. In the 1825 second edition of this classic, Garth castigated the landlords and 'the new system of statistical economy with its cold unrelenting spirit'. By the 1830s, 'the parlous condition of the Highland population . . . began to impinge upon the national consciousness', but this was still a long way from bringing about constructive change in tenant rights.

There was a further wave of departures consequent on the potato famine of the late 1840s. The famine affected part of the west Highlands as well as Ireland, and though the effects were less profound than in Ireland, partly due to 'the strength of the associational culture of civil society', many thousands were destitute in the 1850s, and emigration appeared the only option. Scots from the north-west tended to emigrate, often to Canada and Australia; from the east they were more likely to inwardly migrate to the big cities of the Lowlands, although there was also seasonal migration from the west to the east coast associated with the fishing industry, which helped to sustain some of the west Highland population. Those who emigrated were often placed under pressure to go, and were undoubtedly sometimes forced: 'over 2,500 of Lord McDonald's tenants in Skye and North Uist were shipped out to Canada and Australia between 1849 and 1850'. Native culture flourished anew in these colonies, but unlike the home country they were not romantic locales. In the Highlands Romantic and improved Scotland were in poignant juxtaposition: 'in 1829–30, as Felix Mendelssohn conceived and composed his "Hebrides" Overture, the writing of which began during a visit to Fingal's Cave in Staffa, some miles inland at North Ballachulish and Achintore, the laird of Lochiel was completing the process of "wholesale evictions" which he had begun in 1824'. The price of progress could be high if one were not a tourist, and that this was the case was underlined by the increasing use of land not just for sheep, but also for deer and recreational hunting: by 1884 almost 8,000 square kilometres, 10 per cent of the land area of Scotland, were under deer. The 'image of the Highlands as a wild place full of kilt-wearing neo-brigands' had become a marketing opportunity, where aristocrats and the British haute bourgeoisie could recreationally 'rediscover the primitive blood-lust of the hunt'.

After the Disruption, in which certain Tory landlords had forced some Highland Free Kirk congregations 'to worship for a time in caves and on the bare hillsides', in a manner reminiscent of the Covenanting era, the tide began to turn. In the 1870s 'that part of the Lowland population which was of Highland origin became increasingly active in the cause of the remaining Highland people'. In 1882, there was well-publicised resistance to a clearance at the so-called 'Battle of the Braes' on Skye. Links were made with the Irish land radicals, and five MPs were elected in the crofters' interest in

1885 (by 1895, they had returned to the Liberal Party). The Napier Commission, which began to sit in 1883, examined the issues of Highland landownership and crofters' rights, and in 1886, the Crofters' Act followed. However, despite the Act, which 'conceded much of the . . . claims' of Highland tenants, voluntary emigration continued. From 1881 to 1891, 43 per cent of the natural increase in the Scottish population emigrated; from 1901 to 1911, 47 per cent.[24]

Between 1755 and 1911 the proportion of Scotland's population living in the Central Belt along Forth–Clyde rose from about 35 to about 70 per cent, with the proportion living in west Central Scotland rising from 14 to 46 per cent: a massive shift which must always be borne in mind in characterising Scottish history in earlier periods, where the Central Belt experience is often used as an over-determining factor. By the former date Glasgow had already begun to flourish as a consequence of the rise of the Atlantic trade, and it benefited comparatively during the Napoleonic Wars, when the Royal Navy's blockade of the French Atlantic ports led to Glasgow being given 'a virtually free hand'. In 1815, 'around two-thirds of the tonnage of vessels going from Glasgow was destined for ports in the West Indies and America'. By the Victorian period the expansion of urban Scotland in the west, 'a society in which industrial urbanisation had gone as far as anywhere in the world', led to increased in-migration from the depopulating Highlands. Glass-making in Dumbarton, the coal trade in Dunbar, jute and jam in Dundee and textiles in Paisley were among the specialisms developed by the rising towns of Georgian and Victorian Scotland. Whole areas in Glasgow were dominated by single trades, such as 'spinners and weavers' in 'Anderston and Calton'. In other areas, such as north-east Scotland, whaling developed from the established expertise of the fishing industry, which had been well developed by the seventeenth century: as early as 1680, 'the South Bay' at Peterhead 'could safely hold' several hundred ships. In the Central Belt and Dundee in particular, Irish immigration increased markedly: the Irish-born reached 5 per cent of the population of Scotland in 1841, and rose as high as 10–15 per cent in Lanarkshire. Recent estimates (cited by Tom Devine) put the figure in the west as a whole still higher, at nearly 25 per cent. With this rise grew an intensification in anti-Irish feeling, particularly potent in areas (such as the west) with extensive back-migration from northern Irish Protestants.[25]

POLITICAL SCOTLAND

French and Irish revolutionary activity found some support in the Scotland of the 1790s, with the formation of the 'Scottish Association of the Friends of the People in July 1792', the United Scotsmen and in the 'strikes and worker combinations' of 1794 to 1797. Trees of Liberty, the badge of French Revolutionary sympathy, appeared throughout the country, and there were links to the the radical movement both in England and Ireland, while figures such as Thomas Muir of Huntershill (1765–99), tried for sedition in 1793, encouraged the French authorities to support an (imaginary) mass radical rising in Scotland. Traditional discourses of heroic resistance and patriot valour were once again brought into play: the Scottish Friends of the People distributed material in the Highlands which harked back to the symbolism of Jacobite times, while more than 10,000 people attended a

Covenanting march in Ayrshire in 1815 and the 500th anniversary of Bannockburn the year before, although it is important to note that such symbolism was often deployed in a British context. Nonetheless, some at least among the United Scotsmen seem to have wanted to follow the nationalist road of their Irish counterparts, seeking to dissolve the Union and restore a 'Scottish Assembly or Parliament'.[26]

The most controversial episode of the radical period is the Insurrection of 1820, which various commentators have identified as a nationalist rising on the one hand, or a local piece of British radical protest on the other. Sixty thousand workers were involved in a strike in western Scotland, and armed groups were in conflict with British militia, in a rising which was to be linked to radical disturbances in England, but which, nonetheless, had its own special character. On 4 April, the day after the 'Provisional Government' appeared in west central Scotland, 'banners appeared among the radical military formations round Glasgow bearing the legend "Scotland Free or Scotland a Desert"'. Five thousand troops were sent to Glasgow, and the rising was rapidly defeated, with the main engagement coming at Bonnymuir near Falkirk, where about 40 armed radicals were intercepted by Lieutenant Davidson and Lieutenant Hogson. Although there was a good deal of nationalist language associated with the 1820 insurrection, caution is required in interpreting both its relation to and role in wider British radical disturbances. Nonetheless, 'the balance of probability turns, albeit only slightly, to the nationalist interpretation of at least some of the political activity among Scottish radicals in 1790–1820'. Forty-seven of the participants in the insurrection were tried for treason.[27]

Certainly, radicalism persisted in Scotland. The failure of the 1832 Reform Act to extend the franchise to the working class, despite an increase in the number of Scottish seats, led to Chartist organisation in Glasgow, while in the 1840s the importance of lay patronage to the Disruption revived controversies over the established nature of the Kirk which had been the staple of the seventeenth century and which lay behind the Union settlement; certain Free Kirk figures argued for Home Rule. In 1853, the foundation of the National Association for the Vindication of Scottish Rights provided the first organised evidence of more specifically nationalist unrest. NAVSR was a small (probably under 1,000) and relatively elite body, which was not nationalist in the modern sense. Supported by the Lord Provosts of Edinburgh and Glasgow and the provosts of Perth and Stirling, it aimed for greater parity of esteem for Scotland in the Union. In an 1853 address, the Earl of Eglinton and Wintoun called for such parity between English and Scots heroes, writers and institutions. More specifically, the NAVSR sought a return of the Scottish Privy Council and Secretaryship, the upgrading of Holyrood, Linlithgow and Scotland's heraldic emblems, and the use of the term ' Great Britain' rather than 'England' whenever the country as a whole was being referred to. The Association also attacked levels of spending in Scotland, at that time lower than was the case in England, and sought an increase in the country's MPs from 53 (the Reform Act figure, up from 45 in 1707) to 71, eventually achieved. But this was no narrow nationalism: Patrick Dove argued that Scottish nationality was not based on 'race' but on 'reason', and stated, remarkably, that

> Whoever – whatever man – be he black, white, red, or
> yellow, the moment he identifies with the institutions of
> Scotland, that moment he became a member of the Scottish
> nation. . . .

Made increasingly conscious of national history through the
writing of Scott and other sources, Scottish patriotic
sentiment began to honour its past more stridently, and to
want to be noticed. To an extent this was part of resistance to
increasing British centralisation; in 1827, the management of
Scottish affairs by local magnates had 'effectively ended', and
'Scottish affairs were then entrusted to the Home Office'. This
inevitably led to closer scrutiny of Scottish particularism and
a bias towards measuring what had hitherto been an
administratively devolved country by English norms. The
Scottish boards of Customs and Excise (1843), the Scottish
Mint and the Scottish Household were all abolished in the
early to mid-nineteenth century, while further centralisation
was evident as the century advanced in the field of Scottish
higher education in particular, where there was pressure for
increasing conformity with English practice. Such
centralisation was regarded in some quarters as a breach of
the Union and led some in the NAVSR to begin to argue for
Scottish Home Rule.

At the same time, it is important to point out that a good
deal of local control remained. The Burgh Reform and Police
Acts of 1833 meant that Scottish burghs had both a wide
franchise and extensive self-regulating powers. Local customs
were maintained: the notoriously conservative Old Aberdeen,
a separate burgh until 1891, was reputed to 'regulate its
lamplighting according to the brightness of the moon' as late

as the 1840s. Legislation for Scotland still diverged markedly from English norms, as was the case with the Poor Law Amendment Act of 1845, which created a devolved Scottish model, where 'the localities' were 'balanced' by 'a central body, a Board of Supervision, which exercised general oversight and powers from Edinburgh'. These developments helped preserve a local state, but they did little for a national one. The 1870 Education Act's extension to Scotland in 1872 preserved some administrative devolution, but significantly undermined the independence of the Scottish tradition.

Although the NAVSR, which had only attracted crowds of about 5,000 even in its heyday, had collapsed by 1856, there was a continuing trend to foreground Scottish history in a Unionist context: one of the established views of the time was that the Wars of Independence had preserved Scotland from colonisation and opened the way to an equal partnership. As Noel Paton put it, the 'proposal to build a National Memorial of the War of Independence under Wallace and Bruce' in Edinburgh in 1859 would celebrate a conflict which had 'its results in the Union of England and Scotland'. Statues of Wallace went up at Dryburgh, Falkirk (1820), Ayr (1819, 1833) and Aberdeen (1888). In 1856, plans were begun for the great Wallace Monument in Stirling, opened in 1869.

The extension of the suffrage under the terms of the 1868 second Reform Act almost certainly reinforced the expression of Scottish patriotism, although women were still excluded from voting in national elections (female ratepayers now had 'the local vote'). In 1871, the Gaelic Society of Inverness was founded; in 1883, John Murdoch told the Crofting Commissioners 'that it had been a disaster to tell the Highlander that his culture was valueless and his language a barbarism'. In 1885, continued agitation brought about the reintroduction of the Scottish Secretaryship (an under-Secretaryship had been rejected in 1858), and in the next year, the Scottish Home Rule Association (SHRA) was founded to demand greater autonomy. In 1894, 'the forerunner of the Scottish Grand Committee' was set up in the Commons, becoming 'a permanent body' from 1907. Meanwhile, serious constitutional agitation for Home Rule and the more romantic patriotism of the Celtic Revival were both increasingly visible in Scotland, though neither attracted the mass support of women's suffrage.

Although Gladstone had promised 'Home Rule All Round' in his Midlothian tour of 1879, repeated Liberal promises led only to inactivity, even when in government; after all, Gladstone's attempt to give Ireland Home Rule split his party. It was from the left that a renewed impetus came. In 1888, the Scottish Labour Party was founded, followed in 1893 by the Independent Labour Party, which absorbed the SLP with the agreement of the Scottish Home Ruler Keir Hardie (1856–1915) in 1894. Scottish input to the early years of the Labour Party 'seemed set to increase pressure for a fuller degree of Home Rule to be granted'. Although elected with a landslide majority in 1906, the Liberals concentrated on major British legislation, and the Scottish dimension remained relatively neglected. Active support for constitutional change, though still thin on the ground, was growing. It was argued that Home Rule 'would ease parliamentary congestion at Westminster' and, more radically, that 'it would allow for legislation which was suited to Scottish aspirations and institutions'. By 1914 the Liberal Young Scots Society with fifty-eight branches, the Scottish Patriotic Association, the

Scottish National League and the International Scots Home Rule League were among those organisations either supporting or in competition with the SHRA's role 'as a ginger group within the Liberal party'. Eventually, after 'a second reading for a 1912 Federal Home Rule Bill' the 1913 Scottish Home Rule Bill with considerable Parliamentary support passed its first reading by 204–159, with all but eight Scottish MPs supporting it; 'in May 1914 it was debated again, but without result. Within three months, war had supervened.'

Despite this agitation, it would be fair to say that Unionism remained strong in Scotland in the generation before 1914. There was considerable 'confidence in Scotland's contribution to the imperial partnership . . . Scots were over-achievers in the Union and the British imperial mission'. It was not until both the carnage of the First World War and the industrial decline which followed it supervened that Scotland's position within Britain and the Empire began to change.[28]

SEVEN

MODERN SCOTLAND

POLITICAL SCOTLAND, 1914 TO THE PRESENT DAY

For much of the period since 1914, the history of Scotland and the history of Britain are not distinct. The First and Second World Wars, the General Strike, the Depression, the BBC, the National Health Service and the Welfare State are all British and international developments. So are the stories of nationalisation, devaluation, oil crises, the post-1969 situation in Northern Ireland, accession to the European Union, Maastricht and the Euro. Scotland's local autonomy was in severe decline particularly after 1945, when the United Kingdom centralised at home and lost an empire abroad: for the first time, the country was called a 'region'. For these reasons, what follows will not be a history which regionalises British developments, but one which emphasises the peculiarities of the Scottish situation in politics, culture, economics and the contemporary sense of identity. 'Modern Scotland', if it is to be more than a regional descriptor, must focus on these features.

In the First World War, Scotland lost 110,000 men. Most of these were private soldiers, but statistically the impact was every bit as great among junior officers: some 15 per cent of Edinburgh and Glasgow graduates were killed. Although there was little opposition to the war in 1914, when it was welcomed by crowds, churches and landowners, the absence of the promised 'home fit for heroes' fuelled left-wing politics both north and south of the border by the end of the conflict. Higher wages for American workers and the drafting in of 20,000 munitions workers to Glasgow had an impact on social cohesion, and there was industrial unrest and a major rent strike in the city in 1915/16. This was the background to what appeared to many to be the much greater industrial unrest of 1919, out of which the Red Clydeside myth was born.[1]

During the massive conflict of 1914–18, the 1913 Home Rule Bill was 'quietly forgotten'. Scotland, with a tenth of the population, contributed over 20 per cent of Britain's war dead and 26 per cent of enlisted Scots died. This situation, combined with the social challenges of mobile labour and high inflation (15–20 per cent per annum during 1914–19) and the beginnings of manifest industrial decline (see next section) led to increased working-class political activity. In general, such activity was not connected with Home Rule, although the Scottish Home Rule Association (SHRA) was re-formed in 1918 and seven proposals set before Parliament in 1919–24. Rather, political radicals tended to favour it as one of their aims, if not their highest priority. John Maclean (1879–1923) and James Connolly (1878–1916) indeed linked Communism and nationalism together, but both found, in Scotland and Ireland respectively, that there was little support for this linkage, although Connolly's romanticised 'Celtic Communism' passed into the Irish nationalist mainstream. In Scotland, the Red Clydeside story was born during the January/February 1919 Glasgow strike for a 40-hour week, during which the Red Flag was unfurled. The Scottish Secretary, Robert Munro, dignified this display of working-class frustration with the title of 'a Bolshevist rising', and pressed the Government into sending thousands of troops, together with tanks, to quell it. Munro's absurd over-reaction passed into the mythology of the Scottish Left, perhaps partly because the crisis of 1914–19 really did represent some kind of sea change in Scotland's economic fortunes.[2]

The postwar electoral landscape changed considerably. The Liberal Unionists (who had rejected Irish Home Rule), allied with the Tories since 1895 and merged with them in 1912, thus strengthening the Unionist Party in Scotland at the expense of the Liberals. At the same time, the prospect of power for Labour came closer with the Representation of the People Act of 1918, which 'added women above the age of thirty to the electoral register and increased the number of males entitled to vote by fully a half'. In the increasingly collectivised world of the industrial male working class, the Labour Party made great strides, winning 29 seats in 1922, 34 seats in 1923 and 36 in 1929 in Scotland. In 1918, Labour 'fought the election in Scotland on two distinctively Scottish planks': 'Self-Determination' and land reform. However, as the prospect of UK power drew nearer in 1923, 'within the Labour Party the desire for Scottish autonomy declined', and Ramsay MacDonald's government, despite its Liberal support, failed to put its weight behind the 1924 'Government of Scotland Bill'. It was to become a familiar pattern. British politics were expanding and Scottish autonomy was continuing to contract. In the 1890s, the trade union movement in Scotland was powerfully local, but by 1923 'three out of every five trade unionists in Scotland belonged to a British organisation'. Scotland's relative economic decline (see below) increased the importance of collective bargaining and national wage agreements, while collective action such as the General Strike (1926) helped to coalesce a generically British working class.[3]

The opportunity now existed for a political party to outflank Labour on the Scottish question, though whether there would be any electoral benefit in doing so was another matter. The SHRA was refounded in 1918, but its 1920 Home Rule plan came to nothing. The Celticist and early pro-Irish stance of the Scottish National League (SNL), founded in 1919/20 (an earlier version dated from 1904), was never going to win over mainstream Scottish opinion, despite the fact that in what was still the heyday of the British Empire, there had been some support for the Irish cause in Scotland in 1914–21 – ironically mostly from Catholics of Irish extraction who in Scotland tended to support the Labour Party. Nonetheless, the SNL did a great deal to set a political agenda. In a 1926 rally at the Wallace Memorial in Stirling, the SNL criticised the SHRA for its focus on Westminster, and suggested that, as in Ireland in 1918, 'Scottish MPs should pledge not to cross the border at all but to remain in Scotland and legislate for Scotland'. The SNL's outlook was to underpin what was later to become the fundamentalist wing of the Scottish National Party, just as the SHRA, becoming increasingly discredited in the face of Labour inaction, provided the legacy for a later generation of nationalist gradualists, who favoured home rule rather than instant independence. The SNL, for all its weaknesses (including the tendency to sectarianism endemic in 'purist' organisations which led to the split with the Scottish National Movement (SNM) in 1926) offered a critique of the nature of established Home Rule agitation.

The National Party of Scotland (NPS) evolved in the 1926–8 period from three organisations: the remnants of the SHRA, the SNL and Lewis Spence's SNM. The NPS was inaugurated at Stirling on Bannockburn Day, 23 June 1928. In an editorial in the new nationalist newspaper, *The Scots Independent*, R.B. Cunninghame-Graham (1852–1936) called on Scots 'in the name of Bruce, of Wallace, and of Burns . . . to join the National Party of Scotland'. Relatively few did so, but those who did included figures such as C.M. Grieve ('Hugh MacDiarmid' (1892–1978)) and Compton Mackenzie (1883–1973). The NPS was called by some the SNP, as when MacDiarmid invoked it as 'The Scottish National Party' at the 1928 Glasgow University rectorial election. Former Independent Labour Party (ILP) members such as John MacCormick and Roland Muirhead became among the leading lights in the new party, which sought to distance itself from Celtic cultural enthusiasts and those who looked to the Irish example in favour of a more managerial, bread and butter local politics. In 1932, 'the NPS adopted a three-stage plan involving the establishment of a Scottish National Convention leading to a Scottish National Constituent Assembly, which would then result in a Scottish National Parliament', but despite getting respectable percentages of the vote (10–15) in a few contests, this goal looked a long way off. When the more culturalist (and imperialist) Scottish Party was founded by the Duke of Montrose in 1932, the prospect of a divided nationalist vote loomed.[4]

John MacCormick (1904–61), more given to building the bridges of compromise than celebrating the quarantine of idealism, was able to forge a merger between the Scottish Party and the National Party of Scotland. Sir Alexander

MacEwen was a joint candidate in Kilmarnock in 1933, where he gained one-sixth of the vote. Following this relative success, unity between the two parties was achieved on 7 April 1934, and the Scottish National Party (SNP) was born. On the surface the merger was complete, only a few diehards leaving as a result. But just as the views of the SHRA and SNL continued to retain their distinctive profile within Scottish nationalism, so the SP's Home Rule approach, in concert with the ex-SHRA elements already found in the NPS, had a powerful impact on the SNP, at least up to 1950. Dual membership of the SNP and Unionist political parties continued to be a possibility until the late 1940s.[5]

The new SNP was dominated by instrumental nationalists, who saw self-government as a means of improving material conditions in the Scottish economy and society hit by the Depression, and looking for scapegoats (including the Irish: the Scottish Protestant League had some success in the 1930s). Cultural nationalists, who aimed at a rebirth of the sense of Scottish nationhood, were often treated with suspicion, no doubt not least because of their sympathy with Irish Catholic and Celtic nationalism. Nonetheless, the 1920s and '30s were times of great cultural revival in Scotland, the era of the so-called Scottish Renaissance or Renascence, first mooted by Patrick Geddes in 1895. The Renaissance was a literary and cultural movement which tended to explicitly denigrate Presbyterianism and Scotland's Calvinist inheritance as destructive of national identity, and in contrast to exalt the Scots language (seldom Gaelic) and/or Scotland's oral culture and history against the dowdy inheritance of modernity. It thus held little appeal for those in the SNP (or the electorate) who were the inheritors of Presbyterian social

Christianity or who simply wished to keep local control of a familiar socio-political landscape. Criticising the industrial revolution and the corrupt materialism of a Scottish society 'bought and sold for English gold' since 1560 or 1707 revived the Jacobite world view, but did nothing for those whose politics were sustained by the pragmatic goals of increased living standards and a better material environment for the many who lived in Scotland's cities.

The leading figures of the Renaissance were Christopher Grieve (Hugh MacDiarmid), Edwin and Willa Muir (1887–1959 and 1890–1970), Neil Gunn (1891–1973), James Leslie Mitchell ('Lewis Grassic Gibbon', 1901–35), John Buchan (1875–1940) and (arguably) Sir James Barrie, Catherine Carswell and Nan Shepherd. Many of its leading lights were involved in politics: MacDiarmid and Gunn were both active Nationalists. However, Edwin Muir, Gunn, Buchan, Barrie and Gibbon in particular showed a marked preference for an idealised ruralism over the plight of Scotland's cities, championing ideas of self-discovery and rebirth within a country, not an urban context. Although both Gibbon and MacDiarmid addressed the problems of urban Scotland in *Scottish Scene* (1934), this was in a context where Gibbon thought civilisation itself to be endemically corrupt. Nonetheless, although politically the Renaissance writers might have been an unwelcome distraction, the discussion they provoked was an important one. MacDiarmid argued for the importance of cultural values in any rebirth of national identity, and in this he was arguably right. Cultural analysis of Scotland in the 1930s may have had limited electoral appeal (though such appeal was pretty limited whatever strategy was adopted), but it nonetheless had a vanguard quality which was to come into its own many years later, particularly after 1980, when distinctive cultural values began to be a strong motivating force in Scottish self-articulation.

There was, however, a widening interest in some dimensions of Scottish culture in the 1930s. Middle-class activism in this area helped to result in the establishment of the National Trust for Scotland (1931), the Saltire Society (1936) and other bodies. These added to the 'structure of distinctive Scottish corporations' which 'effectively transformed organic discontent into a sequence of manageable complaints'. For much of the twentieth century, the story of Scottish politics is one of the steady growth of administrative devolution in a series of reforms which exercised a brake on declining local control through an expanding network of patronage and quangos without any central democratic authority, in a manner eerily reminiscent of the governance of Scotland before 1827.

In 1919, an additional Minister of State was added to the Scottish Office; in 1926, the Scottish Secretaryship, regained forty years earlier, was upgraded to a Secretaryship of State; in 1936–7, the Scottish Office departments of Agriculture and Fisheries, Education, Health and Home were moved into St Andrew's House in Edinburgh, 'built on the site of the old Calton Gaol', and the Scottish Office left London. In 1939, the National Government moved staff to Edinburgh. During the Second World War (1939–45), the Labour Scottish Secretary (and founder of the re-formed SHRA in 1917–18) Tom Johnston (1882–1965), in control of the Scottish Office from 1941, allowed 'for meetings of the Scottish Grand Committee to take place in Scotland'. Johnston, whose most significant achievement was 'a comprehensive scheme for the provision of hydro-electricity to the Highlands', used the nationalist threat (which he no doubt exaggerated) to extract concessions from Westminster: such a tactic would form part of the armoury of future Secretaries of State. Johnston also fought to retain jobs in Scotland, and his legacy was arguably considerable. In 1948, a White Paper suggested the administrative devolution of parliamentary business, economic affairs, the machinery of government and nationalised industries. In 1954, the Royal Commission on Scottish Affairs recommended the transfer of responsibility for electricity, food, animal health, roads and bridges to the Scottish Office. Devolution of this kind led to the Scottish Office being empowered during the planning era of the 1960s and thereafter. In 1957, the first Scottish Standing Committee was set up at Westminster, followed in the late 1960s by a Scottish Select Committee. In 1962, a Scottish Development Department was set up in the Scottish Office, and from 1963 the representative peers system set up in 1707 came to an end, and all Scottish peers could sit in the Lords.[6]

Administrative devolution and (arguably) a rising consciousness of 'Scottishness' were accompanied by electoral respectability (if not success) for the SNP in the 1930s. The Second World War, with its focus on far wider horizons, provided a challenge which once again divided the nationalist community into its idealist and pragmatist wings. The SNP was divided between those who joined in the British war effort and those who resisted conscription, and between those who supported a 'federal union' and those for independence; it had mercifully few, if any, outright Nazi sympathisers, though Goebbels tried to enlist some. Following the 1941 National

Service Act, Douglas Young appealed to the High Court that conscription was contrary to the common law of Scotland and to the Union, claiming that English statute law was unknown in Scotland and that British law was null, as Britain 'is deficient in the qualifications of a legal personality by International Law'. Young predictably got nowhere, but the case became a *cause célèbre*. In 1942, the federalists of the Scottish Union (later Scottish Convention) walked out with 500 members, splitting the SNP.

After the end of the war, efforts towards any kind of home rule became increasingly bogged down after the Scottish Labour Party's 1945 pledge of a 'Scottish Parliament for Scottish Affairs' fell by the wayside, as the new Labour Government concentrated its efforts on reconstructing Britain. Labour did little in power to further a devolutionary agenda. The nationalisation of coal, rail, electricity, iron and steel in 1947–9 placed the control of Scottish companies outside Scotland, as the Tories pointed out, while the developing national health (from 1948) and social security systems increased the level of British policy integration. Nevertheless, this did not mean that Scottish affairs were neglected: indeed, they received a surprising amount of attention given the 1 per cent of the vote obtained by the SNP in the 1945 election, in which they lost their sole by-election seat of Motherwell after a few weeks; it had only been won by virtue of the wartime truce between the major parties. The Home Rulers' only real success in the 1945 General Election came from the return of John Boyd Orr (1880–1971) to the Scottish Universities' seat as an independent on a Home Rule ticket. Symbolically, the university seats were abolished by the Labour Government.[7]

John MacCormick, who had long sought cross-party support for Home Rule, including the Liberals, agreed with others the idea of a Covenant for Scottish Home Rule 'in the Inchrie Hotel in Aberfoyle, later renamed the Covenanters' Inn' in 1949. The resulting petition attracted up to 2 million signatures. Turned aside at Westminster on the grounds that political change should come through the ballot box, it was nonetheless a momentous attempt to demonstrate the wide (if arguably shallow) sympathy for Scottish home rule.[8]

With the exception of the Covenant, there was little development in Scottish home rule politics in the 1940s and '50s, decades which remained strongly dominated by the two major parties, themselves frequently converging on a corporatist agenda in which 'post-war economic planning and the development of the welfare state were both based on a centralist strategy'. Home Rule became perceived as an irrelevance, and was formally opposed even by the Labour Party from 1956. In this period, although the SNP evolved a number of policies which would develop later into its characteristics as a mature political organisation, symbolic challenges to the state largely took the place of electoral success. The removal of the Stone of Scone from Westminster Abbey in 1950 by a group of students caused a furore, while John MacCormick's 1953 legal challenge to the royal title 'Elizabeth the Second' invoked 'the principle of Scottish popular sovereignty and challenged Dicey's notion of Parliamentary sovereignty'. MacCormick lost before Lord Guthrie, but on appeal Lord Cooper, the Lord President, upheld MacCormick on one of three counts, that 'the principle of the unlimited sovereignty of Parliament is a distinctively English principle which has no counterpart in

Scottish Constitutional law'. This judgement, amplified in Lord Cooper's verdict that the Parliament of Great Britain potentially inherited 'peculiar characteristics' of both the Scottish and English constitutions (rather than being a mere extension of the second) 'provoked a reaction among legal thinkers on the nature of the Anglo-Scottish Union'. MacCormick's case was typical of Scottish nationalist activity: constitutional and non-violent. Lack of support need be no barrier to separatist criminal activity: so it is one of the positive things that can be said about Scottish nationalism that not one person died or was killed for it in the course of the twentieth century, though there were some thankfully incompetent attempts at violence on the political fringes.[9]

Labour's victory in the 1964 General Election was followed by disillusionment. Regional industrial policy, which had brought motor plants such as Linwood and Bathgate and a steel strip mill at Ravenscraig to Scotland since 1959 had failed to stem rising unemployment or regional disparities within the country, even though Scotland was now receiving more than its fair share of government expenditure. Bill Miller has argued that the 'build-up of the Scottish Office' was 'a Danegeld' which stimulated the 'appetite for self-government', which in the long run is no doubt true. The increased planning powers of the Scottish Office, along with its growing role in patronage, looked as if they might create a new domestic middle-class cadre who could sustain Britishness via the Welfare State, just as the now-declining Kirk or anglicising education system (there was student unrest when Edinburgh became the first Scottish university to enter the British UCCA clearing system in 1962, and it was not until the 1980s that Glasgow, Aberdeen and Strathclyde joined it) had sustained its imperial predecessor. Scottish Office concessions became to an extent a substitute for these local autonomies. But planning could not deliver everything.

In 1965 the Scottish Secretary, Willie Ross, published a National Plan for Scotland, which led to the establishment of a Scottish Development Department, which 'implemented planning on a far more rigorous basis than in any of the English regions'. New towns were founded, and charters of university status were granted to the Royal College of Science and Technology (Strathclyde), Heriot-Watt College and University College, Dundee, while a new university was set up at Stirling, which beat Inverness to the title to concentrate wealth further in the Central Belt, although the Highlands and Islands Development Board (HIDB), set up in 1965, was intended to promote structural change in the north. Public planning and development was taking place on such a scale in a relatively small economy that it began to affect it disproportionately, while not being able to stem Scotland's relative decline. The target of 4 per cent growth was wholly unrealistic, still more so in a planned economy. Arguably, entrepreneurship became devalued in the massive culture of *dirigiste* redevelopment, which had itself 'lost its way' when, in a sign of greater economic incompetence, the Labour government devalued the pound in 1967.[10]

The Scottish Nationalists began to gain ground in the face of dissatisfaction with Labour's failure in government to arrest Scottish decline and (probably) as a result of the final collapse of the British Empire, which removed the international dimension from Britishness. The new international landscape of the Cold War, represented by the siting of Polaris missiles on the Holy Loch, was protested against on the margins, but provided no electoral benefit to the SNP. Other parties had their problems, however. If Labour had promised more than it could deliver, in western Scotland in particular the Tories were in trouble, as the sectarian bases of Protestant unionist support were weakening, though Catholic loyalty to the Labour Party took much longer to begin to dissipate. In 1967 Winnie Ewing won the Hamilton seat from Labour at a by-election. Nationalist membership grew to 60,000, and after earlier flirtations with an electoral alliance with the Liberals, the SNP was now persuaded of the merits of 'going it alone'.

In 1968, Nationalist support touched and then exceeded 30 per cent and the party won 100 seats in the municipal elections in May. The government transferred passenger road and sea transport to the Scottish Office, and set up a Royal Commission under Lord Crowther to 'consider the Constitution': a delaying tactic which was particularly popular in the 1960s. Harold Wilson's 1968 commission took five years to report and 'its members disagreed on the form devolution should take', though the broad conclusion was for reform. Eager to capitalise on the constitutional situation, the Tories (no longer called Unionists in Scotland, but Conservatives) under Ted Heath promised change in the 1968 Declaration of Perth, but did nothing in government when an SNP slippage in polls and local elections dissolved into 11 per cent of the vote at the 1970 General Election. Labour, for its part, remained opposed to devolution up to 1974, describing the Nationalists as 'Tartan Tories', a middle-class party. Both major parties also adopted the tactic of rubbishing the SNP while supporting Scottish public expenditure through concessional subsidy. Although the 1978 Barnett formula, which replaced the Goschen one of the Victorian era, entailed a gradual convergence between Scottish and UK levels of public spending, the pace of such convergence was glacial, and Scotland remained a long-term beneficiary (excluding oil revenues) of the UK Treasury. This was by no means an ineffective arrangement, and it took the Poll Tax debacle of 1988–90 to undermine it and hand the initiative back to supporters of constitutional change.[11]

By 1970, it was beginning to be clear that there were sizeable oil reserves in the North Sea, which transformed the economic prospects of an independent Scotland. In March 1973, the SNP launched the 'It's Scotland's Oil' campaign, the most successful political slogan ever adopted by the Nationalists. Lord Kilbrandon's Royal Commission report on devolution was published on 31 October 1973, and eight days later the SNP won Glasgow Govan at a by-election, while in the February 1974 General Election they picked up seven seats at Westminster. This came as a tremendous surprise to London-based politicians and commentators alike, whose lack of understanding of Scottish affairs arguably led them to exaggerate the scale of the constitutional threat. It was true, however, that the UK as a whole was more unstable in the early to mid-1970s than at any other peace-time period in the twentieth century, with union militancy, minority governments, a collapsing exchange rate, rampaging inflation and an oil crisis. In October 1974, the SNP won 11 seats despite Labour's new-found, if lukewarm, endorsement of a Scottish Assembly; they were second in 42 more. A hard-pressed Labour government with the slimmest of majorities at last moved to legislate seriously on Home Rule.

When the Labour Chancellor Denis Healey had to go for support to the International Monetary Fund in 1976, the credibility of Britain sank to a new low. In this context, constitutional change might seem a necessary breath of fresh air. A new Scottish Labour Party split from Labour under the charismatic leadership of Jim Sillars, the MP for South Ayrshire, in 1976. Its two MPs were a minimal secession, but in the context of a weak government without an effective majority, they constituted a problem. Change seemed inevitable.

Buoyed by Labour's declining popularity, the SNP continued to advance, and had the Liberals not rescued the Prime Minister, James Callaghan, from a no confidence vote in 1977 with the SNP standing at 36 per cent in the polls, modern Scottish history could conceivably have been different. But the Lib–Lab Pact stabilised the government, and although the Winter of Discontent in 1978/9 undermined the recovery of Labour's last two years in office, it was not the SNP who benefited. The devolution legislation was wrangled over and became associated in the public mind with a failing government, while it was a Labour backbencher sitting for a north-eastern English seat, George Cunningham, who, on Burns Night, 25 January 1978, moved a wrecking amendment to the effect that 40 per cent of the registered electorate in Scotland and Wales would have to vote 'Yes' for devolution to be implemented, thus effectively demanding almost two-thirds of the vote in favour in any turnout below 70 per cent. Cunningham's amendment was passed 'against the wishes of more than 80 per cent of Scottish MPs'.

As the referendum on 1 March 1979 approached, other negative factors increased in importance in public consciousness. The establishment of a tier of regional government within Scotland as a consequence of local government reorganisation in 1975 (which had substantially weakened local burgh autonomy, guaranteed in 1707 and reinforced in the nineteenth century) helped to undermine the devolutionary case, as a Scottish Assembly would be a third tier of internal Scottish government in a country where Strathclyde Region already contained almost half the population. Given the limited powers of the proposed non-legislative and non tax-raising Assembly, many doubters turned sceptical. It is instructive to note that when an overwhelming majority was recorded for devolution in 1997, it was in the context of a fresh set of local government changes which had abolished the regions in favour of single-tier authorities. There were other problems: the No campaign was heavily funded, and the largely inactive Alliance for an Assembly, which 'barely existed as a campaigning organisation', specifically excluded the SNP on sectarian grounds, while the SNP dominated the alternative Yes for Scotland. In the last weeks of the campaign, Tory support for change fell significantly following an intervention by Sir Alec Douglas-Home promising a better bill from an incoming Conservative government in the event of a No vote.[12]

Scotland voted 52 per cent Yes, 48 per cent No on a 64 per cent turnout. Only 33 per cent of the electorate voted in favour, and the legislation fell under the terms of the Cunningham amendment. The south-west of Scotland, the Borders and Orkney and Shetland voted No, as did (more narrowly) the north-east. The highest Yes vote, 57 per cent, was in Fife; the lowest, 27 per cent, in Shetland. Turnout varied from 50 per cent in Shetland and the Western Isles to

66 per cent in the Borders, Lothian and central Scotland. Regional disparity and a suspicion of Central Belt dominance under the proposed first-past-the-post voting system for the Assembly were evident, if not the dominant force devolution's detractors claimed them to be.[13]

In 1979, as so often, few understood the fact that economic follows political power. The BBC abandoned its plans to build a large new studio complex in Edinburgh, and interest in Scotland waned. The SNP parliamentary group at Westminster, who had shown their inexperience since being elected in 1974, brought down the Labour government in alliance with the opposition when Labour failed to ignore the 40 per cent rule and press ahead with devolution. In the May General Election, the Labour vote held up well in Scotland, but the SNP lost nine of their eleven seats and Jim Sillars' Scottish Labour Party lost both of theirs and collapsed. The Conservative vote went up from 25 to 31 per cent north of the border, and there was a big swing to them in England. Under the new Prime Minister, Mrs Thatcher, there was some further token administrative devolution in the shape of the 'Select Committee on Scottish Affairs' and occasional meetings of the Scottish Grand Committee in Edinburgh, but otherwise Scotland had put itself off the British political agenda. The Nationalists, like the Labour Party, lurched to the left in spectacular fashion, partly under the influence of defectors from the moribund SLP. The SNP paraded its eroding electoral base as a justification for civil disobedience, and totally failed to address the rise of the Liberal–SDP Alliance in Scotland after 1981. To many, Scottish Nationalism seemed a busted flush.[14]

Why had the SNP broken through at all? Oil was not the major reason, for the first boost to the party's support came in the 1960s, and the oil campaign's long-term effects were negligible. The other parties paid no electoral price for minimising the North Sea's economic potential and ridiculing the SNP's figures and arguments, which were more than borne out by subsequent events. The causes, then, of the Nationalist rise must be sought elsewhere.

As with the Liberals at Orpington in 1962, their success could be read as a third-party protest vote; or it could have been a means of defending Scotland's deteriorating status as a branch economy; or a response to what has been called the 'internal colonialism' of differential rates of development. Most popular has been the view that, ultimately, the rise of the SNP was a response to the decline of the British Empire, and the rapid and public decolonisation which accompanied it. From the beginning, the Union had been about access to imperial markets, and the British Empire had been a strong reason for patriotic Unionism in Scotland. Its loss therefore removed one of the major supports for a British identity north of the border. Perhaps as a consequence, the third-party vote tended to accrue to the Nationalists rather than the Liberals. A rise in the Liberal vote did come in Scotland, but only after 1981; it was subsequently boosted by the Conservative Party entering a fresh phase of decline.[15]

In the 1980s, faced with seemingly interminable opposition at Westminster, the Labour Party became prepared to go further down the Scottish Home Rule route than ever before. Following the 1983 election, in which Labour gained a clear majority of Scottish MPs in the context of a UK Tory landslide, arguments began to be made about a lack of democratic mandate for Conservative rule in Scotland. In 1987, the Tories lost 11 of their 21 Scottish seats, but won by another landslide in England; meanwhile, almost a quarter of Labour MPs came from Scotland. When the 1987 election was followed by the introduction of the Community Charge or Poll Tax in Scotland a year ahead of England, with its regressive per capita rather than income or capital-related levy, pressure on Labour increased. The SNP led a non-payment campaign, which exposed the fact that Labour local authorities (in power in much of Scotland) were collecting a tax which they opposed. Constitutional questions of Scotland's status within the UK acquired a rising profile, and left-wing Labour MPs were reported making quasi-nationalist statements by the press. The Claim of Right of 1988, which led to the setting up of the Constitutional Convention and the beginning of the devolutionary endgame, claimed that 'the Union has always been, and remains, a threat to the survival of a distinctive culture in Scotland', and made claims for sovereignty as residing in the Scottish people. Labour MPs endorsed it, and Labour became wholeheartedly involved in the Convention when Jim Sillars (who had joined the SNP some years previously) overturned a big majority to win Govan for the SNP for a second time in a 1988 by-election.[16]

In 1988–9, the SNP abandoned their anti-Europeanism of the 1970s and returned to their roots in switching to the policy of Independence in Europe. This flagship policy dealt with many of the old separatist and isolationist arguments, with their jibes about a Scottish army and passports at the border. The rising influence of the European Union, and the clear signs of success for small countries within it, may also have played their part. Although the EU became less popular in Scotland as the 1990s progressed, in a poll carried out for the *Economist*'s 'Undoing Britain?' survey in November 1999, 46 per cent of Scots thought that the Scottish Parliament would be the most important political focus for them in twenty years' time, 31 per cent the EU and only 8 per cent Westminster. Rising expectations of EU influence were also evident in England and Wales.[17]

The Scottish Constitutional Convention, based on the Covenants of old and more recently on an idea first circulated in the SHRA by William Mitchell in 1892 and by the Nationalists John MacCormick and Gordon Wilson, was launched on 30 November 1990 (St Andrew's Day) as the successor to the Claim of Right, itself an echo of the Estates' declaration in favour of William of Orange in 1689. Significant concessions had been made to the Labour Party to secure its support, and it was already clear that the Convention, an unelected body of trade unionists, clerics, local government representatives and other political figures would be discussing a limited set of proposals. Nonetheless, the Convention did much to prepare Scottish civic society for constitutional change, and provided a valuable testbed for future Lib-Lab collaboration and coalition, with Labour concessions on proportional representation exchanged for Liberal Democrat abandonment of federalism and a range of other policies.

Despite this, however, much of the Convention's activity was window dressing, in that it had no answer to the Conservative government's refusal to meet its demands, and was unlikely to take any action since its underlying aim was to wait for a Labour General Election victory while officially grounding its case in the sovereignty of the Scottish people. The 'new' consensus politics of the Convention anticipated a future which reinforced Labour hegemony in Scotland with Liberal support while claiming the moral high ground of universal agreement, and extending Labour's claims to be the patriot party. The SNP's withdrawal from the Convention before it was set up anticipated the limited and consensual nature of its remit, and the party was roundly criticised for this. Nonetheless, adroit manoeuvring by Alex Salmond in the mid-1990s allowed the Nationalists to play an effective part in the eventual referendum campaign to endorse a Labour scheme shorn of the rhetoric of Scottish sovereignty which had marked the Convention's own proposals, first unveiled on St Andrew's Day 1995.

Following a fourth Conservative victory in the 1992 General Election, a document called *Scotland in the Union* (1993) was published, which went yet further down the well-trodden path of administrative devolution. It was by this time an inadequate response, and indeed has been called 'the least informed and most insubstantial of government papers reacting to agitation for self-government since the war'. Its consequences were minimal: the 'remit and powers' of the Scottish Grand Committee increased, and it began to meet around Scotland (it had met occasionally in Edinburgh after 1979), while on 30 November 1996 the Stone of Scone was returned to Scotland in a panoply of pageantry but with minimal political effect. The continuous vigil for Home Rule on Calton Hill, manned since 1992, was much more the shape of things to come.[18]

In Labour's General Election victory of 1997, the Conservatives were left without a seat either in Wales (as once before, in 1906) or (for the first time) Scotland. Labour's new Secretary of State, Donald Dewar, a long-time Home Ruler, moved quickly to introduce legislation which provided for a Scottish Parliament exercising power over all areas not reserved to Westminster (foreign policy, macroeconomic policy, social security, broadcasting and a few other specific exemptions). The proposed Scottish Parliament could vary the basic rate of income tax by up to 3 per cent – a separate referendum question provided for this. The Bill went considerably further than its 1977 predecessor in devolving power, although the Parliament's inability to borrow money for capital projects was a major limitation. On 11 September, a referendum took place, in which the Yes vote was 74 per cent (64 for tax-varying powers), with 85 per cent being recorded in West Dunbartonshire and 84 per cent in Glasgow, dropping to 57 per cent in Orkney. Turnout was 60 per cent nationally, only slightly down on 1979 in an era when voter disenchantment with the political process as a whole was markedly more severe than in the 1970s. It ranged from 53 per cent in Orkney and Shetland to 65 per cent in central Scotland. Concern over the Parliament being dominated by the Central Belt had diminished: of its 129 seats, only 73 were to be first-past-the-post, with the remaining 56 allocated proportionately according to the regional vote in the various European Parliament constituencies.[19]

As the public waited for the first elections to the Scottish Parliament in 1999, a wave of exaggerated enthusiasm (soon to be succeeded by an exaggerated sense of disillusionment) swept the country. High figures were recorded for both SNP support and support for independence; it looked for a little while as if the nationalists might win the election. When it finally arrived, the results were less spectacular. The SNP, possibly held back by its leader Alex Salmond's outspoken opposition to NATO action in Kosovo and by its pledge to raise taxes, scored 29 per cent of the vote and gained 35 seats, though only 7 by first-past-the-post. Labour gained 56, and formed a majority administration with Jim Wallace's Liberal Democrats. A high proportion of women were elected, and thanks to the element of proportional representation, the Greens and the Scottish Socialist Party gained a seat each. In July, the Queen opened the Parliament in its temporary headquarters in the General Assembly of the Kirk's debating chamber on the Mound in Edinburgh, with the folk singer Sheena Wellington singing Robert Burns's republican song, 'For a' that and a' that'.

The Parliament's first term has been dogged by ill fortune. The death of Donald Dewar, one of Labour's staunchest Home Rulers, the architect of the devolution bill and Scotland's first First Minister in 2000 was followed by the resignation of Henry McLeish, his successor, in 2001 in connection with a scandal associated with his time as a Westminster MP. Jack McConnell, the first senior figure in the Scottish Parliament with a background solely in Scottish politics, succeeded McLeish. A protracted argument over the siting of the new Parliament building was succeeded by an even more protracted wrangle over costs, while the positive achievements of the Parliament's legislative programme and national profile raising have tended to be undermined by hostile coverage from anti-devolutionary broadsheets and the excesses of tabloid journalism. At the heart of all this lies the key issue over whether the Parliament is a device for local management or the democratic means to fulfil national aspirations. Too many perhaps have expected it to be the latter while criticising it for being anything other than the former. Unlike the situation in the German *Länder* or the major autonomous polities of Spain, Scottish politicians have to suffer being criticised for not standing up to Westminster but being criticised when they do.

Since 1999 it has become more apparent than ever that blame prevails over enterprise in Scottish civil society. Now that Westminster cannot be blamed for everything, Holyrood has taken its place. It is to be feared in the years to come that if this continues Scotland may indeed get the politicians it deserves, devoted to disseminating subsidy rather than innovating policy. But at the same time there are many positive signs. Policies and attitudes fossilised under Scottish Office control are receiving greater scrutiny and debate than ever before, and there are real signs of continuing cultural revival in Scotland. The jury is still out on whether these can be supported by economic growth, and a real national willingness to match the best international standards in business, enterprise, research and cultural practice.

CULTURE, ECONOMICS AND SOCIETY

Emigration continued to be a major problem in twentieth-century Scotland, and the country's population lost ground against other small European nations. In 1911 Sweden had only 16 per cent more people than Scotland; by 1970, 55 per cent and by 2000 close to 70 per cent. Between 1911 and 1980, 23 per cent of those born in Scotland emigrated. On the eve of the First World War, Scotland's unemployment rate was one-fifth of London's; by 1923, the country had a quarter more out of work than the UK average. Many skilled workers lost their jobs at this beginning of a long decline of Scotland's heavy industrial heartland. Hugely invested and narrowly focused, Scottish industry's overcapacity at the end of a prolonged mechanised war inevitably led to contraction. Women, too, became redundant, having been brought into the workplace in numbers for the first time during the war, in which Great Britain had seen a 50 per cent increase in the female labour force, no longer largely confined to domestic service. This social change, however, no doubt compounded the economic shifts being experienced by working-class men, as well as highlighting the middle classes' increasing inability to hire servants.[20]

Even for those in work, comparative wage rates declined. Scotland began to fall clearly adrift of the pace of economic development in southern England, and within Scotland the Highlands became more and more a 'dependent economy': 'between 1911 and 1951 the number of men in work in agriculture in the Highlands almost halved and the population of the Western Isles dropped by 28 per cent'. Seasonal work in Lowland Scotland was increasingly an economic necessity for the declining numbers who continued to live in the crofting counties. It was not until improved communications helped develop both business and tourism in the 1970s that the problems of the Highlands began to be ameliorated, and even then it was at the cost of considerable cultural change, with a major loss in the number of Gaelic speakers between 1931 and 1961.[21]

If the nineteenth century saw forced emigration which contributed to economic growth, the twentieth bore witness to voluntary emigration as a sign of economic decline. On the threshold of the First World War, Scotland's output per capita was almost 20 per cent higher than the UK average; by 2000, it was below it. From 1918 on, there was a lack of creative response to the problems of heavy industry, which had failed to recover fully by the time that the Depression dealt it a second blow. Between 1924 and 1937, UK GDP rose at 2.2 per cent per annum; in Scotland, it rose by only 0.4 per cent: 'by 1931, Scottish industrial production was less than the level achieved in 1913'. The haphazard planning which succeeded the Second World War only slowed the process of relative decline, and obscured the conservative and inward-looking modes of Scottish business formation. The fact that so many Scottish Office civil servants spent their careers in a Scottish educational and professional ghetto, without any time in Whitehall or elsewhere, probably did nothing to speed the circulation of fresh ideas. Technology was not upgraded, and market share fell.

In the 1950s, half a million people left Scotland, half for England. US investment on 'greenfield sites' and the development of New Towns helped the situation, but at the cost of moving Scotland increasingly towards the status of being a branch economy. Declining heavy industry, at first ameliorated by regional policy, finally collapsed in a spate of closures from the Linwood car plant in 1981 to the Ravenscraig steelworks in 1992. Since 1974, the Scottish economy has steadily underperformed its UK counterpart, and the need for a major rethink of the branch economy and subsidy politics outlook of local political management has become increasingly apparent. In a value-added age for the economies of the west, Scottish employment is still often sustained by low-skilled jobs.[22]

After 1918, the Church of Scotland and the United Free Church had launched 'a National Mission of Rededication, an ecclesiastical "new deal" intended to give an avowedly presbyterian direction to the process of post-war reconstruction'. In 1929, the UFC and the Kirk united, but by this stage it was clear that even unity would not help recover a position of influence for Presbyterianism in Scottish society. Social change and the growth of mass leisure activities posed a challenge the Kirk could not meet: 'it was nervous of the new weapons in the armoury of the forces of secularism and lashed out at cinemas, ice-rinks and even ice-cream parlours'. The Kirk was nervous about the growth of Catholicism in the west of Scotland too (not least after the establishment of separate Catholic schools in 1918) and in the 1920s and '30s attacked the Catholic Irish in an unhelpful display of 'a populist strain of Protestantism' which, however, failed to reach critical mass.

The Scottish townscape was becoming more like that of England. In 1917, the Royal Commission on Housing in Scotland had recommended a 'massive house-building programme . . . designed to sweep away the enormous disparity in levels of overcrowding between Scotland and the rest of the United Kingdom'. Scotland had too many families living in 'single ends', one-room tenement accommodation, often windowless. This began to change in the 1920s, although the process was slow. The growth of 'garden suburbs', and the tendency towards the villa, 'flatted villa' or maisonette and bungalow rather than the traditional multi-storey tenement urban building moved closer towards a British norm, although the continued building of 'a novel style of tenement, of no more than three storeys' and the use of traditional harling continued to display some signs of Scottish distinctiveness. One of the other features of the massive rehousing programme between the wars was the extent to which the new build houses were under local authority control: 'no less than 70 per cent of the 344,209 new homes built in Scotland between 1919 and 1941 were owned by local authorities'.[23]

Football became a predominant sport in Scotland as well as in England. The development of a separate Scottish league and cup at the end of the nineteenth century presaged its importance as a moniker of national identity in the twentieth. The percentage of the Scottish population interested in football was unmatched almost anywhere else: as late as 1970 there were 136,000 at the Celtic v. Leeds United European Cup semi-final at Hampden. Scottish football evolved completely separate competitions from those south of the border (some, such as the League Cup, being later adopted in England), and maintained a larger number of senior league clubs per capita. In the Protestant Rangers and Catholic Celtic of Glasgow, it developed two of the largest clubs in the world, whose nationwide support has been consolidated further since the 1970s.

The Boys' Brigade, founded in 1883, became a much more important alternative to the Scouts in Scotland than south of the border. New leisure facilities developed across urban Scotland, and cultural developments included the Edinburgh Festival (1947), Scottish Television (1955) and Scottish Opera (1960). At every level in society, new forms of publicly funded national cultural identity were developing which helped consolidate the concept of Scotland as a separate country, at least to the extent of its being a brand on the UK and international stage. However, while high cultural Scottish organisations tended to be international in outlook and reach, there was equally a tendency for Scotland's public celebration of its own culture to revolve around the stereotypes of the music hall era and the *Sunday Post* newspaper: gloomy ministers, pawky and sly locals *(Scotland the What?)*, community values and egalitarian openness *(Gregory's Girl)* and stereotypical representations of Glasgow as a locale of violence, ignorance and squalor *(Taggart, Rab C. Nesbit)*. Films made outside Scotland, such as *Chariots of Fire* (1981) and *Rob Roy* (1994) paradoxically showed more respect for Scottish historic values than did domestic entertainment. In high culture, Scottishness was incidental; elsewhere, it was celebrated, but in a way too often limited and limiting. In the 1980s, consciousness of the inadequacy of these self-portrayals became more marked.

In the post-1945 era, Gaelic began finally to be rehabilitated as one of the national languages of Scotland. In 1966, a Historical Dictionary of Scottish Gaelic was begun; in 1969, the Gaelic Books Council was set up. In the 1980s, Gaelic medium units began to appear in primary schools in Scotland's cities, and the provision of bilingual signposting began to expand in the Gaidhealtachd. The important Gaelic writer Somhairle MacGill-Eain/Sorley MacLean (1911–96), of limited appeal for much of his life, began to be a famous international figure, was widely translated, and was even nominated for the Nobel Prize in literature. Gaelic broadcasting developed, and more recently pressure has grown for the legal protection of Gaelic in a manner similar to that of the Welsh Language Act of 1993.[24]

In the 1970s, Scotland began a new stage of cultural development. Although Hugh MacDiarmid, the leading figure of the Renaissance, died in 1978, he was no longer the representative of an isolated cultural vanguard. The

Association for Scottish Literary Studies was founded in 1971 to defend and promote the study and teaching of Scottish literature, and it soon gained an important position in universities and schools. Scottish publishers such as John Donald and Canongate began to publish a wide range of the history and literature of the country, while writers such as Edwin Morgan (b. 1920), Alastair Gray (b. 1934), James Kelman (b. 1946) and Liz Lochhead (b. 1947) began to give and utilise voices to and in contemporay urban Scotland, while the country also produced the international talents of Muriel Spark (b. 1918). Although in many cases the work of the new generation of Scottish writers and artists was confined in its appeal to a limited group in Scottish society, this was by no means always the case. Interest in Scottish history in particular became very strong. In 1997 a new National Museum dedicated to the history of the country opened in Edinburgh. By 1999 it was possible for a published work on history by a leading Scottish academic (Professor Tom Devine's *The Scottish Nation 1700–2000*) to be the best-seller in the country, ahead of J.K. Rowling's *Harry Potter*.

The 1960s also saw a revival in Scottish folk music. Groups such as The Corries reached a national and even international audience, and Roy Williamson's 'Flower of Scotland' became and remained an unofficial national anthem for millions, while the academic study of folksong also blossomed in the work of Hamish Henderson (1918–2002) and the establishment of the School of Scottish Studies in Edinburgh. The growth in interest in and performance of traditional music led in the 1990s to the establishment of a Piping Centre in Glasgow and two degree courses in traditional music at the city's higher educational institutions. In the same decade, the

Celtic Connections festival was launched in the city, which sells some 80,000 tickets every January, and a national competition for the young traditional musician of the year was launched there in 2001.

SCOTLAND TODAY

Not only are the Scottish church, banking and educational systems historically distinct: they also attract strong popular support. Scottish Catholicism has been increasingly and strongly seen as native after John Paul II's 1982 visit, to the extent that Thomas, Archbishop Winning's (1925–2001) installation as cardinal in 1994 was seen as a dignity of national significance. Although the Kirk has by contrast continued to lose ground (as in absolute terms have all denominations), a kind of secularised moderate Presbyterianism is deeply rooted in Scottish society, with a commitment to collective values and social improvement, as well as a dislike of perceived pretentiousness and an unwillingness to promote the excellent or exceptional. Thus a 2002 poll could indicate that 47 per cent of Scots regarded themselves as belonging to the Kirk of Scotland, though only around one in eight in fact do so. Scottish professional society also tends to be close-knit, and still has a distinctly national character. The banks, the big investment trusts and the remaining big insurance and investment houses, although gradually being overtaken by globalisation, retain their distinctive character, where anyone who 'matters' is likely to know someone else who does. This is true also of medicine, and especially true of schools and the law, though not higher education. However, even here Scots tend to continue to attend their own universities rather than go south of the border: in 1999, despite the demise of grants in a system which takes a year longer to reach an honours degree, under 9 per cent of Scottish-domiciled students who took up university places went to England and Wales, and the abolition of tuition fees in Scotland may be making this figure fall further. Participation in higher education in Scotland has always been (and remains) higher than in England and Wales: 17 per cent in 1979 (10 per cent in England and Wales), by the beginning of the twenty-first century it reached 50 per cent.

Newer institutions such as the media also have a national basis: indeed, Scotland has a distinctive national media to an extent often unnoticed south of the border. The *Daily Record* had a circulation of 651,000 in 1999 (about 550,000 in 2002), while *The Sunday Mail* had 770,000. *The Sunday Post*, which once reached *The Guinness Book of Records* for its saturation coverage of 1.14 million sales, was by 1999 down to 470,000. Yet together the Scottish tabloid Sundays sold 1.25 million in 1999, as against the 630,000 sold by English titles, even those which sold a Scottish edition. The same situation prevails among the broadsheets. In 1999 *The Times* had 28,000 Scottish sales, *The Guardian* 14,000, *The Independent* 7,500 and *The Daily Telegraph* 24,000, while Scotland's two broadsheet national newspapers, *The Herald* and *The Scotsman*, sold 101,000 and 78,000 respectively (some 91,000 and 80,000 in 2002). The Sunday versions of both these newspapers currently muster over 125,000 sales between them. It must also be noted that many Scots buy one of the big regional broadsheet papers, such as *The (Dundee) Courier* (94,000) or *The Press and Journal* from Aberdeen (102,000), which also prints a separate Highland edition. Only in Lothian do the English papers sell well.[25]

The majority of Scottish exports are sold within the UK. There are differing geographical characteristics within the Scottish economy, such as oil in the north-east and Shetland and 'Silicon Glen' in the Central Belt. Agriculture, forestry and fishing is 67 per cent more important to GDP than is the case in the UK as a whole, while inward investment from US firms alone increased from 6 to 178 per cent between 1945 and 1981. Internationally owned manufacturing accounted in 1996 for 53 per cent of manufacturing jobs in West Lothian and 63 per cent in Inverclyde, an immense reversal from Scotland's position in 1914, and one which has consequences for research and development spending, which is often a 'headquarters' operation: Scottish businesses' R & D spend is less than 45 per cent of the average in the rest of the UK. Low transport costs have helped to ensure Scotland's success in the electronics industry, but prominence here and in financial services have not offset decline elsewhere. GDP per capita in Scotland was 13 per cent lower than the rest of the UK in 1996 (6 per cent higher if 80 per cent of oil revenues are included), and Scotland has a tendency to miss out on economic upswings, house price booms and so on.[26]

The population of Scotland has remained steady at 5 million or so since 1971. The preponderance live in the former Strathclyde region, which had 49 per cent of the population in 1971 and 44 per cent in 1997. The heart of the Scottish economy switched from the east to the west coast after the Union and during the British Empire; following the end of Empire, the pendulum has been swinging slowly back, a process which seems to be accelerating in the context of the re-establishment of the Scottish Parliament. Regional imbalances within Scotland can be stark: between 1977 and 1995, Grampian rose from 114 per cent to 136 per cent of average Scottish GDP, with Edinburgh at 150 per cent. By contrast, there is a serious problem with entrepreneurship and new business growth in parts of the old industrial belt in particular: in 1996, Aberdeenshire had almost three times as many VAT-registered businesses per 10,000 population as Glasgow. Not one of the top ten local authorities for business population per capita was in west central Scotland.[27]

This internal economic imbalance is also reflected in Scotland's major cities. Glasgow city shrank by over a third from 1939–2000, while Dundee declined by 20 per cent in 1960–2000, though boundary changes as well as economic migration have played their part. Meanwhile, Edinburgh and Aberdeen urban areas have increased in size. In recent years, net emigration has declined from its high points in the 1920s, '50s and '60s; nonetheless, it is only since 1990 that there have been small gains in population rather than major net losses. Many Scottish families have at least one relative in the Anglophone countries overseas. Scotland has thus been considerably less successful than Ireland in reducing population loss.[28]

Those Scots who remain tend to see themselves as more 'Scottish' than ever before. The 1999 survey of Scottish opinion showed that whereas in 1979, only 38 per cent of Scots would describe themselves as 'Scottish' rather than 'British' when faced with these as alternatives, twenty years later 77 per cent were prepared to do so. By 2001, this figure was 84 per cent. On the other hand, there was little evidence that this much stronger sense of national identity had any particular political implications.[29]

The rediscovery of Scotland's history adds another dimension to this process. The cultural reputation of Scottish history entered a new phase in the 1980s with the campaign to demythologise it. This process of demythologisation sought to discard the leftover fragments of kitsch Romantic identity (tartan chief among them), by claiming them to be the spurious products of their age, and not part of Scottish identity at all. This demythologisation became quite an industry without anyone appearing to notice that it represented yet a further attack by Scottish history on its own value. It was the Enlightenment construction of Scottish history which left it a mixture of pointless legends shining amid the dross of an irrelevant and forgotten culture; and it is arguably better to re-enter and revalue that culture than waste contemporary energies blaming a caricature drawn by your society of itself, thus caricaturing it in its turn, and setting up a procession of self-abasement and blame.[30]

Scottish society has perhaps not adapted so badly as some parts of England to the demands of multiculturalism: this may be due in part to lower levels of immigration. Racism is nonetheless a considerable problem, even if large-scale urban disruption has been avoided. Dislike of the English, although made much of in certain quarters of the London press (often those quarters themselves unfriendly to multiculturalism), is much less of an issue: it is part of a mythology of Scottishness which can tend to obscure real and pressing discrimination against people from other cultural backgrounds. On the other hand, many Commonwealth immigrants who have made their home in Scotland have adopted Scottish identity.

One of the benefits of the devolutionary era has been an improving understanding of the historic and contemporary distinctiveness of Scottish society on a number of different levels. Some of this recognition is extremely belated. It was only in 1999 that the BBC, in its document *The Changing UK*, acknowledged that Scottish procedures and titles required to be identified separately, despite the long-standing distinctiveness of Scottish institutions. A new country, 'England and Wales', has crept into London news broadcasting as a consequence.[31]

The defence of a distinctive Scottish culture and society is no longer seen as specifically Nationalist, but ironically the 'Scottish society' so defended (both by the SNP and Labour Party) is often largely the creation of British corporate centralisation and the Welfare State of the 1950s and '60s, adopted as a golden age. Neither the entrepreneurial nineteenth-century Scotland of low public expenditure nor the Presbyterian Scotland of earlier days are viewed as the basis of a modern national identity which, as Richard Finlay has observed, is very largely one created by British government policy. Since the Welfare State and a large public sector are both the territory of the Labour Party, Labour unsurprisingly proves to be more credible as a defender of these 'national' values than do the Nationalists. The SNP is extremely vulnerable to any Conservative revival. Except in the context of a politically integrated European Union, Scottish independence seems to be unlikely in the foreseeable future. The devolutionary settlement has won Scotland and Scottish issues more attention and notice, and this is all that many Scots may want.

In the context of the increasing erosion of cultural distinctiveness and the sense of history that supports it in the West, it may seem strange to identify a place called 'Scotland' with a national identity and future. But what this study has attempted to show is that, discrete and fissured as some parts of Scottish culture have been, Scotland, for all that it is a country of cultural hybridity irreducible to ethnic or linguistic unity, is still Scotland. This is a country which in some senses is more, and in others less diverse than in the past (there is now, for example, far less of a Highland–Lowland or Protestant–Catholic divide than obtained in the seventeenth to nineteenth centuries). Its practical (if not always emotional) ideas of itself today may owe more to Nye Bevan and Butskellism than John Knox or Robert the Bruce; but the idea of self is still a collective one, and the lost selves of the past continue to mean a great deal to many Scots. Modern Scottish history no longer sees its country's past as a discarded error or a lost ideal, but increasingly as a past like any other past. Debates over that past can still be fierce, but more than ever Scottish history is studied in an atmosphere of normality; and this is to be welcomed. This history, brief as it is, has set out to be a history both of Scottish distinctiveness and Scottish normality. And this is what a national history is.[32]

CHRONOLOGY

Kings of Scots and Picts

Óengus I mac Forguso (r. 729–61)
Constantín mac Forguso (r. 789/811–20)
Óengus II mac Forguso (r. 820–34)
Cinaed mac Ailpín (r. 840/3–58)
Domnall I (r. 858–62)
Constantín I mac Cinaeda (Constantíne I) (r. 862–77)
Aed mac Cinaeda (r. 877–8)
Giric mac Domnuill (r. 878–89) with Eochaid

Kings of Scots, Picts and possible overlords of Brittonic Strathclyde

Domnall II mac Constantín (r. 889–900)
Constantín II mac Aeda (Constantíne II) (r. 900–43/5)
Mael Coluim I macDomnuill (r. 943/5–54)
Idulb mac Constantín (r. 954–62)
Dub mac Maíle Coluim (r. 962–6)
Cuilen mac Idulb (r. 966–71)
Cinaed II mac Maíle Coluim (r. 971–95)
Constantín III mac Cuilein (Constantíne III) (r. 995–7)
Giric II mac Dubh (r. 997–1005) and Cinaed III mac Dubh

Kings of Scots, Picts, Britons and English

Mael Coluim II mac Cinaeda (r. 1005–34)

Donnchad mac Crínan (r. 1034–40)
Macbethad mac Findláich (Macbeth) (r. 1040–54/7)
Lulach mac Gilla Comgain (r. 1057–8) *in Moray only*
Mael Coluim III mac Donnchada Cinn Moír (r. 1054–7 *south of Dee*; 1057–93 all Scotland)
Domnall III mac Donnchada Báin (r. 1093–4; 1094–7)
Donnchad II mac Maíle Coluim (r. 1094)
Eadgar (r. 1097–1107)
Alexander I mac Maíle Coluim (r. 1107–24)

Monarchs of Scots within mainland Scotland (and sometimes beyond)

David I mac Coluim (r. 1124–53)
Mael Coluim IV mac Henry (r. 1153–65)
William I mac Henry the Lion (r. 1165–1214)
Alexander II mac William (r. 1214–49)

Kings of Scots within Scotland (not Orkney and Shetland)

Alexander III mac Alexander (r. 1249–86)
Margaret (r. 1286–90)
Interregnum (1290–2)
John Baliol (r. 1292–6)
Interregnum (1296–1306)
Robert I FitzBruce (r. 1306–29)
David II FitzBruce (r. 1329–71)
Robert II FitzStewart (r. 1371–90)
Robert III (r. 1390–1406)
James I (r. 1406–37)
James II (r. 1437–60)

Monarchs of Scots within Scotland's present boundaries

James III (r. 1460–88)
James IV (r. 1488–1513)
James V (1513–42)
Mary Stuart (r. 1542–67)
James VI (r. 1567–1625)
Charles I (r. 1625–49)
Charles II (r. 1649/60–85)
James VII (r. 1685–9)
William II and III (r. 1689–1702)
Mary II (r. 1689–94)
Anne (r. 1702–14).
Thereafter as Kings and Queens of the United Kingdom.

NOTES

CHAPTER ONE

1. Michael Prowse, 'Tawdry side to the global pursuit of personal gain', *Financial Times Weekend* (21/22 July 2001), xx.
2. David Ditchburn, 'Who are the Scots?' in Paul Dukes (ed.), *Frontiers of European Culture* (Lampeter: Edwin Mellen, 1996), 89–100 (89–90, 91).
3. For a brief explanation of the ideas of Braudel and Febvre, see John Warren, *The Past and its Presenters* (London: Hodder & Stoughton, 1998), 149–51; Acton, cited in Malcolm D. Prentis, *The Scots in Australia* (Sydney: Sydney University Press. 1983), 1; E.P. Thompson, *The Making of the English Working Class* (Harmondsworth: Penguin, 1963).
4. William Moffat, *History of Scotland*, 5 vols (Oxford: Oxford University Press, 1985), I:5; R.A. Houston and W.W.J. Knox (eds), *The Penguin History of Scotland* (London: Allen Lane/The Penguin Press, 2001), xxv; Ian Armit, 'Prehistory' in Houston and Knox 1–27 (4, 9); Peter G.B. McNeill and Hector L. MacQueen (eds), *Atlas of Scottish History to 1707* (Edinburgh: University of Edinburgh, 1996); Murray G.H. Pittock, *Scottish Nationality* (Basingstoke: Palgrave/Macmillan, 2001), 18; A.A.M. Duncan, *Scotland: The Making of the Kingdom* (Edinburgh: Oliver & Boyd, 1978 (1975)), 1–2; Pat Southern, 'Men and mountains, or geographical determinism and the conquest of Scotland', *Proceedings of the Society of Antiquaries of Scotland* 126 (1996), 371–86; Gordon Barclay, *Farmers, Temples and Tombs: Scotland in the Neolithic and Early Bronze Age* (Edinburgh: Canongate and Historic Scotland, 1998), 9.
5. Norman Davies, *The Isles: A History* (London: Macmillan, 1999), 12; Armit in Houston and Knox, 4, 5, 11; A. Fairweather and I.B.M. Ralston, 'The Neolithic timber hall at Balbridie', *Antiquity* 67 (1993), 313–23; Barclay, 7, 11–13, 15.
6. Magnus Magnusson, *Scotland: The Story of a Nation* (London: HarperCollins, 2000), 6; Moffat I:12; Barclay, 29–36.

7. Moffat I:6–12, 14–17; Davies, 15; Armit in Houston and Knox, 6, 8, 12; Houston and Knox, xiv; Barclay, 37.

8. Armit in Houston and Knox 14–15, 19–20; Moffat I:20–9; McNeill and MacQueen, 12; Lorna Main *et al.*, 'Excavation of a timber round-house and broch at the Fairy Knowe, Buchlyvie, Stirlingshire, 1975–8', *Proceedings of the Society of Antiquaries of Scotland* 126 (1996), 293–417 (405, 409); Barclay, 59–60; Martin Carver, *Surviving in Symbols: A Visit to the Pictish Nation* (Edinburgh: Canongate and Historic Scotland, 1999), 11; Ewan Campbell, *Saints and Sea-kings: The First Kingdom of the Scots* (Edinburgh: Canongate and Historic Scotland, 1999), 28; Olwyn Owen, *The Sea Road: A Viking Voyage through Scotland* (Edinburgh: Historic Scotland/Canongate, 1999), 60.

9. Tacitus, *The Agricola and the Germania*, ed. Harold Mattingley and S.A. Handford (Harmondsworth: Penguin, 1973 (1948)), 20.

10. Tacitus, 20, 22; Davies, 119; Pittock, 20; McNeill and MacQueen, 36; Thomas Owen Clancy and Barbara E. Crawford, 'The Formation of the Scottish Kingdom' in Houston and Knox, 28–95 (30–2).

11. John L. Roberts, *Lost Kingdoms: Celtic Scotland and the Middle Ages* (Edinburgh: Edinburgh University Press, 1997), 2; Tacitus, 60; Houston and Knox, xx.

12. Davies, 4, 131; John Koch, 'The Place of "Y Gododdin" in the History of Scotland', *Celtic Connections: Proceedings of the 10th International Congress of Celtic Studies*, Vol. 1 (East Linton: Tuckwell, 1999), 199–210 (202); Alfred Smyth, *Warlords and Holy Men*, New History of Scotland 1 (London: Edward Arnold, 1984), 2.

13. Roberts, 2, 5, 7; Duncan, 26; Davies, 131–3; Armit in Houston and Knox, 16; Clancy and Crawford, *idem*, 33, 37.

14. Duncan, 29, 36; Davies, 167; Smyth, 9.

15. Duncan, 36, 40, 57; Roberts, 12.

16. Donald Meek, *Celtic Christianity* (Boat of Garten: the Handsel Press, 2000), 135–8, 179; Clancy and Crawford in Houston and Knox, 43.

17. Meek, 157, 181, 184; Davies, 183; Clancy and Crawford in Houston and Knox, 39, 42, 49, 70–1; Kenneth Veitch, 'The Columban Church in northern Britain, 664–717: a reassessment', *Proceedings of the Society of Antiquaries of Scotland* 127 (1997), 627–47; Campbell, 34, 36, 56; Chris Lowe, *Angels, Fools and Tyrants: Britons and Anglo-Saxons in Southern Scotland AD 450–750* (Edinburgh: Canongate and Historic Scotland, 1999), 18–19.

18. Clancy and Crawford in Houston and Knox, 30, 39, 49; Duncan, 45, 47; Roberts, 16; Meek, 150; Campbell, 9, 10, 13, 17–21, 46, 52.

19. Koch, 203, 206–8; Smyth, 39–40; Clancy and Crawford in Houston and Knox, 51, 53; Carver, 7, 9, 30; Lowe, 12, 16.
20. Davies, 183; Smyth, 30, 39–40; Koch, 206–8; Clancy and Crawford in Houston and Knox, 49–50, 56; Carver, 8, 28.

CHAPTER TWO

1. Thomas Clancy and Barbara E. Crawford, 'The Formation of the Scottish Kingdom', in R.A. Houston and W.W.J. Knox (eds), *The New Penguin History of Scotland* (London: Allen Lane/The Penguin Press, 2001), 28–95 (55–7); Martin Carver, *Surviving in Symbols: A Visit to the Pictish Nation* (Edinburgh: Canongate and Historic Scotland, 1999), 8.
2. A.A.M. Duncan, *Scotland: The Making of the Kingdom* (Edinburgh: Oliver and Boyd, 1978 (1975)), 54; Norman Davies, *The Isles* (London: Macmillan, 1999), 248; Murray G.H. Pittock, *Scottish Nationality* (Basingstoke: Palgrave/Macmillan, 2001), 23; Olwyn Owen, *The Sea Road: A Viking Voyage through Scotland* (Edinburgh: Canongate and Historic Scotland, 1999), 53.
3. John Roberts, *Celtic Scotland in the Early Middle Ages* (Edinburgh: Edinburgh University Press, 1999), 19; Peter Marren, *Grampian Battlefields* (Aberdeen: Aberdeen University Press, 1990), 50; Magnus Magnusson, *Scotland: The Shaping of a Nation* (London: HarperCollins, 2000), 93; Clancy and Crawford in Houston and Knox, 75; Owen, 16, 57.
4. Roberts, 37; Christopher Brooke, *The Saxon and Norman Kings* (Glasgow: Fontana/Collins, 1975 (1963)), 92; Duncan, 65; Alfred Smyth, *Warlords and Holy Men: Scotland AD 80–1000* (London: Edward Arnold, 1984), 29; Clancy and Crawford in Houston and Knox, 60, 66.
5. Gordon Donaldson, *Scottish Church History* (Edinburgh: Scottish Academic Press, 1985), 13; Magnusson, 40; Roberts, 15–16; Nick Aitchison, *Scotland's Stone of Destiny* (Stroud: Tempus, 2000), 77, 82; Clancy and Crawford in Houston and Knox, 62–5, 71; Carver, 8; Owen, 48.
6. Magnusson, 40; Duncan, 92–3; Smyth, 199; Pittock, 24; Davies, 267, 269; Brooke, 127; Clancy and Crawford in Houston and Knox, 68–9.
7. Duncan, 93, 95; Davies, 254. For Eadgar and his subject kings, see Vol. 1 of Cassell's *History of the British People* (1923); Clancy and Crawford in Houston and Knox, 71.
8. Roberts, 25; Magnusson, 66; Peter G.B. MacNeill and Hector L. MacQueen, *An Atlas of Scottish History* (Edinburgh: Edinburgh

University, 1996), 30, 336; Michael Lynch, *Scotland: A New History* (London: Century, 1991), 93, 100; Smyth, 230; Donaldson (1985), 17; Judith A. Green, 'David I and Henry I', *Scottish Historical Review* (1996), 1–19 (11); Aitchison, 91; Duncan, 230, 554, 557, 559; Clancy and Crawford in Houston and Knox, 75, 79, 81–4; Frank McLynn, *1066: The Year of the Three Battles* (London: Jonathan Cape, 1998); Gordon Donaldson (ed.), *Scottish Historical Documents* (Edinburgh: Scottish Academic Press, 1974), 17; Roberts, 18; Duncan, 123–5, 128, 132, 134; Davies, 280; David Perry, 'Dunfermline: from "Saracen" castle to "populous manufacturing royal burrow"', *Proceedings of the Society of Antiquaries of Scotland* 129 (1999), 778–815 (790).

9. Green, 18; Donaldson (1974), 36–7; Geoffrey Barrow, *Kingship and Unity: Scotland 1000–1306* (London: Edward Arnold, 1981), 157; Duncan, 589 ff.

10. Barrow (1981), 39, 53, 178; Davies, 347.

11. Barrow (1981), 33, 55, 178; Donaldson (1974), 30; Roberts, 72–3; Magnusson, 84–5; R. Andrew MacDonald, 'Images of Hebridean Lordship in the Late Twelfth and Early Thirteenth Centuries: The Seal of Raonall MacSorley', *Scottish Historical Review* (1995), 129–43 (139).

12. Duncan, 521–2; McNeill and MacQueen, 83; Pittock, 26–7; Barbara W. Tuchmann, *A Distant Mirror: The Calamitous Fourteenth Century* (New York: Ballantine Books, 1979 (1978)), 4.

13. Dauvit Broun, 'The Birth of Scottish History', *Scottish Historical Review* (1997), 4–22 (13); Dauvit Broun, 'Defining Scotland and the Scots Before the Wars of Independence', in Dauvit Broun, R.J. Finlay and Michael Lynch (eds), *Image and Identity: The Making and Re-making of Scotland Through the Ages* (Edinburgh: John Donald, 1998), 4–17 (10, 11); Aitchison, 20.

14. Duncan, 64, 79; Cummins, 40, 43–4.

15. Duncan, 176; Barrow (1981), 20; Roberts, 38–40, 43–4; William Ferguson, *The Identity of the Scottish Nation* (Edinburgh: Edinburgh University Press, 1998), 306.

16. Jean Munro Smyth, 'The Lordship of the Isles' in Loraine Maclean (ed.), *The Middle Ages in the Highlands* (Inverness: Inverness Field Club, 1981), 23–37 (27); G.W.S. Barrow, 'The Sources for the History of the Highlands in the Middle Ages' in Maclean (1981), 11–22 (16–17).

17. McNeill and MacQueen; Duncan, 64; Clancy and Crawford in Houston and Knox, 41, 65.

18. MacDonald (1995), 134–7, 142; Roberts, 18, 38, 95; Barrow in Maclean, 19.

19. Magnusson, 47, 49; Maclean (1981), 143; Geoffrey Barrow, *Robert Bruce*, 2nd edn (Edinburgh: Edinburgh University Press, 1976), 69; Lynch, 94.

20. Donald Meek, *The Quest for Celtic Christianity* (Boat of Garten: Handsel Press, 2000), 106, 202–3; *The Book of Deer*, ed. John Stuart LLD (Edinburgh: Spalding Club, 1869), cxix–cxx; Magnusson, 73; Aitchison, 52; Clancy and Crawford in Houston and Knox, 65.

21. Magnusson, 64; Lynch, 94, 96, 100, 101, 107; plates in Houston and Knox at 100–1.

22. Duncan, 126, 141, 587; Davies, 269; Edward J. Cowan, 'Myth and Identity in Early Medieval Scotland', *Scottish Historical Review* (1984), 111–35 (130); Ferguson, 26–7; Broun (1998).

23. Ferguson, 304–5; Cowan (1984), 120, 129n; Dauvit Broun, *The Irish Identity of the Kingdom of the Scots in the Twelfth and Thirteenth Centuries* (Woodbridge: The Boydell Press, 1999), 1; Broun (1997), 11; Fenton Wyness, *Spots from the Leopard: Short Stories of Aberdeen and the North-East* (Aberdeen: Impulse Books, 1971), 14.

24. Geoffrey of Monmouth, *The History of the Kings of Britain*, tr. Lewis Thorpe (Harmondsworth: Penguin Classics, 1968 (1966)), 10, 258, 261; Cummins, 52.

25. W.F. Skene, *Celtic Scotland* (Edinburgh, 1880), 94; Cowan (1984), 134; Magnusson, 41; Broun, 12; John Bannerman, 'The King's Poet and the Inauguration of Alexander III', *Scottish Historical Review* (1989), 120–49 (149).

26. Alex Woolf, 'The "Moray Question" and the Kingship of Alba in the Tenth and Eleventh Centuries', *Scottish Historical Review* LXXIX (2000), 145–64 (145, 146, 163–4); Roberts, 22, 24, 66–7, 70–1.

27. Roberts, 22–3; Aitchison, 87; Clancy and Crawford in Houston and Knox, 36, 72–3.

28. Lynch, 55–6, 58, 60; Barrow (1981), 33, 56; Duncan, 530–1; M.C. Meston, W.D.H. Sellar and Lord Cooper, *The Scottish Legal Tradition* (Edinburgh: Saltire Society, 1991 (1949)), 34–7; McNeill and MacQueen, 29, 192, 195; Ranald Nicholson, *Scotland: The Later Middle Ages* (Edinburgh: Mercat Press, 1989 (1974)), 14.

29. Alexander Grant, 'Whither Scottish History? To the Medieval Foundations', *Scottish Historical Review* (1994), 4–24 (12, 22); Meston *et al.*, 34–9; Barrow (1981), 56; W. Douglas Simpson, 'The Region before 1700' in A.C. O'Dell and J. Mackintosh (eds), *The North-East of*

Scotland (Aberdeen: British Association for the Advancement of Science, 1963), 67–86 (81); Houston and Knox, li; David Ditchburn and Alastair J. MacDonald, 'Medieval Scotland, 1100–1560' in Houston and Knox, 96–181 (133).

30. Roberts, 33; Barrow (1981), 5, 15, 16; Houston and Knox, xxvi.

31. Moffat, *The History of Scotland*, 4 vols (Oxford: Oxford University Press, 1985), 16, 82–4; Barrow (1981), 3–5; Donaldson (1985), 6, 21; McNeill and MacQueen, 4, 99, 286; William Watt, *A History of Aberdeen and Banff*, The County Histories of Scotland (Edinburgh and London, 1900), 37; *Records of Old Aberdeen*, ed. Alexander MacDonald Munro, 2 vols (Aberdeen: New Spalding Club, 1899, 1909), I: 155; Aitchison, 29; Philip A. Crowl, *The Intelligent Traveller's Guide to Historic Scotland* (London: Sidgwick & Jackson, 1986), 406, 491, 533; *Book of Deer*, cxxvi, cxlix, cli; Nicholson, 3; Ditchburn and MacDonald in Houston and Knox, 134–5, 137.

32. Barrow (1981), 87, 92, 95–7; Duncan, 518; J.D. Bateson, *Coinage in Scotland* (London: Spink, 1997), 40, 44; J. Charles Murray, 'The Archaeological Evidence' in J.S. Smith (ed.), *New Light on Medieval Aberdeen* (Aberdeen, 1985), 10–19 (13).

33. McNeill and MacQueen, 21, 196–7, 300–1.

CHAPTER THREE

1. Geoffrey Barrow, *Robert Bruce*, 3rd edn (Edinburgh: Edinburgh University Press, 1988 (1965)), 1; Geoffrey Barrow, *Robert the Bruce and the Scottish Identity* (Edinburgh: Saltire Society, 1984), 5; Norman Reid, 'The kingless kingdom: the Scottish guardianship of 1286–1306', *Scottish Historical Review* 61 (1982), 105–29 (105–7, 118, 119); Magnus Magnusson, *Scotland: The Story of a Nation* (London: HarperCollins, 2000), 110–11, 115; Fiona Watson, *Under the Hammer: Edward I and Scotland 1286–1306* (East Linton: Tuckwell, 1998), 11–14; Michael Lynch, *Scotland: A New History* (London: Century, 1991), 114–15.

2. Barrow (1988), 39, 46; Peter G.B. McNeill and Hector L. MacQueen, *A Historical Atlas of Scotland* (Edinburgh: Edinburgh University, 1996), 91.

3. Barrow (1988), 40, 42, 47, 50, 51, 59, 161–2; Watson, 16–17; Lynch, 115.

4. Barrow (1988), 63–7, 162; Magnusson, 118–21; Watson, 18, McNeill and MacQueen, 87.

5. Barrow (1988), 76–9, 163–4; Watson, 31.

6. Barrow, *Robert Bruce* (1988), 81, 83–6, 165, also 2nd edn (1976), 97, 113, 119, 167–8; Barrow (1984), 10, 16; Reid, 108; Watson, xix, xxi, 46.

7. Barrow (1988), 85; Watson, 45, 47.

8. Barrow (1988), 86–88, 92–3, 102–3; Reid, 107.

9. Michael Lynch, *Scotland: A New History* (London: Century, 1991), 112; Barrow (1988), 166–7; Magnusson, 143–4.

10. Barrow (1988), 121, 123–7, 167; (1984), 5; Magnusson, 149; Reid, 120, 122; Watson, 17; R. Andrew McDonald, *The Kingdom of the Isles: Scotland's Western Seaboard, c. 1100–c. 1336*, Scottish Historical Review monograph, (East Linton: Tuckwell Press, 1997), 193.

11. Barrow (1988), 127–8, 130–1, 133, 136; Magnusson, 151, 153, 157; Watson, 214.

12. Alexander Grant, *Independence and Nationhood: Scotland 1306–1469* (London: Edward Arnold, 1981), 5; Barrow (1988), 131, 151; Magnusson, 165–7; Watson, xix, xxiii.

13. *The Scottish Parliament Factfile 2* (Edinburgh: HMSO, *c.* 1999).

14. Reid, 105–6; McNeill and MacQueen, 336.

15. Reid, 106, 127; Barrow (1988), 17.

16. Reid, 109–11.

17. Nick Aitchison, *Scotland's Stone of Destiny* (Stroud: Tempus, 2000), 33–5; John Bannerman, 'The King's Poet and the Inauguration of Alexander III', *Scottish Historical Review* (1989), 120–49 (143, 149); Reid, 122; Magnusson, 139; McNeill and MacQueen, 94.

18. John Roberts, *Celtic Scotland in the Early Middle Ages* (Edinburgh: Edinburgh University Press, 1999), 124; Magnusson, 122, 152; Aitchison, 116.

19. Roland Tanner, 'The Lords of the Articles before 1540: A Reassessment', *Scottish Historical Review* (2000), 189–212 (189, 190, 195, 212); Gordon Donaldson (ed.), *Scottish Historical Documents* (Edinburgh: Scottish Academic Press, 1974), 105, 177; Leslie J. Macfarlane, *William Elphinstone and the Kingdom of Scotland 1431–1514* (Aberdeen: Aberdeen University Press, 1985), 217, 267; Jenny Wormald, *Court, Kirk and Community: Scotland 1470–1625* (London: Edward Arnold, 1981), 25; *Extracts from the Council Register of the Burgh of Aberdeen 1398–1570* 413, 417, 425; Grant (1981), 148, 149, 155; Magnusson, 257, 304; McNeill and MacQueen, 213, 215, 233, 235–6; David Ditchburn and Andrew R. MacDonald, 'Mediaeval Scotland, 1100–1560' in Houston and Knox, 96–181 (162–4).

20. David H. Caldwell and Gordon Ewart, 'Finlaggan and the Lordship of the Isles: An Archaeological Approach', *Scottish Historical Review* (1993), 146–66 (146); Richard D. Oram, 'A Family Business? Colonisation and Settlement in twelfth- and thirteenth-century Galloway', *Scottish Historical Review* (1993), 111–45; Geoffrey Barrow, 'The Sources for the History of the Highlands in the Middle Ages', in Loraine Maclean of Dochgarroch (ed.), *The Middle Ages in the Highlands* (Inverness: Inverness Field Club, 1981), 11–22 (19); R.W. Munro, 'The Clan System – Fact or Fiction?', *ibid.*, 117–29 (117); Alexander Grant, 'Whither Scottish History? To the Medieval Foundations', *Scottish Historical Review* (1994), 4–24 (7, 12, 22); McNeill and MacQueen, 183; Barrow (1988), 2–5.

21. Michael Brown, '"Rejoice to hear of Douglas": The House of Douglas and the Presentation of Magnate Power in late Medieval Scotland', *Scottish Historical Review* (1997), 161–84 (184); Alexander Grant, 'The Revolt of the Lord of the Isles and the Death of the Earl of Douglas, 1451–1452', *Scottish Historical Review* 60 (1981), 169–74; Roberts, 64–5; Wormald, 203.

22. *The Book of Deer*, ed. John Stuart LLD (Edinburgh: Spalding Club, 1869), cxxvi; Macfarlane, 200; *Miscellany of the Spalding Club* Vol. II (Aberdeen: Spalding Club, 1842), xlviii; Grant (1981), 91, 93; Tim Thornton, 'Scotland and the Isle of Man, *c.* 1400–1625: Noble Power and Royal Presumption in the Northern Irish Sea Province', *Scottish Historical Review* (1998), 1–30 (14, 20); Donaldson (1974), 88; McNeill and MacQueen, 336–7; Lynch, 96, 98).

23. Macfarlane, xix, 201.

24. John MacInnes, 'Gaelic Poetry and Historical Tradition' in Maclean (1981), 142–63 (160); Barrow (1988), 177, 187; Barrow (1984), 7; Reid, 105.

25. The term 'defensive patriotism' is used by Alexander du Toit in his 2000 Ph.D. thesis on William Robertson (University of London). See also Barrow (1984), 18; Donaldson (1974), 50, 57; Magnusson, 188–9; Keith Brown, 'Reformation to Union, 1560–1707' in Houston and Knox, 182–275 (195); Houston and Knox, xx; Roger Mason, *Kingship and the Commonweal: Political Thought in Renaissance and Reformation Scotland* (East Linton: Tuckwell Press, 1998), 25, 86–7, 96; Edward J. Cowan, 'Identity, Freedom and the Declaration of Arbroath', in Dauvit Broun, R.J. Finlay and Michael Lynch (eds), *Image and Identity: The Making and Re-making of Scotland Through the Ages* (Edinburgh: John Donald, 1998), 38–68 (42, 44).

26. Bruce Webster, 'Anglo-Scottish Relations, 1296–1309: Some Recent Essays', *Scottish Historical Review* (1995), 99–108 (102, 105, 106–7); William Ferguson, *The Identity of the Scottish Nation* (Edinburgh: Edinburgh University Press, 1998), 87; Barrow (1984), 7; Roberts, 150–1; Mason, 44.

27. Dauvit Broun, *The Irish Identity of the Kingdom of the Scots in the Twelfth and Thirteenth Centuries* (Woodbridge: The Boydell Press, 1999), 1–12.

28. James Ritchie, *Some Antiquities of Aberdeenshire and its Borders* (Edinburgh, 1927), 157; *Registrum Episcopatus Aberdonensis* (Edinburgh, 1845), xxix; Roberts, 177, 179.

29. Barrow (1988), 321; Mason, 53.

30. Barrow (1988), 159–64, 171; Roberts, 128–9; Magnusson, 167–9.

31. Barrow (1988), 171, 173.

32. Barrow (1988), 172, 174, 176–7, 182, 190; Roberts, 134–5, 139; Magnusson, 174–5, 177.

33. Barrow (1988), 181, 182, 187, 191; (1984), 3; Roberts, 139; Magnusson, 177, 180; Grant (1981), 21.

34. Barrow (1988), 190, 193–6, 197, 198; (1984), 17; Roberts, 144–5; McDonald, 197–9.

35. Barrow (1988), 195, 207; McNeill and MacQueen, 98.

36. Barrow (1988), 209, 225; Magnusson, 182–5.

37. Barrow (1988), 226–7; McNeill and MacQueen, 98; Magnusson, 185–6; *Barbour's Bruce*, ed. Matthew P. MacDiarmid and James A.C. Stevenson, 3 vols (Edinburgh: Scottish Text Society, 1985), XIII:205 (vol. 3).

38. R.R. Davies, 'The People of Britain and Ireland 1100–1400: II Names, Boundaries and Regnal Solidarities', *Transactions of the Royal Historical Society* (1995), 1–20 (3); Barrow (1988), 198; Grant (1981), 13; Roberts, 149; McNeill and MacQueen, 100–1.

39. Barrow (1988), 316, 317, 322; Roberts, 145, 149; Aitchison, 132; McNeill and MacQueen, 99; McDonald, 186.

40. Aitchison, 35, 132; Barrow (1984), 20; Roberts, 154–5; Grant (1981), 17; Magnusson, 162, 192–3.

41. Geoffrey Barrow, *Kingship and Unity: Scotland 1000–1306* (London: Edward Arnold, 1981), 2; Grant (1981), 69, 73, 74, 87, 90, 201; McNeill and MacQueen, 238–9; Ditchburn and MacDonald in Houston and Knox, 98, 104, 106, 107, 113–16.

42. Grant (1981), 148; Barrow (1988), 9–10; Wormald, 143; McNeill and MacQueen, 239, 263; Ditchburn and MacDonald in Houston and Knox, 99, 113.

43. Lynch, 105–6; Duncan Macmillan, *Scottish Art 1460–1990* (Edinburgh: Mainstream, 1990), 24.

44. Bruce Webster, *Scotland from the Eleventh Century to 1603: Studies in the Use of Historical Evidence* (Cambridge: Cambridge University Press, 1975), 45; Murray G.H. Pittock, *Scottish Nationality* (Basingstoke and New York: Palgrave/Macmillan, 2001), 39; Wormald, 3; Magnusson, 129, 131; See also Macmillan, 15–17.

45. Carol Edington, *Court and Culture in Renaissance Scotland* (Amherst: University of Massachusetts Press, 1994), 97; William Watt, *History of Aberdeen and Banff* (County Histories of Scotland, Edinburgh and London, 1900), 115.

46. Magnusson, 282, 302.

47. *Council Register of Aberdeen 1398–1570*, xxi–xxiii, 166; Grant (1981), 61, 63; *Miscellany of the Spalding Club II*, 77–9; John Bulloch, *Aberdeen Three Hundred Years Ago* (Aberdeen, 1884), 20; Ditchburn and MacDonald in Houston and Knox, 101; Catherine Smith, 'Dogs, cats and horses in the Scottish medieval town', *Proceedings of the Society of Antiquaries of Scotland* 128 (1998), 859–85 (880); Scott Cooper, 'Ornamental structures in the medieval gardens of Scotland', *Proceedings of the Society of Antiquaries of Scotland* 129 (1999), 817–39 (821–2).

48. Grant (1981), 69; Wormald, 166; McNeill and MacQueen, 298–9, 312; Lynch, 173, 175.

49. Roberts, 150, 153; Magnusson, 196–9; Ditchburn and MacDonald in Houston and Knox, 173.

50. Alexander Stevenson, 'The Flemish Dimension of the Auld Alliance' in Grant G. Simpson (ed.), *Scotland and the Low Countries 1124–1994*, The Mackie Monographs no. 3 (East Linton: Tuckwell, 1996), 28–42 (38); Thornton, 3, 5; *Registrum Episcopatus Aberdonensis*, xxixn.

51. Roberts, 153–6; Grant (1981), 21–3, 39; Magnusson, 205; Aitchison, 133; Donaldson (1974), 66; Lynch, 130.

52. Grant (1981), 208–9; Barrow, cited by MacInnes in Maclean (1981), 144; Barrow in Maclean, 16; Jean Munro, 'The Lordship of the Isles' in Maclean (1981), 23–37 (27); *Council Register of Aberdeen 1398–1570*, 75; Wormald, 60–1.

53. Agnes Mure Mackenzie, *Scottish Pageant*, 4 vols (Edinburgh: Oliver and Boyd, 1946–50), I:235–6; Aitchison, 35; Grant (1981), 41, 43–5, 46–7, 55; Magnusson, 227–30; Lynch, 144.

54. Grant (1981), 48–9, 172, 190, 191; Magnusson, 238, 246; McNeill and MacQueen, 113; Lynch, 145.

55. Jean Munro in Maclean (1981), 31; Magnusson, 255; McNeill and MacQueen, 118.
56. David M. Head, 'Henry VIII's Scottish Policy: A Reassessment', *Scottish Historical Review* 61 (1982), 1–24 (3); Wormald, 5–6; Thornton, 19; Magnusson, 261–70; McNeill and MacQueen, 119; Grant (1981), 53.
57. Wormald, 6–7; Magnusson, 248, 279, 287; Lynch, 161.
58. Magnusson, 299; Head, 2–10; Marcus Merriman, *The Rough Wooing: Mary Queen of Scots, 1542–1551* (East Linton: Tuckwell Press, 2000), 167.
59. Wormald, 9; Head, 13–14, 16; Magnusson, 310–11; Lynch, 104; Merriman, 71.
60. Head, 17–19, 21; Magnusson, 308, 311, 321–33; Merriman, 113, 123–4, 135, 140, 154, 164, 167, 181–3, 209, 212, 237–8, 257–9, 262–3, 265, 272, 300, 355.

CHAPTER FOUR

1. David McRoberts (ed.), *Essays on the Scottish Reformation 1513–1625* (Glasgow: Burns, 1962), xiii; Michael Lynch, *Scotland: A New History* (London: Century, 1991), 186; Ian B. Cowan, *The Scottish Reformation: Church and Society in Sixteenth-Century Scotland* (London: Weidenfeld and Nicolson, 1982), 2, 7, 8, 11, 185, 188.
2. Anthony Ross, 'Some Notes on the Religious Orders in Pre-Reformation Scotland' in McRoberts, 185–244 (213, 220, 234); Lynch (1991), 186–7; Cowan, 71; Keith M. Brown, 'Reformation to Union, 1560 to 1707' in R.A. Houston and W.W. J. Knox (eds), *The Penguin History of Scotland* (London: Allen Lane/The Penguin Press, 2001), 182–275 (189–90).
3. McRoberts, xii, 417 ('Material Destruction Caused by the Scottish Reformation', 415–62); Cowan, 7–8, 195; Jenny Wormald, *Court, Kirk and Community: Scotland 1470–1625* (London: Edward Arnold, 1981), 167; Revd John Davidson DD, *Inverurie and the Earldom of the Garioch* (Edinburgh and Aberdeen, 1878), 142; Lynch (1991), 200.
4. Carol Edington, *Court and Culture in Renaissance Scotland* (Amherst: University of Massachusetts Press, 1994), 163; Ian Cowan, 72, 76–7, 90.
5. McRoberts, xvii–xviii; J.H. Burns, 'The Political Background of the Reformation, 1513–1625' in McRoberts (1962), 1–38 (11); Brother Kenneth, 'The Popular Literature of the Scottish Reformation' in

McRoberts, 169–84 (169); Lynch, 187–8, 204; Marcus Merriman, *The Rough Wooings: Mary Queen of Scots 1542–1551* (East Linton: Tuckwell Press, 2000), 209, 211 for Wishart's status.

6. Burns in McRoberts, 13, 16; Bruce McLennan, 'The Reformation in the Burgh of Aberdeen', *Northern Scotland* (1975), 119–44 (140); Magnus Magnusson, *Scotland: The Story of a Nation* (London: Hutchinson, 2000), 332; Cowan, 111.

7. McRoberts xix; Burn in McRoberts, 15; Cowan, 108, 162; Lynch (1991), 191; Magnusson, 336; Merriman, 71, 215; Brown in Houston and Knox, 182; Gordon Donaldson and Robert S. Morpeth, *A Dictionary of Scottish History* (Edinburgh: John Donald, 1977), 69; Tertullian, cited in Henry Bettenson (ed.), *The Early Christian Fathers* (Oxford: Oxford University Press, 1987 (1956)), 166.

8. Burn in McRoberts, 17; Gordon Donaldson, *Scottish Church History* (Edinburgh: Scottish Academic Press, 1985), 139–41; Lynch (1991), 196–7, 216, Magnusson, 335–8; Peter McNeill and Hector MacQueen, *An Atlas of Scottish History* (Edinburgh: University of Edinburgh, 1996) 129; Brown in Houston and Knox, 189–90; Cowan, 124.

9. Burn in McRoberts, 19–22; Gordon Donaldson, 'The Parish Clergy and the Reformation' in McRoberts, 129–44 (144); Ross in McRoberts, 412–13; William James Anderson, 'Rome and Scotland, 1513–1625', in McRoberts, 463 ff (463); Michael Lynch, 'Mary Stewart: Queen in Three Kingdoms', *Innes Review* 38 (1987), 1–29 (4); Lynch (1991), 212–19, 223; Magnusson, 360–1; Cowan, 140.

10. Burn in McRoberts, 22–6; Donaldson in McRoberts, 144; Michael Lynch, 'Queen Mary's Triumph', *Scottish Historical Review* (1990), 1–21; Lynch (1991), 218, 219, 223; Magnusson, 372.

11. McRoberts, xxiv–xxv; Anthony Ross in McRoberts, 185–244 (212); McRoberts, 417, 420, 436, 439, 442–5, 448–50, 451, 452, 455–9, 461; Cowan, 192.

12. McRoberts, 402, 404; Lynch, 199; McNeill and MacQueen, 382–3; Arthur Williamson, *Scottish National Consciousness in the Age of James VI* (Edinburgh: John Donald, 1979), 17.

13. McRoberts xxvi–xxvii; Matthew Mahoney, 'The Scottish Hierarchy, 1513–1565' in McRoberts, 39–84 (80, 82); Gordon Donaldson, 'The Parish Clergy and the Reformation' in McRoberts 129–44 (131); Anthony Ross, 'Reformation and Repression' in McRoberts, 371–414 (377–8); John McQuaid, 'Music and the Administration after 1560', *Innes Review* 3 (1952), 14–21 (15); Gordon Donaldson, *Reformed by Bishops* (Edinburgh: The Edina Press, 1987), x; Norman Davies, *The*

Isles (London: Macmillan, 1999), 464, 466; Donaldson (1985), 111, 141, 144, 170, 175, 177, 206, 267; Lynch (1991), 199; Cowan, 183.

14. Wormald, 134, 139; Ian Cowan, 183.

15. Fenton Wyness, *Spots from the Leopard: Short Stories of Aberdeen and the North-East* (Aberdeen: Impulse Books, 1971), 23, 44; Leslie J. Macfarlane, 'St Machar's Cathedral Through the Ages' in John S. Smith (ed.), *Old Aberdeen* (Aberdeen, 1991), 14–37 (20); *Fasti Aberdonienses* (Aberdeen: Spalding Club, 1854), xxvi–xxviii; McLennan, 128, 133, 137–40; *Registrum Episcopatus Aberdonensis* (Edinburgh, 1845), lxvi; *Selections from the Records of the Kirk Session, Presbytery and Synod of Aberdeen* (Aberdeen: Spalding Club, 1846), 22, 52; 'Homage to Schir John Blak: Maister of the Sang Schuill of Saint Nicholace Paroche Kirk', City of Aberdeen Archives AL12; Henry George Farmer, *Music Making in the Olden Days: The Story of the Aberdeen Concerts 1748–1801* (London, 1950), 10; John Durkan, 'Early Humanism and King's College', *Aberdeen University Review* 163 (1980), 259–79 (271–2); Cowan, 185.

16. McRoberts, xxii–xxiv, xxviii–xxix; John Kerr, *Scottish Education: School and University* (Cambridge: Cambridge University Press, 1910), 39; Cowan, 174, 180; Murray G.H. Pittock, 'From Edinburgh to London: Scottish Court Culture and 1603' in Eveline Cruickshanks (ed.), *The Stuart Courts* (Stroud: Sutton, 2000), 13–28; Donaldson and Morpeth, 140, 184.

17. Cowan, 168–9, 173–4, 183; Burn in McRoberts, 33–4, Donaldson, *idem*, 144; Ross, *idem*, 406; Davidson (1878), 320, 423; *Miscellany of the Spalding Club* I (Aberdeen: Spalding Club, 1841), 151–2; Revd David McRoberts, 'Provost Skene's House in Aberdeen and its Catholic Chapel', *Innes Review* 5 (1954), 119–24; Wormald, 134; Ian Bryce and Alasdair Roberts, 'Post-Reformation Catholic symbolism: further and different examples', *Proceedings of the Society of Antiquaries of Scotland* 126 (1996), 899–909 (899).

18. Cowan, 187–90; *Spalding Miscellany* I:49–55; *Kirk Session*, 33, 84; Ross in McRoberts, 397; Kerr (1910), 181; Revd Robert Wodrow, *Collection upon the Lives of the Reformers and Most Eminent Ministers of the Church of Scotland*, 2 vols (Glasgow: Maitland Club, 1834), 165.

19. *Extracts from the Council Register of the Burgh of Aberdeen 1398–1570*, 459; *Kirk Session*, xxvii, lxix, 8, 13, 29; Ian Cowan, 194–5.

20. John Durkan, 'Education in the Century of the Reformation' in McRoberts, 145–68 (154); Julia Buckroyd, *The Life of James Sharp* (Edinburgh: John Donald, 1987), 8; Ian Cowan, 197–9; Kerr, 76–7,

181; H.M. Knox, *Two Hundred and Fifty Years of Scottish Education 1696–1946* (Edinburgh: Oliver and Boyd, 1953), 3, 5.

21. *Fasti Aberdonenses*, xliv–xlv; David Stevenson, *King's College, Aberdeen, 1560–1641: From Protestant Reformation to Covenanting Revolution* (Aberdeen, 1990), 106; Murray G.H. Pittock, *Scottish Nationality* (Basingstoke: Palgrave/Macmillan, 2001), 44; Donaldson and Morpeth, 204.

CHAPTER FIVE

1. Murray G.H. Pittock, 'From Edinburgh to London: Scottish Court Writing and 1603' in Eveline Cruickshanks (ed.), *The Stuart Courts* (Stroud: Sutton, 2000), 13–25; M.A. Bald, 'The Anglicisation of Scottish Printing', *Scottish Historical Review* 23 (1926), 107–15 and 'Contemporary References to the Scottish Speech of the Sixteenth Century', *Scottish Historical Review* 25 (1928), 163–79; Allan Macinnes, 'Politically Reactionary Brits? The Promotion of Anglo-Scottish Union, 1603–1707' in S.J. Connolly (ed.), *Kingdoms United? Great Britain and Ireland since 1500* (Dublin: Four Courts Press, 1999), 43–55 (43); Jeremy Black and Donald M. MacRaild, *Studying History*, 2nd edn (Basingstoke: Macmillan, 2000 (1997)), 163.

2. J.H. Burns, 'The Political Background of the Reformation, 1513–1625' in David McRoberts, *The Scottish Reformation, 1513–1625* (Edinurgh: Oliver and Boyd, 1962), 1–38 (28–31); Magnus Magnusson, *Scotland: The Story of a Nation* (London: HarperCollins, 2000), 372–5, 387; Michael Lynch, *Scotland: A New History* (London: Century, 1991), 222; Peter McNeill and Hector MacQueen, *Atlas of Scottish History to 1707* (Edinburgh: University of Edinburgh, 1996), 221; Keith M. Brown, 'Reformation to Union, 1560–1707' in R.A. Houston and W.W.J. Knox (eds), *The Penguin History of Scotland* (London: Penguin, 2001), 182–275 (196).

3. Jennifer Wormald, *Court, Kirk and Community: Scotland 1470–1625* (London: Edward Arnold, 1981), 156; Magnusson, 375–81, 391–2.

4. Wormald (1981), 166; A.J.S. Gibson and T.C. Smout, *Prices, Food and Wages in Scotland 1550–1780* (Cambridge: Cambridge University Press, 1995), 8; Brown in Houston and Knox, 199; T.M. Devine, *The Scottish Nation, 1700–2000* (London: Penguin, 2000), xx.

5. Aberdeen City Archives, Kennedy Index I: 301/XXXVII; T.F. Henderson, *James I and VI* (Paris and Edinburgh, 1904), 13, 301; R.D.S. Jack, *Alexander Montgomerie* (Edinburgh: Scottish Academic Press, 1985),

11; Maurice Lee, Jr, 'King James's Popish Chancellor', in Ian Cowan and Duncan Shaw (eds), *The Renaissance and Reformation in Scotland: Essays in honour of Gordon Donaldson* (Edinburgh: Scottish Academic Press, 1983), 170–82 (174).

6. Henry George Farmer, *A History of Music in Scotland* (London: Hinrichsen edition, n.d.); R.D.S. Jack (ed.), *A Choice of Scottish Verse 1560–1660* (London: Hodder & Stoughton, 1978), 12; R.D.S. Jack (1985) 2, 126; R.D.S. Jack and Kevin McGinley (eds), *Of Lion and of Unicorn: Essays on Anglo-Scottish Literary Relations in Honour of Professor John MacQueen* (Edinburgh: Quadriga, 1993), 85; Wormald (1981), 186, 193; Duncan Shaw, 'Adam Bothwell: A Conserver of the Renaissance in Scotland' in Cowan and Shaw (1983), 141–69 (143); W. Douglas Simpson, *The Earldom of Mar* (Aberdeen, 1959), 94 ff; Bald (1926, 1928).

7. Lee in Cowan and Shaw, 170–82 (175); Magnusson, 397–9; Lynch, 234–6.

8. R.D.S. Jack (ed.), *The History of Scottish Literature Volume I: Origins to 1660* (Aberdeen: Aberdeen University Press, 1988), 3; Keith Brown, 'Scottish identity in the seventeenth century' in Brendan Bradshaw and Peter Roberts (eds), *British Consciousness and Identity: The making of Britain, 1533–1707* (Cambridge: Cambridge University Press, 1998), 236–58 (253); Michael J. Enright, 'King James and his island: an archaic kingship belief', *Scottish Historical Review* 55 (1976), 29–40 (32).

9. Macinnes (1999), 44; Tim Thornton, 'Scotland and the Isle of Man, c. 1400–1625: Noble Power and Royal Presumption in the Northern Irish Sea Province', *Scottish Historical Review* (1998), 1–30 (29); Norman Davies, *The Isles* (London: Macmillan, 1999), 555–6; Agnes Mure Mackenzie, *Scottish Pageant* (Edinburgh and London: Oliver and Boyd, 1946–50), III: 8; Miles Glendinning, Aonghaus MacKechnie and Ranald MacInnes, *A History of Scottish Architecture* (Edinburgh: Edinburgh University Press, 1996), 75; Jenny Wormald, 'James VI and I: Two Kings or One?', *History* LXVIII (1983), 187–209 (190); Wormald (1981), 192; Lynch, 237–9; Murray G.H. Pittock, *Scottish Nationality* (Basingstoke: Palgrave, 2001), 47; Magnusson, 401–3.

10. Julian Goodare, 'The Statutes of Iona in Context', *Scottish Historical Review* (1998), 31–57 (31–33, 39, 50); Brown in Houston and Knox, 237; Michael Fry, *The Scottish Empire* (East Linton and Edinburgh: Tuckwell and Birlinn, 2001), 10.

11. Allan I. Macinnes, *Clanship, Commerce and the House of Stuart, 1603–1788* (East Linton: John Tuckwell, 1996), 89, 94.

12. Wormald, (1981), 207; Lynch, 242; McNeill and MacQueen, 154–5; Fry, xxi, 21, 34.

13. Brown, 237; Mackenzie III:9, 244; Brown in Houston and Knox, 205.

14. *Passages from the Diary of General Patrick Gordon of Auchleuchries AD 1635–AD 1699* (Aberdeen: Spalding Club, 1859), xxiii–xxiv; Jonas Berg and Bo Lagercrantz, *Scots in Sweden* (Stockholm: The Nordiska Museet, Swedish Institute, 1962), 7, 13, 45; Patrick Mileham, *The Scottish Regiments 1633–1996* (Staplehurst, 1996 (1988)), 10, 22, 42, 66.

15. Magnusson, 422; Lynch, 268.

16. *Antiquities of Aberdeen and Banff II* (Aberdeen: Spalding Club, 1847), 373; Magnusson, 422–3.

17. Macinnes (1999), 47; Lynch, 264.

18. Magnusson, 424–5; *Extracts from the Council Register of the Burgh of Aberdeen 1625–1642* (Edinburgh: Scottish Burgh Records Society, 1871), 128, 133–4.

19. Magnusson, 427–33.

20. Macinnes (1999), 47–9; Magnusson, 433.

21. Gordon Donaldson, *Scottish Church History* (Edinburgh: Scottish Academic Press, 1985), 213, 217, 234–5; Magnusson, 435–49, 461; Lynch, 276–9; Brown in Houston and Knox, 250–1.

22. Macinnes (1999), 50; Davies (1999), 592, 595, 596; Magnusson, 470–2; Lynch, 280; Brown in Houston and Knox, 252; Fry, 23.

23. Davies (1999), 598; Lynch, 288; Brown (1998), 237n; Pittock (2001), 51; Magnusson, 472–3; Gordon Donaldson and Robert S. Morpeth (eds), *A Dictionary of Scottish History* (Edinburgh: John Donald, 1977), 153.

24. Allan I. Macinnes, 'Repression and Conciliation: The Highland Dimension, 1660–1688', *Scottish Historical Review* (1986), 167–95 (189, 193); Magnusson, 478; Brown in Houston and Knox, 254.

25. Hon. G.A. Sinclair, 'The Scottish Progress of James VI', *Scottish Historical Review* 10 (1913), 21–28 (21); Magnusson, 485, 492–9; Lynch, 295; Brown in Houston and Knox, 213–14.

26. Macinnes (1986), 185; Macinnes (1996), 140; Macinnes (1999), 50–2; Lynch, 291–5; Brown in Houston and Knox, 205.

27. Murray G.H. Pittock, *Jacobitism* (Basingstoke: Macmillan, 1998), 15–16; Magnusson, 502.

28. Zwicker, 88; Pittock (1998), 15–22.

29. Cf. Sinclair (1913), 23; Steven N. Zwicker, 'The Paradoxes of Tender Conscience', *English Literary History* (1996), 851–69 (855).

30. Mark Dilworth, 'Jesuits and Jacobites: the *cultus* of St Margaret', *Innes Review* (1996), 169–80 (178, 180); *Passages from the Diary of General Patrick Gordon*, 39.

31. National Archives of Scotland GD 95/11/11(2); NAS RH15/105/3; NAS RH 15/201/18; Scottish Catholic Archives BL3/293/11; Lynch, 304; *Inverurie and the Garioch*, 423; Revd John Pratt, *Buchan* (Aberdeen, Edinburgh and London, 1858), 85; Watt, *History of Aberdeen and Banff* (Edinburgh and London: County Histories of Scotland, 1900), 276; *Miscellany of the Spalding Club* I: 57; G.D. Henderson (ed.), *Mystics of the North East* (Aberdeen: Third Spalding Club, 1934); Macinnes (1996), 176.

32. Pittock (1998), 29; Christopher A. Whatley, *Scottish Society 1707–1830* (Manchester: Manchester University Press, 2000), 1, 25, 29; Jeremy Black, *Eighteenth-Century Britain 1688–1783* (Basingstoke: Macmillan, 2001), 77; Lynch, 309; Fry, 26–9; Devine, 25.

33. Whatley, 1, 6, 17–18, 23, 37; Pittock (1998), 24; Bruce Lenman, 'From the Union of 1707 to the Franchise Reform of 1832' in Houston and Knox, 276–354 (280, 285); Devine, xxii; Brown in Houston and Knox, 206–7.

34. Macinnes (1999), 52–4; McNeill and MacQueen, 152; Lynch, 319; Mackenzie III: 329; Daniel Szechi (ed.), *Scotland's Ruine?: Lockhart of Carnwath's Memoirs of the Union* (Aberdeen: Association for Scottish Literary Studies, 1995), xvii, 148–9, 160, 177–9; P.W.J. Riley, *The Union of England and Scotland* (Manchester: Manchester University Press, 1978), 283, 285, 304; John S. Gibson, *Playing the Scottish Card: The Jacobite Rising of 1708* (Edinburgh: Edinburgh University Press, 1988), 74; Whatley, 55; Fry, 29–30; Donaldson and Morpeth, 93.

35. Black, 209; Whatley, 54; Gordon Donaldson (ed.), *Scottish Historical Documents* (Edinburgh: Scottish Academic Press, 1974); Donaldson (1985), 237–8; Lynch, 321; Athol L. Murray, 'The Scottish Mint after the recoinage, 1709–1836', *Proceedings of the Society of Antiquaries of Scotland* 129 (1999), 861–86 (861); Devine, 69.

36. Mackenzie IV: 189; Lynch, 320, 323; Gibson and Smout (1995), 365; Whatley, 57; Pittock (1998), 35; Patricia Dickson, *Red John of the Battles* (London, 1973), 157–9; Devine, 22.

37. Gibson (1988), 93–4; Pittock (1998), 32–3; Daniel Szechi, *The Jacobites* (Manchester: Manchester University Press, 1994). I believe that Professor Szechi will strongly endorse this account of Scottish networking in his forthcoming book on the Rising of 1715.

38. Lynch, 327; Pittock (1998), 38–9, 48.

39. Alistair and Henrietta Tayler, *1715: the Story of the Rising* (Edinburgh and London, 1936), 311, 313; Pittock (1998), 36–46.
40. Mackenzie IV: 172, 175–6.
41. Whatley, 59–61, 142, 155, 157, 162–4, 184; Jacob M. Price, 'Glasgow, the Tobacco Trade, and the Scottish Customs, 1707–1730', *Scottish Historical Review* 63 (1984), 1–36 (1); Lynch, 331; Brown in Houston and Knox, 203; Lenman in Houston and Knox, 290–1; Devine, 142, 147–50.
42. Pittock (1998), 93–4; Lynch (1991) 332; Whatley, 152, 160.
43. Pittock (1998), 97–118; Michael Hook and Walter Ross, *The 'Forty-Five* (Edinburgh: HMSO, 1995), 26.
44. Alastair Livingstone of Bachuil, Christian Aikman and Betty Stuart Hart, *Muster Roll of Prince Charles Edward Stuart's Army 1745–46* (Aberdeen: Aberdeen University Press, 1984).
45. Macinnes (1996), 211–12, 217; Bruce Lenman, *Integration, Enlightenment and Industrialisation: Scotland 1746–1832* (London: Edward Arnold, 1981), 65–6; James Michael Hill, *Celtic Warfare 1595–1763* (Edinburgh: John Donald, 1986), 168.
46. Mackenzie IV: 185; *The Life and Works of Dr Arbuthnot*, ed. George A. Aitken (Oxford: Clarendon Press, 1892), 396–408.
47. Whatley, 1; Black, 97–8; Brown in Houston and Knox, 210.
48. *Spalding Miscellany* II, (Aberdeen: Spalding Club, 1842), 96; Black, 38–9; Whatley, 68, 70, 72, 219; R.J. Brien, *The Shaping of Scotland: Eighteenth Century Patterns of Land Use and Settlement* (Aberdeen: Aberdeen University Press, 1989), 11, 22.
49. Lenman (1981), 45–6; Brien (1989), 4–5, 8–9; Lynch, 383.
50. *Spalding Miscellany* II: 97, 100; Whatley, 60–1, 66, 112, 220–1; Lenman (1981), 40, 43, 46; G.J. Bryant, 'Scots in India in the Eighteenth Century', *Scottish Historical Review* (1985), 22–41 (23, 27, 33); Fry, 25; Devine, 26.
51. Mackenzie IV: 284; *Spalding Miscellany* II: 99; Macinnes (1996), 226; Black, 39, 76–7.
52. Gibson and Smout (1995) 167, 275–9.
53. Whatley, 75, 96, 99, 101–2, 118; Paul Langford, *Public Life and the Propertied Englishman* (Oxford: Clarendon Press, 1991).
54. *Spalding Miscellany* II: x, xi, 100; Black, 163.
55. Lynch, 353; Glendinning, MacInnes and MacKechnie (1996), 102, 106, 170; Alexander Murdoch, 'The Importance of being Edinburgh: Management and Opposition in Edinburgh Politics, 1746–1784', *Scottish Historical Review* 62 (1983), 1–16 (3); Whatley, 226.

56. John and Muriel Lough, 'Aberdeen Circulating Libraries in the Eighteenth Century', *Aberdeen University Review* XXXI (1944–6), 17–23 (18); John Laird, 'George Dalgarno', *Aberdeen University Review* XXIII (1935–6), 15–31 (19); Alexander Broadie, *The Scottish Enlightenment* (Edinburgh: Birlinn Books, 2001), 10–11; Aberdeen City Archives Mi 21/I; Whatley (2000), 124; H. Lewis Ulman, *The Minutes of the Aberdeen Philosophical Society* (Aberdeen: Aberdeen University Press, 1990), 15, 20; Lynch, 350.
57. National Library of Scotland MS 17505 f. 65.

CHAPTER SIX

1. Murray G.H. Pittock, 'Historiography' in Alexander Broadie (ed.), *The Cambridge Companion to the Scottish Enlightenment*, forthcoming.
2. R.A. Houston and W.W.J. Knox, *The Penguin History of Scotland* (London: Penguin, 2001), xxxi; William R. and C. Helen Brock, *Scotus Americanus* (Edinburgh: Edinburgh University Press, 1982), 13, 92–3, 113, 127; Michael Fry, *The Scottish Empire* (East Linton and Edinburgh: Tuckwell and Birlinn, 2001), 59; Gordon Donaldson and Robert S. Morpeth, *A Dictionary of Scottish History* (Edinburgh: John Donald, 1977), 229; Lewis Ulman (ed.), *Minutes of the Aberdeen Philosophical Society* (Aberdeen: Aberdeen University Press, 1990), 12.
3. A.J. Youngson, *The Making of Classical Edinburgh* (Edinburgh: Edinburgh University Press, 1988 (1966), 1–10; Alexander Broadie, *The Scottish Enlightenment* (Edinburgh: Birlinn Books, 2001); Richard B. Sher, *Church and University in the Scottish Enlightenment* (Edinburgh: Edinburgh University Press, 1985), 3; Ulman, 20; Sydney and Olive Checkland, *Industry and Ethos: Scotland 1832–1914*, 2nd edn (London: Edward Arnold, 1997 (1984)), 153; T.M. Devine, *The Scottish Nation 1700–2000* (London: Penguin, 1999), 333; for Scottish casualty figures in Seven Years' War see James Michael Hill, *Celtic Warfare* (Edinburgh: John Donald, 1986); Bruce Lenman, *Integration, Enlightenment and Industrialisation: Scotland 1746–1832* (London: Edward Arnold, 1981), 30, 40, 46, 65–6; John Dwyer and Alexander Murdoch, 'Paradigms and Politics: Manners, Morals and the Rise of Henry Dundas, 1770–84' in John Dwyer, Roger Mason and Alexander Murdoch (eds), *New Perspectives on the Politics and Culture of Early Modern Scotland* (Edinburgh: John Donald, n.d. [1983]), 210–48 (217).
4. Ulman, 15; Marinell Ash, *The Strange Death of Scottish History* (Edinburgh: Ramsay Head Press, 1980), 34, 149; Henry George

Farmer, *Music Making in the Olden Days: The Story of the Aberdeen Concerts 1748–1801* (London, 1950), 1, 13, 57 and *passim*; Graeme Morton, *Unionist-Nationalism: Governing Urban Scotland 1830–1860* (East Linton: Tuckwell Press, 1999), 176; Murray G.H. Pittock, *Scottish Nationality* (Basingstoke: Palgrave, 2001), 75–6.

5. David Allan, 'Protestantism, presbyterianism and national identity in eighteenth-century Scottish history' in Tony Claydon and Ian McBride (eds), *Protestantism and National Identity: Britain and Ireland* c. 1650–c. 1850 (Cambridge: Cambridge University Press, 1998), 182–205; Eric Duncan, 'James Ramsay 1733–1789 – Abolitionist', *Aberdeen University Review* 182 (1989), 127–35 (129); Pittock (2001), 73; Anand Chitnis, *The Social Origins of the Scottish Enlightenment* (Edinburgh: Edinburgh University Press, 1986), 66, 70; Lenman (1981), 88, 89, 93, 95; Fry, 77.

6. W.H.G. Armytage, 'David Fordyce: A Neglected Thinker', *Aberdeen University Review* XXXVI (1955–6), 289–91 (290); John Kerr, *Scottish Education: School and University* (Cambridge: Cambridge University Press, 1910), 174, 179, 209, 264; Donaldson and Morpeth, 75, 85, 149; Houston and Knox, xlv, xlvi.

7. John McCaffrey, 'Thomas Chalmers and Social Change', *Scottish Historical Review* 60 (1981), 32–60 (46–8); McCaffrey, *Scotland in the Nineteenth Century* (Basingstoke: Macmillan, 1998), 23; T.C. Smout, *A Century of the Scottish People 1830–1950* (London: Collins, 1986), 220; Checklands (1997), 75, 112, 114, 122, 123, 126–7, 205; Kerr, 211; Devine, 285–6; Fry, 23.

8. Christopher Whatley, *Scottish Society 1707–1830: Beyond Jacobitism, towards industrialisation* (Manchester: Manchester University Press, 2000), 228; Joyce M. Ellis, *The Georgian Town 1680–1840* (Basingstoke: Palgrave, 2001), 148–50; McCaffrey (1998), 3; Brock, 91; Donaldson and Morpeth, 18, 163; Devine, 62, 161, 249, 329; Houston and Knox, xlvi; Bruce Lenman, 'From the Union of 1707 to the Franchise Reform of 1832' in Houston and Knox, 276–334 (287–9).

9. David Wootton, annual lecture, British Society for Eighteenth-Century Studies Conference, 4 January 2002; Lenman (1981), 85; Checklands (1997), 5.

10. Checklands (1997), 31, 106, 146–9; Donaldson and Morpeth, 13, 18.

11. R.H. Campbell, 'Scotland' in R.A. Cage (ed.), *The Scots Abroad* (London: Croom Helm, 1985), 1–28 (20–1); Checklands (1997), 13, 16, 20–2, 27, 173; Fry, xxiv; Devine, 249–51.

12. Maisie Steven, *Parish Life in Eighteenth-Century Scotland: A Review of the Old Statistical Account* (Aberdeen, 1995), 75; Malcolm Gray, 'The Processes of Agricultural Change in the North-East, 1790–1870' in Leah Leneman (ed.), *Perspectives in Scottish Social History: essays in honour of Rosalind Mitchison* (Aberdeen: Aberdeen University Press, 1988), 125–40; Devine, 166, 264, 334, 337–8, 340.

13. Robert Burns, *Poems and Songs*, ed. James Kinsley, (Oxford: Oxford University Press, 1992 (1969)), 102; Keith Robbins, *Nineteenth-Century Britain: Integration and Diversity* (Oxford: Clarendon Press, 1988), 38.

14. Katherine Haldane, 'Imagining Scotland: Tourist Images of Scotland, 1770–1914', unpublished Ph.D. (University of Virginia, 1990), 6, 283, 292–3; Murray G.H. Pittock, *The Invention of Scotland: The Stuart Myth and the Scottish Identity 1638 to the Present* (London: Routledge, 1991), chs 3 and 4.

15. Lenman (1981), 102, 132; Sydney and Olive Checkland, *Industry and Ethos: Scotland 1832–1914* (London: Edward Arnold, 1984), 7, 138; John Prebble, *The King's Jaunt* (London: Collins, 1988); Haldane, 30 ff.; Angela Morris and Graeme Morton, *Locality, Community and Nation* (London: Hodder & Stoughton, 1998), 12–13, 23–5, 31; Norman Davies, *The Isles* (London: Macmillan, 1999), 865–6; Ash (1980).

16. Pittock (1991), ch. 5

17. Checklands (1997), 142; Duncan Macmillan, *Scottish Art 1460–1990* (Edinburgh: Mainstream, 1990), 114, 118, 150, 165; McCaffrey (1998), 117; Devine, 358, 361.

18. Lenman (1981), 80–3; Morton (1999), 11; Checklands (1997), 159; Devine, 198; Fry, 326 pl. 67.

19. Robbins (1988), 175; Fry.

20. Checklands (1997), 162; Donaldson and Morpeth, 29, 34, 136; Fry, xxii–xxv, 31, 108, 197–8, 326 pls 61 and 73, 390 pl. 95; Brock, 68; Houston and Knox, xxxii; Graeme Morton and Angela Morris, 'Civil Society, Governance and the Nation, 1832–1914' in Houston and Knox, 355–416 (362); *Scotland & Africa* (Edinburgh: National Library of Scotland, 1982), 6–8; Malcolm D. Prentis, *The Scots in Australia* (Sydney: Sydney University Press, 1983), 47, 198, 205.

21. David S. Macmillan, 'Scottish Enterprise and Influences in Canada, 1620–1900' in Cage, 46–79 (57, 66); Tom Brooking, 'Tom McCanny and Kitty Clydeside – The Scots in New Zealand' in Cage 156–90 (172); James G. Parker, 'Scottish Enterprise in India, 1750–1914' in Cage, 191–219 (193); Checklands (1997), 45; Devine, 474; Fry, 390

pl. 89; John Foster, 'The Twentieth Century, 1914–1979' in Houston and Knox, 417–93 (420).

22. Manuel A. Fernandes, 'The Scots in Latin America: A Survey' in Cage, 220–50 (225–6); Checklands (1984), 166; Donaldson and Morpeth, 64.

23. Lenman (1981), 45–6; Checklands (1997), 56; Eric Richards, *A History of the Highland Clearances*, 2 vols (London, 1985), II: 181, 184–5, 186.

24. Richards, II: 45–6, 68, 239; Iain Fraser Grigor, *Mightier than a Lord* (Stornoway, 1979), 14, 21, 33; Whatley, 254, 293; T.M. Devine, 'Highland Migration to Lowland Scotland, 1760–1860', *Scottish Historical Review* 62 (1983), 137–49 (140, 143–4, 148); R.H. Campbell, 'Scotland' in Cage, 1–28 (10); Malcolm MacLean and Christopher Carrell, *As an Fhearann* (Glasgow, 1986), 21, 39; Cage, 'The Scots in England' in Cage, 29–45 (33, 42); Olive Checkland, 'The Scots in Meiji Japan' in Cage 251–74 (260); Checklands (1997), 61, 64; McCaffrey (1998), 12–13; Devine, 283, 299, 301, 427, 435; Lenman in Houston and Knox, 293–4; Morton and Morris in Houston and Knox, 376.

25. Ellis, 42, 45, 111; Whatley, 220–1; David W. Summers, *Fishing off the Knuckle: The Fishing Villages of Buchan* (Aberdeen, 1988), 2, 6, 46, 49; Campbell in Cage 1–28 (9, 11); Elaine McFarland, *Protestants First* (Edinburgh: Edinburgh University Press, 1990); Checklands (1997), 28–9, 41; Devine, 163.

26. Whatley, 290, 302–3; Pittock (2001), 88–90; James D. Young, *The Very Bastards of Creation: Scottish International Radicalism 1707–1995: A Biographical Study* (Glasgow: Clydeside Press, n.d.), 39; Morton, 191–2; Devine, 205; McCaffrey (1998), 22.

27. Pittock (2001), 90–1; Peter Berresford Ellis and Seamus MacGhiobhainn, *The Scottish Insurrection of 1820* (London: Gollancz, 1967); Colin Kidd, *Subverting Scotland's Past* (Cambridge: Cambridge University Press, 1993); Frank Andrew Sherry, *The Rising of 1820* (Glasgow, n.d.), 15–19; Devine (1999).

28. Morton, 12, 21, 68, 79–81, 116, 135–9, 140, 146–8, 149–53, 155, 176–7, 181, 196; George Davie, *The Democratic Intellect* (Edinburgh: Edinburgh University Press, 1961); Pittock (2001), 93–102; Keith Webb, *The Growth of Nationalism in Scotland* (Glasgow: Molendinar Press, 1977), 40; Checklands (1997), 71, 79–80; Checklands (1984), 166; Michael Fry, *Patronage and Principle* (Aberdeen: Aberdeen University Press, 1987), 82, 102, 105, 128, 206; *The Scottish*

Parliament: factfile 2; Richard J. Finlay, 'Unionism and the Dependency Culture', in Catriona M.M. MacDonald (ed.), *Unionist Scotland 1800–1997* (Edinburgh: John Donald, 1998), 100–16 (101–2); McCaffrey (1998), 26–7, 36, 42–3, 68, 125; Devine, 229, 289, 397, 401, 538.

CHAPTER SEVEN

1. Murray G.H. Pittock, *Scottish Nationality* (Basingstoke: Macmillan, 2001), 103; Christopher Harvie, *No Gods and Precious Few Heroes: Scotland 1914–1980* (London: Edward Arnold, 1981), 24; Michael Lynch, *Scotland: A New History* (London: Century, 1991), 422, 424–5.

2. William L. Miller, *The End of British Politics?* (Oxford: Oxford University Press, 1981), 14; Harvie (1981), 17, 22, 24; James Mitchell, *Strategies for Self-government: The Campaigns for a Scottish Parliament* (Edinburgh: Polygon, 1996), 74; Douglas Young, *The Treaty of Union Between Scotland and England 1707* (Perth: Tannahill & Methven, 1955), 27–8; T.M. Devine, *The Scottish Nation 1700–2000* (London: Penguin, 1999), 309.

3. Keith Webb, *The Growth of Nationalism in Scotland* (Glasgow: Molendinar Press, 1977), 45; Lynch, 428, 429, 433; Harvie (1981), 32, 94; Mitchell, 79; Devine, 302, 313.

4. H.J. Hanham, *Scottish Nationalism* (London: Faber, 1969), 133; Richard Finlay, *Independent and Free: Scottish Politics and the Origins of the Scottish National Party 1918–1945* (Edinburgh: John Donald, 1994), 30; Ian Paterson, 'The Activities of Irish Republican Physical Force Organisations in Scotland, 1919–21', *Scottish Historical Review* (1993), 39–59; Harvie (1981), 99; Mitchell, 81–4, 177, 181–9; Francis Russell Hart and J.B. Pick, *Neil M. Gunn: A Highland Life* (London: Murray, 1981), 108; *The Scots Independent* II: 2, 169; II: 9, 129, 131–2.

5. Harvie (1981), 99; Mitchell, 115, 122, 182–4, 186–7; Alan Bold, *Hugh MacDiarmid* (London: Murray, 1988), 228; *Scots Independent* IV, 100.

6. Lynch (1991), 435; Richard Finlay, 'Unionism and the Dependency Culture', in Catriona MacDonald (ed.), *Unionist Scotland 1800–1997* (Edinburgh: John Donald, 1998), 100–16 (105); Christopher Harvie, *Scotland and Nationalism* (London: Allen and Unwin, 1977), 51; Mitchell, 44–5, 307, 309, 311, 313; Miller (1981), 10; *The Scottish Parliament: factfile* 2; Devine, 319, 552–3; John Foster, 'The Twentieth

Century, 1914–1979' in R.A. Houston and W.W. J. Knox (eds), *The Penguin History of Scotland* (London: Penguin, 2001), 417–93 (453); Gordon Donaldson and Robert S. Morpeth, *A Dictionary of Scottish History* (Edinburgh: John Donald, 1977), 110; Ian G.C. Hutchinson, 'Government', in T.M. Devine and R.J. Finlay (eds), *Scotland in the 20th Century* (Edinburgh: Edinburgh University Press, 1996), 46–63 (49); also Roderick Watson, 'Maps of Desire: Scottish Literature in the Twentieth Century', *idem*, 285 ff.

7. Mitchell, 85, 309; Douglas Young, *An Appeal to Scots Honour* (Glasgow: The Scottish secretariat, 1944), 2; Devine, 557.

8. Harvie (1981), 107; Mitchell, 144–8.

9. Mitchell, 192–200, 260–8; Andrew Murray Scott and Ian Macleay, *Britain's Secret War: Tartan Terrorism and the Anglo-American State* (Edinburgh: Mainstream, 1990); T.M. Devine, 'Introduction' in Devine and Finlay, 1–12 (7).

10. Miller, 10; Lynch, 443–4; Devine in Devine and Finlay, 6; Ewan A. Cameron, 'The Scottish Highlands: From Congested District to Objective One' in Devine and Finlay, 153–69 (163).

11. Harvie (1981), 82; Mitchell, 35–8, 199, 315; *Scots Independent* II, 1; 18 November 1967, 1; 2 March 1968, 8; 13 April 1968, 5; 11 May 1968, 8; 15 June; 20 July; 17 May 1969; Miller, 33, 55; Gordon Brown (ed.), *The Red Paper on Scotland* (Edinburgh, 1975), 7–21; Lynch, 445; James Mitchell, 'Scotland in the Union, 1945–95: The Changing Nature of the Union State' in Devine and Finlay, 85–101 (95).

12. Mitchell, 100–1, 209, 318; Harvie (1981), 161; Lynch, 447; Devine, 576; Callum G. Brown, 'Popular Culture and the Contemporary Struggle for Rational Recreation' in Devine and Finlay, 210–29 (218).

13. Christopher Harvie, *No Gods and Precious Few Heroes*, 3rd edn (Edinburgh: Edinburgh University Press, 1998).

14. Mitchell, 47.

15. Mitchell, 312–16; Harvie (1981), 165; Webb (1977), 75, 81, 86, 95.

16. Mitchell, 152–8, 271–7; Devine, 611; Foster in Houston and Knox, 478.

17. *The Economist* (6–12 November 1999), 'Undoing Britain' survey, 4.

18. *Scottish Parliament factfile 2*; Mitchell, 47–8, 122, 127, 128, 131, 133, 297–8; *Sunday Herald election 99*, 4 April 1999, 1, 11.

19. Harvie (1998).

20. Harvie (1981), vii; Lynch, 423–4; Ewan A. Cameron in Devine and Finlay, 162.

21. Lynch, 423, 439.

22. Harvie (1981), 1; Hutchinson in Devine and Finlay, 49, 53; Peter L. Payne, 'The Economy', *idem*, 13–45 (17, 24, 35); Foster in Houston and Knox, 455, 457; Devine, 318, 570–1.

23. Lynch, 437–8; Devine, 347.

24. Kenneth Mackinnon, *Language, Education and Social Processes in a Gaelic Community* (Cambridge, 1977), 3; Callum G. Brown in Devine and Finlay, 214, 217; Devine, 562–3, 609. The Meek Report on the future status of Gaelic was released in May 2002, and at the time of writing is under consideration by the Scottish Executive.

25. *Sunday Herald*, 20 January 2000, 25; *Herald*, 27 January 2000, 1; Magnus Linklater and Robert Denniston (eds), *Anatomy of Scotland* (Edinburgh and New York: Chambers, 1992), 122, 131, 133, 134, 144; Roderick Watson in Devine and Finlay, 290; Lindsay Paterson, 'Liberation and Control: What are the Scottish Education Traditions of the Twentieth Century?', *idem*, 230–49 (233); Devine, 609. The Kirk of Scotland membership figure is from the Catholic-commissioned poll discussed in *Platform* and in *The Evening Times*, 23 May 2002.

26. Jeremy Peat and Stephen Boyle, *An Illustrated Guide to the Scottish Economy* (London: Duckworth, 1999), 1, 3, 4, 7, 12, 17, 82–3; Neil Hood in Peat and Boyle, 38–53 (38, 44, 49).

27. Peat and Boyle, 54–85.

28. Peat and Boyle, 21, 23, 55–7, 76–7.

29. John Curtice, *Newsnight Scotland*, 18 December 2001; *Sunday Herald*, 20 February 2000.

30. Cf. Angus Calder, 'Scott and Goethe: Romanticism and Classicism', in *Cencrastus* 13 (1983), 25–8, and Murray G.H. Pittock, *Scottish Nationality* (London: Palgrave, 2001), 169n and *The Myth of the Jacobite Clans* (Edinburgh: Edinburgh University Press, 1999 (1995)), ch. 4.

31. Harvie (1981), 155; Houston and Knox, 1.

32. Norman Davies, *The Isles* (London: Macmillan, 1999), 1037–8; Tom Nairn, *After Britain* (London: Granta, 2000), 241, 259; Finlay in MacDonald (1998), 112–13.

FURTHER READING

Barclay, Gordon, *Farmers, Temples and Tombs: Scotland in the Neolithic and Early Bronze Age*, Edinburgh: Canongate and Historic Scotland, 1998.

——, ed., *The Peoples of Scotland*, Edinburgh: Canongate and Historic Scotland, 1999 (contains books by Martin Carver, Ewan Campbell, Chris Lowe and Olwyn Owen).

Barrow, G.W.S., *Kingship and Unity: Scotland 1000–1306*, London: Edward Arnold, 1981.

——, *Robert Bruce*, 3rd edn, Edinburgh: Edinburgh University Press, 1988.

Broadie, Alexander, *The Scottish Enlightenment*, Edinburgh: Birlinn Books, 2001.

Broun, Dauvit, *The Irish Identity of the Kingdom of Scots in the Twelfth and Thirteenth Centuries*, Woodbridge: The Boydell Press, 1999.

Broun, Dauvit, Finlay, R.J. and Lynch, Michael, eds, *Image and Identity: The Making and Re-making of Scotland Through the Ages*, Edinburgh: John Donald, 1998.

Checkland, Sydney and Olive, *Industry and Ethos: Scotland 1832–1914*, 2nd edn, London: Edward Arnold, 1997 (1984).

Cowan, Ian B., *The Scottish Reformation: Church and Society in Sixteenth Century Scotland*, London: Weidenfeld and Nicolson, 1982.

Craig, Cairns, gen. ed., *A History of Scottish Literature*, 4 vols, Aberdeen: Aberdeen University Press, 1987–8.

Davies, Norman, *The Isles*, London: Macmillan, 1999.

Devine, T.M., *The Scottish Nation 1700–2000*, London: Penguin, 1999.

Devine, T.M. and Finlay, Richard, eds, *Scotland in the 20th Century*, Edinburgh: Edinburgh University Press, 1996.

Donaldson, Gordon, ed., *Scottish Historical Documents*, Edinburgh: Scottish Academic Press, 1974.

Donaldson, Gordon, *Scottish Church History*, Edinburgh: Scottish Academic Press, 1985.

Duncan, A.A.M., *Scotland: The Making of the Kingdom*, Edinburgh: Oliver & Boyd, 1978 (1975).

Ferguson, William, *The Identity of the Scottish Nation*, Edinburgh: Edinburgh University Press, 1998.

Fry, Michael, *The Scottish Empire*, East Linton and Edinburgh: Tuckwell/ Birlinn, 2001.

Gibson, A.J.S. and Smout, T.C., *Prices, Food and Wages in Scotland 1550–1780*, Cambridge: Cambridge University Press, 1995.

Glendinning Miles, Macinnes, Ranald and MacKechnie, Aonghus, *A History of Scottish Architecture*, Edinburgh: Edinburgh University Press, 1996.

Grant, Alexander, *Independence and Nationhood: Scotland 1306–1469*, London: Edward Arnold, 1984.

Harvie, Christopher, *Scotland and Nationalism*, 3rd edn, London: Allen & Unwin, 1998 (1977).

——, *No Gods and Precious Few Heroes*, 3rd edn, Edinburgh: Edinburgh University Press, 1998 (1981).

Houston, R.A. and Knox, W.W.J., eds, *The Penguin History of Scotland*, London: Penguin, 2001.

Kidd, Colin, *Subverting Scotland's Past: Scottish Whig Historians and the Creation of an Anglo-British Identity, 1689–c. 1830*, Cambridge: Cambridge University Press, 1993.

Lenman, Bruce, *Integration, Enlightenment and Industrialisation: Scotland 1746–1832*, London: Edward Arnold, 1981.

Lynch, Michael, *Scotland: A New History*, London: Century, 1991.

McClure, Derrick, *Why Scots Matters*, Edinburgh: Saltire Society, 1988.

McCrone, David, *Understanding Scotland: The Sociology of a Stateless Nation*, London: Routledge, 1992.

MacDonald, Catriona, ed., *Unionist Scotland 1800–1997*, Edinburgh: John Donald, 1998.

Macfarlane, Leslie, *William Elphinstone and the Kingdom of Scotland, 1431–1514*, Aberdeen: Aberdeen University Press, 1985.

Macinnes, Allan, *Clanship, Commerce and the House of Stuart, 1603–1788*, East Linton: Tuckwell Press, 1996.

MacLean, Lorraine, ed., *The Middle Ages in the Highlands*, Inverness: Inverness Field Club, 1981.

Macmillan, Duncan, *Scottish Art 1460–1990*, Edinburgh: Mainstream, 1990.

McNeill, Peter G.B. and MacQueen, Hector L., *Atlas of Scottish History to 1707*, Edinburgh: Edinburgh University, 1996.

McRoberts, David, ed., *Essays on the Scottish Reformation 1513–1625*, Glasgow: Burns, 1963.

Mason, Roger, *Kingship and the Commonweal: Political Thought in Renaissance and Reformation Scotland*, East Linton: Tuckwell Press, 1998.

Meek, Donald, *Celtic Christianity*, Boat of Garten: The Handsel Press, 2000.

Merriman, Marcus, *The Rough Wooings: Mary Queen of Scots 1542–1551*, East Linton: Tuckwell Press, 2000.

Mitchell, James, *Strategies for Self-government: The Campaigns for a Scottish Parliament*, Edinburgh: Polygon, 1996.

Morton, Graeme, *Unionist-Nationalism: Governing Urban Scotland 1830–1860*, East Linton: Tuckwell Press, 1999.

Nairn, Tom, *After Britain*, London: Granta, 2000.

Nicholson, Ranald, *Scotland: the Later Middle Ages*, Edinburgh: The Mercat Press, 1989 (1974).

Pittock, Murray G.H., *Jacobitism*, Basingstoke: Macmillan, 1998.

Prebble, John, *The King's Jaunt*, London: Collins, 1988.

Richards, Eric, *A History of the Highland Clearances*, 2 vols, London, 1985.

Smout, T.C., *A Century of the Scottish People 1830–1950*, London: Collins, 1986.

Smyth, Alfred, *Warlords and Holy Men: Scotland AD 80–1000*, London: Edward Arnold, 1984.

Whatley, Christopher A., *Scottish Society 1707–1830*, Manchester: Manchester University Press, 2000.

Withers, C.W.J., *Urban Highlanders: Highland–Lowland Migration and Urban Gaelic Culture, 1700–1900*, East Linton: Tuckwell, 1998.

Wormald, Jenny, *Court, Kirk and Community: Scotland 1470–1625*, London: Edward Arnold, 1981.

INDEX